AROUND THE WORLD IN EIGHTY YEARS

AROUND THE WORLD IN EIGHTY YEARS

Kenneth M. Scott, M.D.

PROVIDENCE HOUSE PUBLISHERS
Franklin, Tennessee

Printed in the United States of America

02   01   00   99   98   5   4   3   2   1

Library of Congress Catalog Card Number: 97-75781

ISBN: 1-57736-077-X

Cover by Gary Bozeman

Scripture references are based on: (1) Holy Bible, New International Version. Copyright © 1973, 1978, 1984 International Bible Society. Used by permission of Zondervan Bible Publishers; (2) King James Version. Copyright © 1976 by Thomas Nelson, Inc., Nashville, Tennessee; and (3) Revised Standard Version of the Bible. Copyright © 1946, 1952 Division of Christian Education of the National Council of the Churches of Christ in the United States of America. Used by permission.

PROVIDENCE HOUSE PUBLISHERS
238 Seaboard Lane • Franklin, Tennessee 37067
800-321-5692

TO
ANN AND
OUR CHILDREN

CONTENTS

FOREWORD

AMONG AMERICA'S PROMINENT PRESBYTERIAN missionary families none has a more distinguished record than the Scott family. The parents of Dr. Kenneth M. Scott—Charles E. and Clara H. Scott, left for China in 1907. All five of their children, three daughters and two sons, followed them in answering the call of God to serve with their spouses as missionaries. The oldest, Elisabeth Alden Scott, with her husband, John Stam, paid the supreme price, laying down their lives in 1934 to a murderous band of Chinese Communists and leaving behind an infant daughter, which story is of itself one of the heroic chapters in mission history.

The reader will find in the story of Dr. Kenneth Scott a clue to the building blocks of the kind of sturdy Christian living, nurtured by a close-knit family and by a supportive community with strong beliefs and a common goal, that made the modern Christian missionary movement a pivotal part of the transformation of Asia from nineteenth century impotence into what may well be the power center of the twenty-first century.

This book will disabuse the reader of the caricature of missionaries as somber, humorless eccentrics obeying a sense of duty, displaying a self-righteous, superior attitude to people they are called to live among. Missionaries and their children, however, are subject to the same weaknesses and temptations faced by all people. Dr. Scott does not gloss over certain elements of his own character over which he has felt cause to repent before the Lord. He is quick to acknowledge, however, the inestimable blessing of having loving Christian parents who prayed for their children daily and who passed on to them a heritage of faith in Jesus Christ far richer then gold.

Kenneth Scott was blessed with great natural gifts undergirded by the gifts of the Spirit, all of which have been developed through discipline. His remarkable musical talent at piano and organ has enriched all who have been graced by it, including the writers of this foreword for whose wedding he played so beautifully.

This is the story of an outstanding career. Scott's obedience to his Lord took him back to the vast continent on which he was born, first as an army officer in World War II on the Burma Road and then as a missionary. He combined surgical skill with a rare capacity for medical administration and a compassionate heart for evangelism to make a highly significant Christian medical witness towards the improvement of the public and private health practice of two strategic Asian countries, Korea and India. His wife Ann's nursing skills completed the partnership. His stories of the life of a doctor in mission hospitals are moving and heart-warming. They bring a glow of happiness and promise into the dark corners of a world in pain and suffering, with the good news that in the most hopeless of circumstances, in Christ there is healing and love and hope.

Reading this book is not only inspiring, it is fun. Dr. Scott's life has been an adventure throughout his first eighty years. There have been intensely trying times, tense times, frustrating times, joyous times, sad times, funny times. The book sparkles with love for his wife, Ann, their three children and spouses, and their grandchildren. It is abundantly clear that his life has been a response of love to his faithful Savior and that his highest desire is to stand at the door of the Kingdom of God inviting people to feast at the table of the Lord. It has been our great privilege to call him partner and friend.

Eileen and Samuel Moffett

PROLOGUE

THIS PERSONAL ACCOUNT OF MY LIFE'S EIGHTY years has been written primarily for my own beloved children and grandchildren. They have been curious to know, and have said so. Some acquaintances have asked me to share this with them also, provided it is not too lengthy. I have promised I would if they will overlook my not mentioning hundreds of wonderful friends and colleagues who have enriched my life along the way. I have never kept a diary and therefore have omitted many situations the memory of which is not clear enough to be factual.

Yes, I have traveled around the world—completely around the world six times and at least halfway around another twenty-one times, not counting the trips made between the United States and Europe and between India and Europe.

If there is a common thread running through this narrative, it should be the goodness and mercy of our Heavenly Father, for these have followed me all the days of my life. Most of the crucial determinants of my life's course have come undeserved and quite unanticipated—out of the blue, so to speak. I have become impressed more and more by the practicality of Solomon's words (and my life's motto), "Trust in the Lord with all your heart and lean not on your own understanding; in all your ways acknowledge him, and he will make your paths straight" (Prov. 3: 5–6 NIV). As I look back over the years, I can see His guiding hand in it all, even when I have fallen short time and again.

AROUND THE WORLD IN EIGHTY YEARS

CHAPTER ONE

EARLY CHINA YEARS

MY FATHER, CHARLES ERNEST SCOTT, AND MY mother, Clara Heywood Scott, agreed they would provide a good *American* home for whatever children God gave them, when they first sailed to China in 1907, along with their one-year-old firstborn Elisabeth Alden. The name Alden was given in memory of John and Priscilla Alden, Clara's ancestors on the *Mayflower*.

Charles and Clara had been assigned by the Presbyterian Mission to Tsingtao (Quingdao, modern spelling) in Shantung (Shandong), North China, because of their versatility with the German language, since Tsingtao was at that time a German crown colony. Once a quiet fishing hamlet on the Yellow Sea and then recognized by Germans as being potentially the finest natural harbor in all Asia, Tsingtao had become German property as indemnity following the Boxer Uprising of 1900.

Charles and Clara did not believe that the gospel was always best served by foreign missionaries "going native," and so they had brought along to China all their best American possessions—books, paintings, their numerous wedding gifts, and their piano. They themselves arrived at Tsingtao safely, but all their household effects, coming by another ship, were lost when the other ship foundered during a typhoon and sank. They took this loss hard. Recovering from the blow of this loss, they realized that God was weaning them from material "things." Ultimately, this proved a blessing, for when later on in life they lost everything they had, not once but three times, the subsequent losses of "things" did not devastate them.

It was in Tsingtao, in 1916 during World War I, that I was born—in the Faber Krankenhaus, the only hospital in this German crown colony. Two other sisters (Helen and "Bunny")—my oldest sister Betty was born in Michigan—and my brother Francis (known as "Laddie") had already been born in this same Faber Krankenhaus. All of us were ushered into the world by Herr Doktor Weischer, chief physician within the German crown colony. (In 1935, when I met Doktor Weischer in Tsingtao again, I was soundly shocked to hear this good physician extol the praises of Adolph Hitler and the Nazi movement.)

The Scott children in Tsingtao, China, 1916. Left to right: Bunny, Laddie, Betty holding me, and Helen.

When I was two years old, the family was transferred to Tsinan (Jinan), the capital of Shantung Province. This was to be our home for the next two decades. Like all mission houses in China in those days, it was surrounded by a nine-foot-high brick wall which enclosed a spacious garden, a playground, and the servants' quarters, and could be entered only through a massive, Chinese-style front gate. Half of the garden space was planted with flowers, the other half with peanuts. The playground was the scene of soccer games, pom-pom-pull-away ("come away or I'll fetch you away"), and all manner of family cavorting. Daddy was an athlete, and he insisted, when he was not out itinerating in the country, on leading the whole family, Mother included, in regimented calisthenics. ("Throw your chest out, chin and shoulders back, tummy in, breathe deeply—then exhale.") In later years the playground was converted into a tennis court.

In February 1923, our family began its furlough return to America, which normally began after every seven years of service on the mission field. This was my first trip out of China, and it was a very special one for all of us, for we took the long way home. Boarding a Peninsular and Oriental Steamship company ("P & O") boat from Shanghai, we sailed to Suez, stopping at Singapore and Colombo on the way. I remember Cairo and the pyramids and the nightly howling of hyenas outside Jerusalem. I remember Venice— who can ever forget Venice?—with all the pigeons at St. Mark's Square and the iron men striking the hour by the Doge's Palace. I clearly remember standing on a balcony overlooking the Grand Canal and watching, with crowds of other people, a strutting Benito Mussolini ride by on a lavishly-decorated motor-barge, followed at a little distance by King George V and Queen Mary on a second barge, and then trailing behind, as an afterthought, a third barge bearing King Victor Emmanuel and his queen.

Switzerland was so delightful to be in that we prolonged our visit there by doubling the time Daddy had scheduled for it. I remember seeing the impressive Lion of Lucerne and also innumerable milk-chocolate replicas of that famous statue, two or three of which we kids persuaded Daddy to buy to give Mother, knowing she would "share" them with us. I will never forget climbing Mount Pilatus on a cog-wheel railroad from a warm summer valley below to the snowy winterland above.

Eventually we sailed across the Atlantic on the huge SS *Leviathan*. Midway across, President Warren Harding died, and for an hour the ship stopped its engines and rolled with the swells, while Daddy, apparently the only clergyman on board, conducted the memorial service for the deceased president.

That trip to America took six months and was marred only by the news received while we were in Cairo, that my last surviving grandparent, Mother's mother, had died. I have, therefore, never known a grandparent of my own.

Our furlough year was spent in Springfield, Massachusetts—nine miles south of Holyoke, where Mother grew up and where her brother Fran Heywood and his wife Harriet and baby daughter were living. My sister Betty had rheumatic fever that year and had to spend many months at home in bed. During that winter, I came down with lobar pneumonia and almost died. The Rev. William Reed, pastor of the First Congregational Church of Springfield, spent all night in prayer for my recovery the night my "crisis" occurred and my fever broke—so I was told. So our house on Union Street was an infirmary for much of our furlough year. Daddy was away most of the time, in big demand to speak all over the United States. That year Laddie attended the Stony Brook School for Boys, on Long Island, during its second year of existence—the same school I was to graduate from years later, as would also my two sons.

Betty recovered enough from her rheumatic fever to enter Wilson College in Pennsylvania in the fall of 1924, and our family returned to China. Our ship across the Pacific was the SS *President Lincoln*, which withstood a typhoon that reportedly sank more than one ocean liner—it was exciting enough for us, anyway.

Back in China, Helen, Bunny, and Laddie headed for the North China American School, a boarding school in Tungchow (Tongxian), near Peking (Beijing). I was still too young to leave home, so I stayed at home the next two years, tutored by Mother, who also tried to teach me to play the piano. She began with hymns, and the first I ever learned was "By Cool Siloam's Shady Rill." By then my sisters had already introduced me to that chestnut, "Chopsticks."

While in China, our summers were spent in Pei Tai Ho, a beach resort for foreigners not far from where the Great Wall reaches the Yellow Sea. Pei Tai Ho Beach stretched from East Cliff southward to Rocky Point. Temple Bay, in between (also known as the British Legation), was where our family owned a cottage, complete with our own tennis court, which was always in use. There, in the very first tennis game I ever tried to play, my opponent was Frank Tucker, the same age as I, and he trounced me good and hard, even though this was also his first try at tennis. Years later, during World War II, we were to sail overseas as U.S. Army medical officers, in the same ship and cabin, live in the same tent in India, cross the Hump in the same airplane, ride down the Burma Road in the same truck, and teach in the same Chinese Army medical "refresher" course in Tali, in Yunnan Province.

Pei Tai Ho Beach's best attraction was the swimming, always excellent except for the one week or so in the summer when jellyfish abounded—some as large as five feet in diameter and with stingers. It was also there that I saw my first dead human body—three pirates had been shot in a skirmish and their bodies had washed ashore onto our beach.

Pei Tai Ho days were idyllic. One general fact I remember about them was this: We never went bounding down to the beach or scooted to the tennis court until we first had our family "worship" together, which always followed immediately after breakfast and which included singing a hymn, reading Scripture (each person reading around the family circle in turn), and prayer. Though as kids we often chafed impatiently to get on our way, much of our lasting family solidarity and wholesomeness I now attribute to this family practice, wherever we might be living.

Those two years alone with Mother in Tsinan (Daddy was most of the time out in the country) were turbulent years in China. The Communists began a concerted attempt to discredit Christianity and its missionaries as tools of western imperialism, and they were quite successful in agitating the people against Christians and Americans. For months I was forbidden to leave our compound walls even if accompanied by our wonderful collie Ginger. Whenever I should expose myself, it was to invite a chorus from ever-present Chinese kids of, "Shiao yang gwer, shiao yang gwer!" meaning "little foreign devil." But even then, the kids were always smiling and playful, and I never at any time felt threatened by them.

People have asked my impressions of the Chinese as I remembered them during my childhood. As a youngster I always liked the Chinese and felt at home among them. They were uninhibited in their curiosity, and they always found foreign kids highly entertaining. Even during periods of stepped-up anti-foreign propaganda, I always found them friendly toward me, smiling even while calling me a little foreign devil. Very rarely did I encounter any personal hostility, and then it was only when Communist anti-foreign agitation was at its height.

So what were my impressions of the Chinese people I knew as a boy? Above all else, most were very poor and underfed. They had to be frugal, and they threw nothing away. Even human excrement was carefully collected and applied as fertilizer to grow food. I remember once riding in a rickshaw through a crowded street eating a banana; when I tossed the banana peel overboard, immediately a man picked it out of the dirt and ate it down. I also remember, not far from our home, seeing two men skinning a dog they said had died of rabies, in order to make leather and to recover some flesh to cook; they explained to me that they were being very careful about it.

Trees had long ago disappeared from the landscape, except for those few protected within temple walls or in our compound. The Chinese generally used grass as fuel for their woks; and when no more grass was to be found, they would often dig up the grass roots for fuel. When drought and famine struck, as it often did, I saw people strip the reachable leaves and even the bark from the acacia trees growing inside our compound wall. These would be chopped up and made into a gruel to eat, sometimes with dirt added to thicken it.

Desperate want for food would, understandably, lead to apparent callousness toward others. I remember telling our servants about a current famine somewhere else in China that had left fifteen million Chinese dead, expecting these kindly people to respond with shock and sorrow. Instead, they simply commented, "Too many Chinese; population too dense," the implication being that with fifteen million fewer mouths to feed, those remaining should then have better chances at survival.

We Americans had to be careful about the food we ate. Cooked food that was still too hot for flies to walk about on it was all we were permitted to eat, with few exceptions. Water had to be brought to a rolling boil before it became potable. Watermelons could be very dangerous because they were always sold by weight; to fetch a better price they were apt to be cleverly plugged with contaminated water added to make them heavier.

We were dependent on local milk supply, which meant that milk must always be boiled, not just pasteurized. Once, when we noticed that our milk was gradually getting thinner and more watery, we confronted our dairyman. With complete aplomb he reminded us that it had been raining a lot lately and that the cows had had to eat very wet grass. We knew that his excuse for selling diluted milk was specious, and he knew that we knew that his excuse was specious; but by it he was able to save face, and our conversation concluded with everyone smiling. The milk suddenly improved—for awhile.

We had no refrigerator. If we wanted fish to eat, our cook had to find and bring a live fish home in a pan of water and present it to Mother. If the fish moved spontaneously, it was edible; if it didn't move, it was returned to the vendor. If we wanted chicken, the cook would bring home a live hen, not a rooster, and we would fatten her up for two or three weeks before making her into dinner. One of those hens, whom we soon named Biddie, endeared herself to us kids by laying two eggs before the planned date of execution; also she would come running to us whenever we called her. Biddie became a wonderful pet after we persuaded Mother to spare her life. But months later, when it was time to leave Tsinan for our summer cottage on the Yellow Sea, Mother said we would have to eat Biddie before we went away. It was a wrenchingly sad dinner we sat down to. Eyes brimmed and choking sobs interrupted the silence of that meal. Parts of Biddie remained untouched on each of our plates.

It was the custom in our mission station to rotate from house to house for the monthly station meeting and the dinner that followed. One year, well before our turn was due, Mother, feeling everyone was getting tired of eating only chicken, asked our cook, "Do you think we could get some beef for that night?"

"Let me find out," replied the cook. Several days later he reported that it could be done. But when the dinner finally came, the meat dish was chicken.

"You told me we would have beef tonight," Mother reminded the cook. The cook replied, "I thought so too. But the cow hadn't died yet."

Our servants—there were four of them—were mostly uneducated and were all related to each other; they lived as a close-knit family in quarters adjoining our house. This was the only way one could insure harmony among the servant help. The gardener ("outside man") was the father of the cook. The cook's wife was the "amah" and sewing woman. When we needed a fourth servant to do laundry and clean the house ("inside man"), a country cousin who was unmarried, was offered by the family. I remember when this new man was first introduced to us. He had never been in a city before, much less in a foreigner's house, and he was ill-at-ease and blushing, which made the pockmarks that covered his face a livid red. In his confusion he spat on our living room rug and then rubbed it out of sight with his muddy shoe. But Chou Tran-Giang learned fast and soon showed he had good common sense and great resourcefulness.

A person cannot live in China, even as a kid, without soon becoming oriented in terms of the compass. The Chinese word for *thing* is "dong xi," literally "east-west," or anything east or west.

"Beijing" means "northern capital," "Nanjing" means "southern capital." "Shandong,"the province where I was born and brought up, means "east of the mountains." Of course, there is another province, "Shanxi," which means "west of the mountains." If you go down a hallway, you don't say, "Take the last door on the left." That would be confusing to a Chinese person because if you were facing the opposite way, it would actually be the first door on the right. But the compass never changes, and so you say instead, "Enter the door to the northwest room of the house, and in the southwest corner of the room is a bureau. If you open the top drawer to the east, you'll find my pocketbook in the southeast corner. It's simple; you can't miss."

But most serious in those days was the complete chaos caused by bandit warlords overrunning the whole land. The predominant bandit-warlord controlling most of Shantung, with his headquarters in Tsinan, was General Chang Tsung-Ch'ang, a strapping six-foot native of Shantung who had many wives and some two hundred concubines. His favorite wife, a lovely cultured woman, was simply referred to as Number Seventeen. Mother was asked to teach English to Number Seventeen, and she was glad to do so. Predictably, Mother used for her textbook the King James New Testament.

General Chang "taxed" the people forty years in advance, but gave no service in return. He kept a complete train of the *Blue Express* (stolen from the fleet of American trains donated to China) on track one of the Tsinan railroad station for over a year, to be ready at any hour to spirit him and his entourage away to safety if the need arose. The need never came while I was in Tsinan. Passengers trying to reach other trains on other tracks had to crawl under the *Blue Express* or around it or hazard the small iron foot-bridge to get beyond track one.

Sometime during my last year in Tsinan there was a rebellion among General Chang's concubines, details of which were never clear to me—rumors run rife among the oppressed. All I know is that General Chang had about two hundred concubines executed and their bodies hung along the city wall for a week before letting relatives remove them for burial.

Since boarding school at Tungchow began only with the sixth grade, it was 1926 before I was sent there. I was one of the three sixth-graders whom the mighty seventh-and eighth-graders loved to goad into homesickness by the antics of what they called "the mercy band." Health in those days was thought to be enhanced by sleeping in outdoor air, and so we grade school boys (there were no grade school girls then) slept on a wide screened-in porch. In the winter we slept in sleeping bags and wore flannel hoods to protect our heads from bitter winds and drifting snow. Tungchow got mighty cold in winter. The athletic field would be flooded over around Thanksgiving and would serve for ice hockey until almost Easter.

But we never got to Easter that one year I was at Tungchow. The so-called "Nanking Incident" occurred in early 1927. As a young boy, I had no idea what the "Nanking Incident" was all about; I only knew that at that time, China was dangerous and threatening for all foreigners and that all westerners, in particular, were suddenly and urgently ordered by their governments to get out of China immediately. Even to adults, China is full of complex-ities and enigmas; nothing is simple and straightforward. In later years, we understood something of the tremendous power struggle being waged unrelentingly between the Soviets and the West for the "soul" and geopolitical bonding of China, first felt in the clash between the left and right wings of the Kuomintang in South China, in which the key figure was Chiang Kai-Shek—who had been strongly wooed by the Kremlin and even given a Russian wife while in Moscow. It was when Chiang Kai-Shek broke with the Communists in a bloody coup in early 1927 that the fireworks erupted and the struggle between Communism and the West intensified. The details of that "Nanking Incident" showdown are still somewhat shrouded in a haze. At the time, we heard that one American living in Nanking escaped with his life from a hostile crowd by stripping to his shorts, painting himself with Mercurochrome, and rushing to safety screaming like a banshee.

Overnight our school was disbanded. Bunny, Laddie, and I headed to Tientsin (Tianjin), the major port near the Yellow Sea, where we were met by Mother arriving from Tsinan. Daddy, who had been out in the country, joined us two days later, having providentially caught the very last train between Tsinan and Tientsin. Where to go now? All transportation leaving China was quickly booked solid. Mercifully, our family was together, and we were fortunate to book a steamer from Tientsin to Korea, a country I had never heard of before. The day before we were to sail, my parotid glands became swollen, and a misdiagnosis of mumps compelled us to swap bookings with a family leaving three days later. We were most fortunate to evacuate China together, for one of my schoolmates never caught up with his family for the next eight months.

CHAPTER TWO

EARLY KOREA YEARS

ONE OF DADDY'S CLOSEST FRIENDS AND A classmate in Princeton Seminary days was Dr. John Fairman Preston, a Southern Presbyterian missionary in Soonchun, near the southern coast of Korea. In seminary, Dr. Preston was "Brer Rabbit" and my father was "Brer Wolf." So for the spring and summer of 1927, we Scotts (Daddy, Mother, Bunny, Laddie, and I) lived with the Prestons.

That fall, Bunny, Laddie, and I attended the Pyengyang Foreign School (PYFS) in what is today the capital of North Korea. Like ourselves, many students who had been attending Tungchow the previous school year also enrolled at PYFS, where we were referred to as the "China Flees" (or "China Fleas"). Ours was a happy, wholesome school in an outstanding community of American, Canadian, and Australian missionaries.

With a sudden influx of "China Flees" that fall, PYFS was initially strapped for dormitory space for all its boarding students. Bunny and Laddie, being in high school, got into the dormitory. It was still too dangerous for Mother to return to China that fall with

Daddy; so for that first year she and I lived with the Stacy L. Roberts family. Our family already knew them because our furlough years had coincided and we had crossed the Pacific together on the same ship of the Dollar Steamship Line. Dayton Roberts, one year younger than I, would in later years become a prominent leader in the Latin American Mission and a brother-in-law to Kenneth Strachan.

Dr. Samuel A. Moffett was the first Protestant missionary to settle in North Korea. That was around 1890. He and his family lived in Pyengyang. I well remember seeing many hundreds of Korean Christians come from near and far to pay homage and express their loving appreciation of this great missionary pioneer during the celebrations of his fortieth year in Korea. His son Sam (Samuel H. Moffett) was my classmate at PYFS. Sam and his younger brother Howard would in later years become fellow missionaries of ours in Korea. In fact, most of my PYFS school-mates entered some form of full-time Christian ministry in years to come, many of them in Korea, like myself.

In this large community were some very talented musicians, so music flourished in this school. Fully three-fourths of the students took private music lessons. My four years in Pyengyang (now spelled Pyongyang) saw much progress in music for many of us students, thanks to the inspiration and encouragement of the community and the school we were in.

While in school in Korea, none of us Scott children returned to China, though our parents did. Instead, Daddy and Mother came to Korea for our summer vacations. We rented a cottage at Sorai Beach, on the southern coast of what is now North Korea. It was here that most of the Korea missionaries spent their summers. Sorai Beach had the finest sand to be found anywhere in the world, and ships would come from Europe to buy sand from the Japanese sand company (which employed Korean diggers and paid half of their wages in sake) for the finest glassmakers in Europe.

Swimming at Sorai was excellent. There were tennis courts and even the semblance of a golf course. Laddie, who reached the finals in tennis, couldn't quite beat the perennial champion Dr. McAnliss, the mission dentist, who was the only person in Korea with a metal tennis racket. There were community chowder picnics on the beach—clam and clamless—with Mrs. Harry Rhodes as the chief chowder chef, later to become Laddie's mother-in-law. Sunset worship-on-the-point every Sunday evening, sitting on the grassy cliff overlooking the Yellow Sea, was an unforgettable experience.

A memorable recollection of Sorai Beach was Daddy's readings of *Kenilworth* in our cottage. Evening after evening our cottage would be crammed, floor space and all, with older kids attracted from all around to hear Daddy read this Walter Scott classic with his clear, rich, dramatic voice.

One summer at Sorai, Ruth Paxson, a popular Bible lecturer with missionary communities around the world, gave a week of morning lectures. Except for the smaller children, everybody attended. Miss Paxson had severe asthma, and I still remember hearing her, in the still of the night, coughing and wheezing and fighting for air. She would have spasms of coughing up to the moment she rose to speak, but as soon as she began to speak, all coughing stopped. Her messages were understandable even to us youngsters, and they were always powerful. Some years later, when she was a speaker at the Keswick Conferences in New Jersey and I was their pianist, I was to appreciate even more the power and authority of her Bible teaching.

In Korea, which had been completely under control of the Japanese since 1910, we all could see how intent the Japanese were to absorb the Koreans as a people and make them indistinguishable from the Japanese. Pyengyang was named Heijo, Seoul was named Keijo; Soonchun was Junten, Syenchun was Sensen; Kangkei became Kokai, and so on. All schools had to teach in Japanese. Eventually it was forbidden to speak in Korean even in one's own home. Korean culture and aspirations were systematically suppressed and enforcement became progressively more brutal. Thought police were everywhere. A Korean man whom we students often saw at school and was known among us as Crazy Paul had graduate degrees from Oxford University. Because he had shown great promise for national leadership and therefore posed a threat to the Japanese, the police had imprisoned him and over many months tortured him out of his mind permanently. Crazy Paul, now broken and gentle and harmless, would ask us for a pair of trousers and then would slip the pair we gave him over the four pairs he was already wearing. Even youngsters like us would feel the pathos of such a great man now destroyed. Even in this sad state, he was still able to speak five languages fluently.

We students in Pyengyang readily noticed that only the Christians in Korea would dare stand up to the Japanese, even when it landed them in prison; the other Koreans seemed to knuckle under to avoid unpleasantness. It was no wonder that the Japanese authorities bore down hard on Christian institutions as being the prime obstructers to Japanization. A diabolic quandary for Christians was the Japanese requirement in every school (for Koreans, that is) to assemble all students and teachers every Monday and have them bow to the emperor's shrine. Some church leaders in America argued that this was no big deal—like saluting the flag. But to Korean Christians, this was blatant idolatry. "You missionaries liberated us from worshipping idols," they would say; "Why return us now to what we have been saved from?" And so over the years, many Christian schools were closed, many Christian pastors and elders were imprisoned for months and even years. As students in our warm and safe American school, we would often send blankets, warm clothing, and food for students and faculty members of nearby Soongsil Christian College or Pyengyang Theological Seminary who were enduring bitter winter cold in unheated prisons.

During my fourth and last year in Pyengyang—my sophomore year—my roommate Dwight Thompson and I were invited to spend our Christmas vacation with a missionary family in Kangkei, far to the north near the Manchurian border. My brother Laddie had spent the previous Christmas there and had bagged a deer then. Dwight and I were warned that it got cold there, and it surely was. Every night the temperature reached forty degrees below zero (Celsius and Fahrenheit). On sunny days the tempera-ture would climb to fifteen below zero or possibly to as high as ten below zero. The Byram family in Kangkei had two small girls. When Dr. Byram shot a black bear early that winter, he let it freeze stiff standing on all fours in their backyard so that his girls could play on it. Around Easter, when things began to thaw, the bear was butchered and the meat given to friends to eat.

During that same school year, the entire high school learned and twice performed Gilbert and Sullivan's H. M. S. *Pinafore*. I was given the part of Tom Tucker, a minor role. Its first public performance was scheduled for a Saturday night during the spring. Tracy Logan, one of our high school teachers, had the part of Sir Joseph Porter, KCB. Friday morning, the day before we were to give it, Mr. Logan was found to have the mumps. They grabbed me out of classes, put the admiral's score in my lap, and told me to learn it. That really wasn't such a big deal, because by that time everybody in the operetta was familiar with everybody else's lines; the major performers already had their parts and couldn't be spared. At any rate, the show went on as scheduled, and I still have a photograph of myself dressed in a bona fide admiral's dress uniform, medals and all, including the Order of Chrysanthemum conferred by the emperor. It appears that the Japanese army had adopted German uniforms and the Japanese navy had adopted British uniforms; so the uniform I wore was authentic, because the Governor-General had graciously loaned his own navy uniform for the occasion. We understand that he sat quietly in the back of the auditorium soothed with sake, and was there mostly to see his uniform on stage. Later on, when H. M. S. *Pinafore* was again performed at commencement time, Tracy Logan played his regular admiral's role and I was out of everything with the mumps.

Also during that year in Pyengyang, another event of even greater importance for us occurred at school. It seems that a quartet of men students from Asbury College in America, none of whom were Christians before they attended Asbury, felt constrained to "thumb" their way across the Pacific and to give brass concerts, sing, and give their Christian testimonies wherever the opportunity opened. These men arrived unexpectedly in Pyengyang, and for a full week our principal Ralph Oliver Reiner turned over to them the daily morning assembly hour. We students were fascinated. God used these men that week to bring most of us, myself included, to a personal commitment to Christ. I emphasize the word "personal," because as children in missionary communities, we kids had always considered ourselves to be Christians. After all, our parents were missionaries and naturally we kids expected to ride into heaven as a family. I consider it a miracle that as a result of this quartet's visit, at least two-thirds of us high schoolers were persuaded of our own need for a personal Christian commitment, and we made those personal commitments, not in days to come, but that week. Many fellow students wept openly with love and joy and expressed in unembarrassed, heartfelt words what was happening to them. All this was quite new to us and quite unexpected. My own commitment to Christ was unemotional. The only difference I noticed for myself was a strong resolve to read the Bible regularly every day and to delight in doing so. This practice, usually the first thing every morning, has now been a habit since that eventful week in the spring of 1931. I have now read the whole Bible dozens of times, the New Testament twice as often as the Old Testament. I would feel dislocated and adrift if I were ever to miss a day. I wholeheartedly recommend this particular habit to everyone.

There was also another life habit or attitude which, as I look back, began that same week. That attitude was not apparent during my high school years, because both Pyengyang years and Stony Brook years (which followed Pyengyang) were sheltered years, where I was surrounded by Christian people with Christian outlooks and standards and lifestyles, people whom I admired for their upbeat integrity and strength of character. This particular attitude, which has become most liberating to me over the years, is freedom from peer pressures, freedom from pressures to do wrong just because "everybody is doing it," like cheating, stealing, lying, and also activities that in the 1930s were considered in Christian circles as worldly, such as the classical triad of drinking, smoking, and dancing.

Please don't get me wrong. I am no paragon of goodness. I have repeatedly been reminded of the admonition, "Let him who thinks he is standing beware lest he fall." Only through God's mercy have I been prevented, time and time again, from falling off the deep end. I am still a sinner, and I know it; and so I can't point a finger at others who sin. But I am a forgiven, freed sinner.

Speaking of Bible study, I would add that Bible courses were a part of the curriculum for every high school student in Pyengyang Foreign School (as it would also be at Stony Brook). Perhaps our most popular teacher was Elsa Logan, Tracy Logan's elder sister, who taught French and Bible and whose classes were fascinating and memorable in both subjects. Miss Logan taught us how to study the Bible. Not only that, but God undoubtedly used her to instill in me, at least, if not the rest of her students, an eagerness to discover for ourselves its treasures, finding something new and poignant whenever it was read. This sense of expectation persisted even during periods of spiritual spinelessness.

As I look back, the convergence of this saintly teacher's influence and the sudden input of the quartet's visit was providential for me. Some thirty years later I was privileged to meet one of those men from Asbury College, J. B. Crouse Sr., the father of a fellow missionary in Korea, and tell him what happened in my life that week in Pyengyang when he was there.

CHAPTER THREE

STONY BROOK SCHOOL

I T WAS IN THE SUMMER OF 1931, RIGHT AFTER MY sophomore year in Pyengyang, that my parents began their furlough in America, which in those times came after every seven full years of service on the mission field. I went to America with them—my brother and my three sisters were already there. That July and August were spent in Ventnor, New Jersey, in one of the seaside cottages provided by the Pennsylvania Medical Missionary Society. That delightful stay in Ventnor was memorable because it was the first time our entire Scott family had been together in seven years, and it was to be the last time we would all be together this side of heaven. It was also the only time I ever saw my future brother-in-law John Cornelius Stam, who together with my eldest sister, Betty, would be beheaded by the Chinese Communists only three years later.

Sometime during that summer, a kind lady drove several of us in her Lincoln car to nearby Keswick Grove for the day. My memory of what happened that particular day is clear on only two things. The first had to do with the ride itself. As an adolescent car

At Ventnor, New Jersey, 1931. This was the last time our entire Scott family was together. Left to right: Helen, Mother, Daddy, Bunny, Betty, Laddie, and me.

enthusiast, I was startled (and somewhat worried) to see that whenever this dear lady came to a railroad crossing, she always drove right up onto the track and stopped there, the more clearly to see if anything was coming, before driving on. In those days of gear-shifting, she would often stall the engine, but seemed unperturbed by it. My second memory of that day was that during the one meeting we attended at this conference center, I made a public commitment to God to become a missionary. Betty and Helen were not there then, but some six years before, Betty, while a college girl, had surrendered her complete life to Christ at that very place.

That fall I entered the Stony Brook School, a private Christian preparatory school for boys on the north shore of Long Island. The headmaster was Frank Ely Gaebelein, a man who next to my own father was to exert a more profound influence on my life than any other man. Dr. Gaebelein, in his early thirties at that time, was gifted in many areas of life. He even wrote a mystery novel, entitled *The Hollow Queen*. He was a scholar, an accomplished concert pianist, a track star, and alpinist; his brilliant mind was disciplined. To me he

was character personified, with an unbending commitment to
Christian principles and to excellence. During my junior and senior
years at Stony Brook I came to appreciate also how humble and self-
giving he was despite the no-nonsense aura he bore.

On Good Friday of 1932, while my parents were still on
furlough, Dr. Gaebelein and Daddy and Bunny and I attended
Wagner's *Parsifal* together at the Metropolitan Opera House in
New York (Bunny was a senior at Wilson College). Many weeks
before this, Dr. Gaebelein had taken the time to teach me on the
piano in his home all the significant *leit motifs* of this impressive
opera. As a result, to this day the magnificent music of this opera,
especially its "Prelude" and "Good Friday Spell," brings me to
tears with its beauty every time I hear it. At Stony Brook I was just
one of his students; he took time with other students as well.

Then the next year, my senior year, Dr. Gaebelein taught a class
in New Testament Greek, even though there were only two of us
taking it. This he offered to do in addition to his teaching the
Gospel of Luke to the whole senior class. Such was his love of
Scripture and of his Lord. One can easily see why he had placed on
the lectern of Hegeman Chapel, where no visiting minister could
miss it when he rose to speak, the words in John 12:21 (KJV), "SIR,
WE WOULD SEE JESUS." During my two years at Stony Brook,
Sunday-morning preachers included Samuel Zwemer, Robert E.
Speer, J. Ross Stevenson, Donald Grey Barnhouse, Daddy Hall, and
many like them. I still remember when Daddy Hall, the inimitable
Episcopalian priest who worked among the down-and-outers in
the Bowery, got down from the pulpit and taught us boys from the
central aisle the poem which ran

> Tobacco is a filthy weed
>> And from the Devil doth proceed.
> It picks your pockets, burns your clothes,
>> And makes a chimney out of your nose.

My roommate throughout my senior year was Paul McClanahan,
the son of missionaries in Assiut, Egypt. Paul was the most popular

boy in school. This was attested to by the fact that during his senior year he was president of the student body, president of our senior class, president of the Christian Association, captain of the football, wrestling, track, and tennis teams, and also—to break the camel's back—editor-in-chief of the yearbook, *Res Gestae Classis*. I worried that all these responsibilities would overwhelm Paul, hamstring his schoolwork, and jeopardize his graduating, and so did the faculty. When spring break and Easter arrived and nothing had even begun on the yearbook, Dr. Gaebelein called me aside and asked me to produce the yearbook. Paul would continue to be editor-in-chief, but I would carry the ball, make the decisions, and do whatever had to be done. I suddenly acquired a lot of work which would have to be completed before graduation. This meant my making plans and assignments, doing layout work, arranging for photographs, soliciting advertisers, plus numerous trips to the printer in lower Manhattan.

Everybody was relieved when Paul successfully passed his final examinations and the complete volumes of *Res Gestae Classis* all arrived for distribution, but only the day before commencement. If they had arrived two days later, boxes of yearbooks would have been piled somewhere for storage with nobody to belong to. The suspense of all this, plus the pressure to prepare and deliver the valedictory address, was such that immediately after commencement exercises, I lost my voice for two days. But all this effort was well compensated when I received a gracious, heart-warming letter of appreciation from Dr. Gaebelein, which I still have and treasure. In years to come, I was to appreciate this great man all the more.

The next year the school made regulations limiting the number of offices a student could hold at one time, so as not to impair his progress in school.

CHAPTER FOUR

CAMP CHENANGO

THE HEADWATERS OF THE GREAT SUSQUEHANNA River is Lake Otsego in upstate New York, the setting for James Fenimore Cooper's *Deerslayer* and *The Last of the Mohicans*. Cooperstown, where baseball was invented, lies at the southern end of this beautiful lake that is roughly a mile wide and extends twelve miles to the north. Midway along the eastern shore was Camp Chenango, the private boys camp where I spent four summers as a counselor. The first summer occurred between my two years at Stony Brook. My brother-in-law Gordon Mahy had been a counselor there some years before and had recommended me to its owner and director, "Pop" Fisher, a public high school English teacher in Maplewood, New Jersey. Very wet behind the ears, I was accepted there as counselor because Gordon had been a legendary hero while there and because they wanted someone who could play the piano, "Cap" Mattoon, the codirector, being strong on camp singing. (Gordon had authored the words of a rousing camp song; eventually I composed the tune for some rousing words authored by "Cap" Mattoon.)

My summers at Camp Chenango were delightful. Every morning began with a bugle call and regimented calisthenics outside the tents, followed immediately by a yippee-yahoo swim-in-the-buff in the lake and then a hearty breakfast, bed-making, policing the tents, and morning assembly, followed by a wide assortment of crafts, horseback riding, baseball, tennis, sailing, then another swim (this time with trunks) before lunch, then rest period, then on and on with more supervised fun. Camp lasted during the eight weeks of July and August. It was great, and I loved it.

Toward the end of my first summer at Camp Chenango (1932) my sister Betty was on her way to China. I obtained permission to leave the camp in order to see Betty once more on her train going west. I rode by bus to Albany, joined Betty on her New York Central train, and rode with her as far as Utica where I said good-bye and got off. I then proceeded by a Toonerville cross-country trolley back to Cooperstown. Little did I realize, during the some two hours we visited together, that I would never see Betty again.

That August day turned rainy and cold, and I was not dressed for either. I reached camp later that day drenched and shivering and the next day had to be taken to the Mary Imogene Bassett Hospital in Cooperstown with pneumonia. I was hospitalized there for a week. This was in the days before sulfa drugs and penicillin.

Subsequent summers at Camp Chenango were halcyon days. Water sports were always a major activity, fortified by a large armada of canoes, by two sailboats called Barnegat Bay sneak boxes (cat boats), and by "Pop" Fisher's motorboat (which could carry many passengers if they all sat down and didn't jump around). Lake Otsego was deep and usually calm, but one could usually expect a nice afternoon breeze for sailing, which would die down toward dusk. There were races and canoe tilts. During two summers I was there, the annual Central New York Racing Regatta was held on Lake Otsego, and it was a magnificent sight to see more than a hundred star-class sailing yachts racing at one time.

We counselors were permitted to take the canoes on the evenings we had off, and we made good use of them. On the shore to the north of us was a patrician girls camp comparable to ours for boys. To the south of us was a Scout camp—for boys during July and for girls during August. It was at the latter that I came near to moral calamity during my last summer at Camp Chenango, at a time when the air and the surface water had become comfortably warm and I was vulnerable to romantic stimulations.

A fellow-counselor and I had begun dating two Girl Scout counselors who were sisters. Eventually the four of us arranged to have our day off together when the moon was to be full. We two men were to paddle to the Scout camp that afternoon in our canoes, pick up our dates, and proceed to a lovely secluded spot along the lake to enjoy a picnic, spread our blankets, and when it was quite dark, hopefully go skinny-dipping in the lake. The day came—gorgeous weather—and my colleague and I paddled to the girls camp. The sisters were waiting for us. They climbed in and we shoved off. We had paddled out about a hundred yards or more when a counselor was seen running down out of the woods toward the dock, waving her arms wildly. We were already far enough from shore so that we could barely hear her yelling, "Come back, come back, come back!" We did come back, wondering what could be so urgent. Then we heard her tell us, "We're all under quarantine for scarlet fever, and nobody can leave camp." So ended our evening plans.

Later my fellow-counselor assured me that he and the sisters were counting on having sex that night. I am convinced that had that dramatic interruption not taken place, I would surely have lost my virginity then. I soon realized that only God's providential intervention at that moment forcibly pulled me free from an over-powering temptation I would have been too weak to resist. I can't think of a better example than this particular experience, of what Scripture says in 1 Corinthians 10:13 (NIV), when Paul wrote, "No temptation has seized you except what is common to man. And God is faithful; he will not let you be tempted beyond what you can bear. But when you are tempted, he will also provide a way out so that you can stand up under it." In this instance, I would have been too weak to have stood up under this temptation. When

I think of the possible consequences of that night and how it could have altered my whole future life, I break out in perspiration and I thank God for delivering me. I am also convinced that it was the faithful, earnest prayers in my behalf by my godly parents far away on the other side of the world in China that God was hearing and answering, because I certainly was not asking for deliverance then. Through the years since then I have repeatedly thanked God for this mercy, so that I could enjoy the full happiness of having had sex with only one person in my life, my wonderful wife Ann.

No doubt there will be some reading this who will wonder why all the angst about this, why be such a prig by giving this a second thought now that extramarital sex is today so commonly accepted and practiced. My reply must be that fornication, whether homosexual or heterosexual, is still as offensive to God today as it was when the Bible was written.

CHAPTER FIVE

COLLEGE YEARS

WHERE SHOULD I ATTEND COLLEGE? WHILE A senior at Stony Brook, I spent my Christmas vacation with my sister Helen and her husband George Gordon Mahy Jr., and their infant son George Gordon Mahy III, known to us as Don. Gordon was attending Yale Divinity School preparing for a graduate degree. He took me to some of his classes, and I also visited the university. One of Mother's closest friends, Fannie Reed Hammond (whose husband chaired the Department of Music at Mount Holyoke College), had a brother on the Yale University staff, Edward Bliss Reed, who encouraged me to apply to Yale. I did this and was accepted; they even offered me a full scholarship.

At the time, my brother Laddie was attending Davidson College in North Carolina and liked it much. But Davidson had no music department at all and I wanted to continue in music while in college, if at all possible. However, during that summer, word reached me that Davidson College was beginning a music department that fall. I immediately applied to Davidson and was accepted.

I roomed that freshman year with Laddie, who was a senior. The Great Depression was at its height, and I had no scholarship at Davidson except for the fifty percent tuition reduction the college gave to all sons of clergymen and missionaries. This meant that instead of one hundred dollars for tuition, I had to pay only fifty dollars. Laddie, known on the campus as Pon, and I were able to save somewhat on expenses by living in the cheapest dormitory, a small wooden shack built during World War I known as North Barracks, which now no longer exists. Laddie was on the college tennis team. He earned much of his way as student assistant to Dean Sentelle correcting Bible-course examinations and also correcting German papers for Professor Guy Vowles.

The Department of Music did indeed begin that fall and rushed full speed ahead. I found myself involved in it up to my eyebrows from the first day. The department chairman was Professor James Christian Pfohl, a musical dynamo from a highly musical family. His father was the Moravian bishop in Winston-Salem. In this account I will refer to Professor Pfohl as Jim, simply because he was only twenty years old at the time—my brother's age. Jim was a born leader and soon wielded more influence in college than the athletic director. He knew music well. He was an accomplished organist and a brilliant cornet and trumpet player. Most importantly, he was an effective administrator and music director. Within two years he had organized a symphonic band that was second to none in the South—an incredible accomplishment for a small college that had no music department at all only two years before.

During my freshman year I took organ lessons under Jim and in a few weeks became the college student organist. In those days daily chapel attendance was compulsory; each student sat every week-day morning in his own alphabetically-assigned seat and his attendance was checked by student monitors sitting in the balcony overlooking the auditorium. The three-manual console of the Skinner-Aeolean pipe organ sat in front of the center aisle below a large stage, with the organist's back to the audience. My responsibility as student organist was to play for the college chapel service once or twice each week. The organist always played a prelude, the name and composer of which appeared on a board above the console, and then everyone joined in singing the morning hymn. Jim Pfohl usually played the rest of the week.

Decorum usually characterized the chapel services. But one day, later on in college in a moment of youthful exuberance, I yielded to peer pressure by playing for the chapel prelude a classical-style arrangement I devised on the then-popular tune, "Music Goes Down and Around." The signboard above the console bore the title "Aria on a Submitted Theme." The students all recognized the theme, but none of the faculty did; in fact, President Walter L. Lingle seemed to like it and complimented me on it. To this day, whenever I meet a college mate I have not seen for some years, remembrance of the "Aria" performance is sure to surface.

Jim Pfohl's wife, Louise Nelson Pfohl, ten years older than Jim, was an exceptionally gifted concert pianist. Throughout my last three years at Davidson, Mrs. Pfohl graciously gave me piano lessons. Regrettably, I could not find time to practice more than two hours every day, often not that much; for to do justice to what she had to offer me would have meant my practicing eight hours every day. Even so, I did save some time for practice (and some college expenses) by eating two meals a day during most of college. The South lost an outstanding artist and Jim Pfohl a devoted wife when Louise Nelson Phohl died of cancer not long after I graduated from Davidson.

To this day I have never given a piano recital. The nearest I came to doing so was during the spring of my junior year at Davidson, when Carlton Chapman and I were scheduled to give a joint concert—he on the organ and I on the piano. Carlton was a senior then and the president of the student body and of the Student Council. Carlton became a Rhodes scholar at Oxford, studied medicine, became Dean of the Dartmouth University School of Medicine, and ultimately the top executive of the Commonwealth Foundation. I felt privileged to share the program planned with him at Davidson. Unfortunately, on the day the concert was to be given, President Lingle's brother, Professor Thomas Lingle, suddenly died and the concert was canceled. Due to the busy college spring programs, it was never rescheduled.

Music occupied my time and energies also in related areas such as the mens' chorus (called "glee club" in those days), which I accompanied, and the football band, where I played the glockenspiel, and the ROTC band, of which I was the cadet captain (my senior year). When the Davidson College band played its spring concert my senior year, I counted five different instruments I had to play with the band during the program—a xylophone, a celeste, kettle drums, a glockenspiel, and the pipe organ. So much for music at Davidson.

Within Davidson's student body we had many men, mostly sons of missionaries, who were brought up in countries where soccer was the national sport. Most of these men were themselves good at soccer. So we organized our own college soccer team with members from China, Korea, and Brazil, and we did quite well. In fact, we tied one year with Duke University for the state championship with a final score of 3–3. At Duke, soccer was a letter sport and had a full-time coach; we at Davidson simply coached ourselves. We were excused from classes, however, to compete on other campuses. As captain, it was my lot to schedule games and make travel arrangements, and it was fun except for one sore experience. During the play-off game with Duke to break the tie, Duke players repeatedly kicked my shins instead of the ball—I was playing left fullback and they beat us by one goal. I spent the next several days in the infirmary with my legs elevated, both shins a black-and-blue swollen pulp. (After that experience I always wore shin guards to play soccer—I never had to before.)

I did not join a social fraternity, nor did I feel any need to, even if I had had the money. Dormitory life was my main social life, for all students lived in the dormitories. Paul McClanahan, my roommate at Stony Brook, was again my roommate when he transferred to Davidson our sophomore year; but he later returned to Monmouth College to graduate. John Stephen Brown, another classmate at Stony Brook, also transferred to Davidson our sophomore year and was my roommate our senior year. John was to be my best man at my wedding, and I was to be his best man at his wedding. In later years, John was to become the senior pastor of the Ginter Park Presbyterian Church in Richmond, Virginia, adjacent to Union Theological Seminary.

During those college days, thumbing a ride was not only an economical way to reach one's destination, but was quite proper and was widely practiced by the best people. It was safe and among college students was reliable for getting around. At that time the only road between Charlotte (Queen City of the South) and Davidson, which was twenty miles north of Charlotte, was a winding, two-lane, tree-lined blacktop built before highway curves were banked. The Eighteenth Amendment was still in effect. North Carolina was a dry state, but there was heavy bootleg traffic from wet Kentucky which reached Charlotte mostly by way of this one road through Davidson. Drivers of "rum runners" evaded lawmen by cruising too fast for highway patrols to catch them. The usual vehicle used was an ordinary-looking two-door sedan with the back seat removed and replaced by the payload secured to the floor by large bolts. With heavy-duty rear springs to accommodate the payload, southbound vehicles normally rode level. But when returning to Kentucky, the rear end would ride conspicuously high, making an empty "rum runner" easy to detect.

I well remember the night when the three of use—Paul McClanahan, Johnny Brown, and I—were returning to Davidson from Charlotte and waited for some kindhearted driver to pick us up. A two-door Model A Ford sedan stopped for us and the driver invited us aboard, and off we went. I sat in the middle between the driver and Paul. It was only when Johnny, the heaviest of us three, observed there was no back seat to sit on that we realized we were in for a fast ride with a bootlegger. Obviously he needed ballast to weigh the car down. We made the twenty miles to Davidson in exactly sixteen minutes, and that included one full minute's stop along the highway to confer with a loaded bootlegger on his way to Charlotte. We heaved a sigh of relief when we walked into our dormitory intact, but the next day my right foot was still sore from pressing hard against the floorboard the night before.

When Laddie graduated from Davidson at the end of my freshman year, our sister Bunny appeared on campus to help represent the Scott family at commencement. Bless her! After she arrived, she deliberately waited a full hour before she told us that she was just engaged to a surgeon, Dr. Ted Stevenson, son of Princeton Seminary's President J. Ross Stevenson, and she informed us that they would be married in three months in Princeton and would depart immediately after that for China, where Ted would direct the Hackett Medical College and Hospital in Canton. She said she and Ted wanted me to play the organ for their wedding.

That wedding took place on September 8, 1934, in Princeton Seminary's Miller Chapel. Dr. J. Ross Stevenson performed the ceremony. Daddy and Mother were in China and so could not attend. Mrs. ("Aunt Florence") Stevenson hosted the large wedding reception in Springdale, their home on the seminary campus. A lovely garden party was planned, but a devastating Atlantic storm swept through New Jersey that afternoon with torrential rain and high winds that blew down trees and power lines and sank the *Morro Castle* off the New Jersey coast. A downpour apparently caught Dr. Albert Einstein, a neighbor who lived across the street, and made him seek shelter in Miller Chapel during the wedding. I was too preoccupied with the organ to notice all that happened, but friends reported seeing Dr. Einstein in the chapel dressed in a turtleneck sweater and canvas sneakers. Bunny and Ted sailed for China the next month.

On December 13 of that same year (1934) I received a telegram from my Uncle Fran Heywood (Mother's brother) which read: "JUST RECEIVED CABLE FROM UNITED STATES CONSUL AT SHANGHAI SAYING BOTH BETTY AND JOHN'S DEAD BODIES FOUND BUT BABY MISSING." A few hours later a telegram came from Laddie at Princeton Seminary: "VERIFIED CABLES SAY BETTY'S AND JOHN'S BODIES FOUND MURDERED BY BANDITS BABY NOT MENTIONED FOLKS NEED OUR PRAYERS LOVE LADDIE."

The next day, large headlines and the portraits of Betty and John were spread across the front page of the *Charlotte Observer*, our local newspaper, telling the news that they had been decapitated and that the fate of their three-month-old baby girl was unknown. We learned that the same kind of news coverage reached everywhere around the world. Follow-up stories gave more details and told of the remarkable escape—the word miracle was most often used—of little Helen Priscilla.

Betty and John's life and death have been best told in the biography written by Mrs. Howard Taylor (Hudson Taylor's daughter-in-law) titled *The Triumph of John and Betty Stam*. This book has been reprinted many times and has been translated into a score of languages. Briefly told, Betty and John, missionaries under the China Inland Mission, were living in Tsingteh, in Anhwei Province, when a large armed force suddenly burst into the city without warning, making any escape impossible. Initial reports called the attackers bandits, but subsequent information identified them as a well-armed band, three thousand strong, part of the Nineteenth Route Red Army, famous for being especially hostile to foreigners and at that time being pursued by the Nationalist Army's 78th Division. These Communist soldiers seized Betty and John and their infant Helen Priscilla, kept them in jail that night, bore them the next day to Miaosheo, a village fifteen miles away, and the next morning (December 8) beheaded them in front of villagers rounded up to witness the executions—John first, then Betty.

Helen Priscilla, not yet three months old, was left in an empty house unattended for about thirty hours before being found by Chinese evangelist Lo. She had escaped execution herself only because a Chinese stranger protested against the soldiers killing her, saying the baby had done no harm to anyone. When the Communist leader rhetorically asked, "Well, would you give your life for the baby?" The man said he would and was immediately decapitated. It took six days for Pastor Lo and his wife to carry the baby, mostly at night for fear of discovery, to the large city of Wuhu, where she had been born. They found her to be in good health, thanks to compassionate wet nurses they encountered along the way.

The Inventor

Kenneth, he knows
How the aeroplane goes,
He watches the workings of all things in
                                        motion;
P'raps someday he'll find,
In the back of his mind,
An auto that flies and that swims in the
                                        ocean.

Love from Betty

Betty's poem given to me for Christmas, 1926.

The background circumstances leading to Betty and John's deaths have never, to my knowledge, been explained publicly. Chinese Communist dogma, being militantly atheistic, regarded the Christian religion as a superstitious propaganda arm of foreign imperialism. And because America was pro Chiang Kai-Shek and therefore their enemy, there could be no worse enemy of the people than the American Christian missionary. An effective means to eliminate this enemy should be to kidnap missionaries one by one, and hold them for large money ransoms; thus they could bleed the Christian missions to death financially, so that missionaries would all eventually have to leave China. Nobody need be harmed, and it could all be blamed on bandits, of whom there were many. The first victims of this strategy were Hayman and Bosshart, two bachelors serving with the China Inland Mission, who were captured early in the 1930s. They were held for ransom and moved about incessantly for over a year awaiting ransom payment. But all Christian missions in China had agreed that no ransom would ever be paid, and Hayman and Bosshart's captivity, month after month without a single ransom payment being made, proved that missions were adamant in their policy. This Communist strategy obviously was failing to do what was intended, and Communist coffers were not being replenished as hoped.

Betty and John Stam on their honeymoon in Tsingtao, 1933.

What to do to get the missionaries out of China? The next step was to actually kill missionaries one by one, on the assurance that "skin for skin! All that a man has he will give for his life" (Job 2:4 RSV). This was calculated to thin missionary ranks in a hurry. Betty and John were the first victims of this new stepped-up strategy. Other missionaries had already died violently, such as John W. Vinson at the hands of Chinese bandits, and the world had taken no note of it. But Betty and John's deaths occurred at a time when newspapers around the world had relatively little news to publish, and this incident was seized upon and reported so extensively and with such widespread condemnation that, in God's plan, this strategy of violent attrition of missionaries stopped dead in its tracks. It was not tried again. Furthermore, God has used Betty and John's story to

JOHN CORNELIUS STAM

AND

ELISABETH ALDEN SCOTT STAM

"Faithful unto death" (Rev. 2:10)

"Beheaded for the witness of Jesus, and for the Word of God."   (Rev. 20:4)

On the 8th of December, 1934, from Eagle Hill, outside the town of Miao Sheo, Anhwei, China they entered into glory.

Memorial brochure, 1934.

sharpen and strengthen Christian commitment around the world to such a degree that its blessing has far exceeded its tragedy.

Betty and John's deaths brought an aching trauma to Daddy and Mother which needed something to assuage it before it over-whelmed them permanently. So it was decided that all of us Scotts must get together for a family reunion the coming summer (1935). This would be held in Tsingtao, the city where we remaining children were born and where Betty and John had had their honey-moon, a seaside city readily accessible to frequent ocean going ships. Bunny, already in China, would leave Ted in Canton and sail to Tsingtao. Helen and Gordon, who had volunteered to replace Betty and John as missionaries to China, would be arriving in China that summer, anyway, under Presbyterian support. Laddie in Princeton Seminary and I in Davidson College were to get there as best we could.

I was able to buy a round-trip ticket across the Pacific with the Canadian Pacific Lines for $166 and sailed from Vancouver on the *Empress of Japan*, the same ship John Stam had gone to China on less than three years before. I disembarked at Yokohama and took a night train to Shimonoseki, where I boarded a small ship to Tsingtao. Daddy and Mother and little Helen Priscilla and Laddie were already there when I arrived. Soon Bunny came, and then Helen and Gordon with their two small children Don and Carol.

Being all together that summer was great medicine for Daddy and Mother. In spite of the awesome pressures of Betty and John's deaths and the thousands of letters they kept receiving from every-where, Daddy and Mother responded beautifully to the savoring again of united-family joys. For we have always been a close-knit family even when scattered across the world over many years.

Laddie and I returned to America together on the *Empress of Canada*. (Incidentally, all four *Empress* ships of the Canadian Pacific Lines were torpedoed and sunk during World War II.) Going east by bus across the United States, we were able to meet and visit Minnesota uncles and aunts and cousins for the first time—blood relatives of Daddy's whom he himself had met for the first time only four years earlier. (Daddy's mother had died when he was born, and a childless couple by the name of Scott had adopted him almost immediately.)

While a student at Wilson College in Pennsylvania, Betty had been very active in the Student Volunteer Movement, an agency most effective in sparking foreign mission advancements early in this century. Betty would have been saddened if she had lived to see the virtual demise of this great student movement, which happened about a year after her death. I happened to be there at the time. It was during the Christmas vacation of 1935–1936 that the quadrennial convention of the Student Volunteer Movement took place in Indianapolis. Many illustrious speakers and leaders were there: John R. Mott, William Temple (later to be Archbishop of Canterbury), Robert E. Speer, Toyohiko Kagawa, and others well known. The man scheduled to play the organ for the convention singing had the flu, we heard. Somehow I was asked to pinch-hit at the organ, which I did. But somehow the leaders of the liberal Student Christian Movement were also there in force and dominated the proceedings to such an extent that, before the convention ended, they had swallowed up the Student Volunteer Movement. I remember the consternation at the snubbing of honored persons and the insidious power plays that characterized those convention days. Ever since, the Student Volunteer Movement has become an ineffective, pathetic, bleary shadow of what it once was.

It was not until between my sophomore and junior years at Davidson that I decided to go into medicine rather than into the ministry. I had already determined in high school to become a foreign missionary. Thus it was that I had two majors, chemistry and philosophy, when I graduated. There were four in my class who graduated *summa cum laude*, including myself, but I was not at the top at commencement, though I did receive the Algernon Sydney Sullivan Award then. Our Class of 1937 was Davidson's centennial class, and an elaborate, costly pageant celebrating the history of Davidson's hundred years was planned for the night before commencement. This pageant was to utilize the entire football field for the stage. There were to be Indian ambushes and Civil War scenes with cavalry and rebel shouts, all with period costumes and equipment. The finale was to introduce Davidson's new alma mater hymn, the words written by English Professor "Jap" Cumming and the music by myself. (Davidson already had a first-rate football song, "O Davidson," composed by E. H. Hamilton while a student before he went to China as a Presbyterian missionary, but no alma mater hymn.) But after all those many months of preparation and rehearsals, when the day came to perform it, heavy, continuous rain deluged the football field, and the performance was canceled.

When I graduated in 1937, no family member was able to be present. That was because every member of my family was then in China except my brother Laddie, who was graduating from Princeton Seminary at the same moment that I was graduating at Davidson. But the family of Dr. R. Morrison King of nearby Concord graciously acted as my family to give me support in many heartening ways, for which I will always be grateful.

Laddie and his high school sweetheart Helen Rhodes were married June 25 that summer and immediately sailed to China as missionaries just as Japan's war with China was gaining full force. After language study in Peking, they were able to reach their Hunan mission station in central China only by going through French Indo-China's port of Haiphong and through Hanoi. After reaching Hunan, they were then to be subjected to almost daily bombing raids by the Japanese for many months.

Looking back at my four years at Davidson, I realized that, for me, they were not years of any particular spiritual growth. But Davidson College did provide something every spring which was strongly positive in its spiritual impact. It was called Spiritual Emphasis Week. One of the most outstanding Presbyterian speakers available anywhere was obtained to speak in chapel each morning that week. Chapel time, compulsory for every student, was extended to a full hour. During my four years at Davidson, the four speakers we had were Clarence E. Macartney of Pittsburgh, Robert E. Speer of New York, Donald Grey Barnhouse of Philadelphia, and Peter Marshall of Atlanta (later to become U.S. Senate Chaplain). These men, all well-known, were well received by the student body members, and their powerful Christian witness raised us high above our usual chapel fare.

CHAPTER SIX

MEDICAL SCHOOL YEARS

WHEN I FIRST TOLD MY FATHER DURING college days that I planned to go into medicine, he knew that I was already committed to the mission field, and he was most supportive of my decision. He said to me then, "Ken, you know that I will do everything in my power to help you, and my love and prayers will always be with you. But to be realistic, you must know at the outset that with only a missionary salary for income and with our having spent all Mother's and my resources to get all you five children through college, I just don't have any money left to help with your medical educational expenses. You'll have to depend on the Lord to see you through on this."

I knew Daddy was right, and I appreciated his frankness in not promising financial support I knew he could not give. Although I had no idea where my support might come from, I had the inner assurance that God was leading me in this direction and would provide what I needed. I can honestly say that at no time did I ever worry about my future or have second thoughts about my decision, for every detail, almost always unanticipated, seemed to open up before me in astonishing and timely fashion. It turned out that even though Daddy could not help me directly with money, time after time a crucial help would materialize because of someone who happened to be one of Daddy's friends.

I applied to only one medical school, the University of Pennsylvania, and was accepted. Then one of Daddy's good friends, Dr. Howard Atwood Kelly, one of the four original faculty pioneers of Johns Hopkins School of Medicine, offered to pay all my tuition expenses for my first two years at Penn. Dr. Kelly had operated on Betty while she was a student at Wilson College. He was the first physician in the United States to make obstetrics and gynecology a separate specialty of its own. He was an earnest Christian and always carried a Greek New Testament in his vest pocket, pulling it out and reading it while waiting, say, for a taxicab (he never owned or drove an automobile himself). As Daddy's friend, he had earlier, during my freshman year at Davidson, sent me a copy of his book *A Scientific Man and the Bible*, published by Harper and Brothers, along with a kindly personal letter (which I still have), not knowing that I would someday choose to enter medicine myself. In earlier years, he had brightened the pages of the *Baltimore Sun* with his running battle with H. L. Mencken, who scoffed at Dr. Kelly's Christian faith. When I first visited Dr. Kelly in his home in Baltimore, it was crammed with historic mementos and even had a few snakes around—his hobby was herpetology (he had earlier designed the reptile building for the Philadelphia Zoo). I was to know him much better during my medical school years when he was a guest speaker at the Keswick Conferences in New Jersey and I was their pianist.

The summer before medical school started, I had the vague hope of earning some necessary income by becoming a church organist somewhere around Philadelphia to help me through medical school. Amazingly, such a job flew into my lap before I even started looking. Another friend of Daddy's known to me as Uncle Will Gehmann, a banker in the Philadelphia National Bank, was also chairman of the music committee of the Presbyterian

Church-of-the-Covenant in Bala-Cynwyd on the outskirts of Philadelphia. Uncle Will informed me that their organist was going to leave soon for another church, and would I be at all interested to apply for that position? I applied and got the job and held it for all four years I was at Penn.

When medical school first began in September 1937, I lived in a rented room. But during my second week there, a faculty member came to me and said that his elderly aunt, who lived two blocks from the medical school, was offering me a room completely free if I would be willing to tend her coal furnace when the weather was cold; she said her daughter could handle the fire during the day while I was in class. I eagerly accepted, and this turned out to be perfect for my needs. The furnace (there were two of them to tend during the very coldest weather) was easy to bank at bedtime and easy to start up again early the next morning. This very nice old Philadelphia home on a quiet street was next door to the home of Dr. Josiah Penniman, then Provost of the University of Pennsylvania.

My experience in medical school was different from that of my classmates only in this respect: most of my classmates hit the books throughout the weekends, since courses were demanding and were taken seriously, whereas church responsibilities in Bala-Cynwyd required that I spend Saturday afternoons and evenings practicing for morning and evening worship services of the next day.

But I usually needed more practice Sunday mornings and came to church before anybody else arrived—I couldn't practice during Sunday School because the adult Bible class always used the church sanctuary then. During the Sunday School hour I usually joined the Sunday School upstairs where the high school and junior high kids were; I enjoyed that, because the kids were great. I remember one Sunday when the subject of Christ's coming again came up. The leader asked, "How many of you would like to see Jesus come today?" All hands went up but one. "Eddie, don't you want to see Jesus come?" the leader asked.

"Yes, of course," Eddie replied, "but I'd rather he not come today."

"Why not today?"

"Well, you see," Eddie said, "I've got my first date tonight with the cutest girl in our school, and I don't want to miss that." To most, that reason was unanswerable. Then, as a medical student preparing for the mission field, I thought of Jesus' words in Matthew 24:14 (NIV), "And this gospel of the kingdom will be preached in the whole world as a testimony to all nations, and then the end will come." In other words, each day that goes by without His returning is mute testimony to the fact that we have *not yet* preached the gospel in the whole world. I realized that we Christians cannot control such things as earthquakes and famines, wars and rumors of war—these are mostly out of our control—but one thing we *can* do to hasten His coming is to get the gospel preached in the whole world. This seemed to me to be a fair indicator of how eager we are to see Jesus return.

Weekly involvement with the church and the friendships there were good for me and did not divert too much time from my medical studies. Fortunately for me, the volunteer choir, which had existed before my coming to Bala-Cynwyd and would have consumed more time than I could have afforded, was mercifully replaced by a precentor (one-man choir). Over the four years I served as organist there, we had several good precentors, then a fine duet, and finally a very good quartet my last two years. One of our quartet vocalists used to sing on Charles E. Fuller's "Old-Fashioned Revival Hour." My memory of these fine vocalists was always a happy one, and I enjoyed working with them. Sundays were therefore always a complete day of rest as far as medical studies were concerned, spent in the company of church friends, and someone among them was sure to drive me home that night in time to roll out the barrels of ashes from the basement into the back alley for collection the next morning.

The Church-of-the-Covenant, whose minister was Dr. Herbert Walter Bieber in those days, kindly released me each summer during July and August, and this permitted me to accept the job of pianist for the Victorious Life Conferences held in Keswick Grove, New Jersey, a job I had each summer while I was in medical school. The conference grounds had begun originally with a colony for rehabilitating alcoholics and drug addicts through the power of Christian witness and prayer and surrender to Christ. To this Colony of Mercy, as it was named, was added a conference center known as America's Keswick, patterned somewhat after England's Keswick. Conference after conference was held all summer, led by outstanding Christian speakers, to know whom was one of the richest blessings of my life.

I have already mentioned Dr. Howard A. Kelly, exuberant even in his nineties and always wearing a red rose in his coat lapel. I can see him now, standing on the conference platform, holding aloft his little Greek New Testament and explaining that the Greek verb *aphorontes* in Hebrews 12:2 means "look away," that is, looking away from ourselves to Jesus. Then, almost hopping up and down for emphasis, he would give a big smile and tell everybody, "Stop stewing in your own juices. Look away at *Him*."

Another speaker at Keswick whom I always loved to hear and to be with was Dr. Robert C. McQuilkin, founder of Columbia Bible College in Columbia, South Carolina, another dear friend of my father's and a man who attributed his own great missionary vision to my father. He was Uncle Bob to me and in many ways has been a role model in my life. Dr. and Mrs. McQuilkin had repeatedly tried to get to the mission field and were dramatically blocked each time. On their last try, on the very night before they were to board their ship to sail overseas (and with all their freight already on board), their ship caught fire in the harbor and sank.

I last saw Dr. McQuilkin when he was a patient in Johns Hopkins Hospital shortly before his death. His sister was a missionary in Korea; her husband, Lloyd Henderson, was mysteriously killed near Manchuria in 1930 while I was a student in Pyengyang, probably by the Japanese. Mrs. McQuilkin's brother, Dr. Tom Lambie, was a medical missionary in Ethiopia when the Italians occupied that country, at which time he became a doctor without a country, because he had taken Ethiopian citizenship in order to register hospital property. It was my privilege to be Dr. Lambie's roommate for a full week during one of Keswick's conferences. His knowledge of hymns was prodigious. I remember him singing, as he sat on the edge of his bed, from memory all twenty-some stanzas of Annie Cousin's lovely hymn, "The Sands of Time are Sinking."

Probably Daddy's closest friends on earth were Phillip E. Howard and his brother-in-law Charles G. Trumbull and Dr. Howard's son Phillip E. Howard Jr., all of them editors of the *Sunday School Times*, a Philadelphia-based weekly journal no longer published. While a medical student, I was privileged to visit these gracious people a number of times in their homes in New Jersey. Dr. Phillip E. Howard Sr., an alumnus of the University of Pennsylvania himself, very kindly took the time to accompany me to the office in the University of Pennsylvania responsible for student scholarships and with his quiet prestige and persuasiveness successfully obtained for me a tuition scholarship for my final two years of medical school. Years later, while I was in Korea as a missionary, Phillip E. Howard Jr., the father of Thomas and David Howard and Elisabeth Elliott (whose husband Jim was killed by Auca Indians in Ecuador), would be the first to inform me of my own father's death and would ask me to write a biographical sketch about Daddy for publication in the *Sunday School Times*.

Even though I was preoccupied with medical studies—and properly so—somehow my love of music would get me involved in extracurricular situations in addition to my church organ responsibilities. A radio preacher and conference speaker who lived in Bala-Cynwyd, Rowan Pearce, had regular early-morning devotional broadcasts over Philadelphia's radio station WFIL. His wife sang, his son Rowan and daughter Jean played trumpets, and his twelve-year-old son Bill a trombone. For a number of weeks I played the piano for their broadcasts. Those were the days before programs could be prerecorded, and I remember our riding to the studio through freezing predawn darkness to make it in time for the live broadcasts.

For many months I also played the piano for another Christian broadcast. E. Schuyler English, a minister and editor, had a weekly Bible program broadcast during the daytime. Most people remember him as the Editorial Committee Chairman for the New Scofield Reference Bible (Dr. Frank E. Gaebelein was also on that committee).

Early in the spring of my first year at Penn I did something which in retrospect seems rather foolish. I felt the need for some exercise and bought a pair of roller skates, my first ever. I had done much ice skating in Korea, but I soon learned there were some differences. What I did for weeks was to skate on the residential streets of West Philadelphia at night before bedtime, a time when it was cool and the streets were deserted—I had them all to myself, and it was free. Unlike ice skating, where the surface is always level, West Philadelphia has rolling terrain and skating on inclined streets presented a situation I had little experience with, especially going downhill. I tried to be careful. But one night while coasting downhill and enjoying the exhilaration of it, a delivery van came up the hill toward me and its headlights blinded me. I tried to get out of the way, took a spill against the curb, and landed on a pile of broken glass bottles, cutting myself in a few places. Since horse-drawn milk wagons regularly traversed those residential streets, I reported next morning to the university infirmary. In those days tetanus toxoid had not yet become available generally, and I was started cautiously on tetanus antitoxin, which is made of horse serum. Because I am allergic to horse serum, I spent almost a week in the infirmary with serum sickness. A couple of days after I rejoined my classmates in school, the professor of microbiology happened to lecture on the tetanus bacillus. When he stated that tetanus commonly threatens irresponsible little boys who go roller skating on city streets, everyone turned around and looked directly at me; all I could do was grin back. I gave my skates away and thereafter got my exercise by swimming in the university pool.

Between my second and third years at Penn, Daddy and Mother came home from China on their scheduled furlough, together with Betty and John's little girl Helen Priscilla. They then lived in Payne Hall in Princeton, the missionary furlough apartments across Alexander Street from the Seminary. I visited them when I could, but it was not always easy. One weekend, rather than take a late train to Philadelphia Saturday night, I studied the railroad schedule and figured that connections would be just right for me to leave Princeton early Sunday morning, catch a local Philadelphia train at Princeton Junction, get off the local at Trenton, catch an express train at Trenton a few minutes later, and arrive at Philadelphia Thirtieth Street Station in good time to take the Norristown commuter train to Bala-Cynwyd, where I would walk up the street to the Church-of-the-Covenant in time to begin playing the chimes at 10:45.

I started out as planned. But at Princeton Junction, the local train was late and, to my horror, the express train I was to catch in Trenton flew by, having track priority, and was followed a few minutes later by the local train. I was truly worried, because there was no way I had of reaching anyone at church to warn them I couldn't be there. I explained my predicament to the conductor. To my astonishment, the local train not only made up for lost time but arrived in Thirtieth Street Suburban Station well ahead of schedule. Not only so, but the conductor had phoned for the Norristown commuter train to wait for me, which it did. When I stepped off the train, the Norristown commuter had already delayed its run by twenty minutes. Its conductor, watch in hand, asked me, "Are you the man we're waiting for?" I said weakly, "Yes," and hopped on. Even this train made up some of its lost time, and I arrived, panting up the hill, just in time to start playing the chimes at 10:45 and the organ prelude at 10:55 as scheduled. Needless to say, I never tried that plan again.

Early in the summer of 1940, after completing my third year at Penn, I bought a secondhand 1935 two-door Ford sedan, drove to Ishpeming, Michigan, (on the northern peninsula) to see Bunny and Ted and their two boys following their return from Canton on furlough. Daddy was traveling all over America speaking. While in Denver, he was injured in a traffic accident and was hospitalized for weeks. So I left Bunny and Ted and drove Mother and Helen Priscilla out to Denver to visit Daddy, then came back east to keep my commitment at Keswick.

When Helen and Gordon returned from China on furlough that same summer and settled for the year in Lansdowne, outside Philadelphia, I lived with them in their home that final medical school year. In September, I remember I registered for my first presidential election by walking into the local fire station in Lansdowne, giving my address and signing my name—nothing was needed for identification besides my driver's license. That one act was to lift me out of a serious frustration two years later when I was to apply for permission to take the state medical licensing examination.

At that same time, I was able to find a small apartment for Daddy and Mother in Ardmore, since by then the ominous war threats in the Far East made it clear that they would not be returning to China right away. It had been difficult to find apartments for rent. But when I learned that my friends Jim and Betsy Crothers were planning to leave their apartment in Ardmore, we arranged it so that Daddy and Mother could walk into it after them. Jim had been in Laddie's class in the Pyengyang Foreign School and Betsy had been my classmate there. At PYFS Jim had a piano-playing style that I greatly admired and tried to emulate at school, and so it was that I learned to play hymns the way he did— firm and full-chorded without frivolous embellishments. In Ardmore Jim was just completing his time in the Ardmore Presbyterian Church as its assistant minister. The apartment he and Betsy vacated had the advantage of being within walking distance of that same church. And since Daddy and Mother were close friends of its pastor, Ardmore became their church home.

T. Edward Ross, a leading elder in that Ardmore church, taught its Adult Bible class. Each Christmas season he used to invite his class to a sumptuous dinner and program in his home. That Christmas (1940), Mr. Ross arranged to have George Beverly Shea come from Chicago—Shea was then with Moody Bible Institute's Radio Station WMBI—to sing at his dinner party. Mr. Ross also asked me to play to accompany Shea. That was when I first met Bev Shea and had the high privilege of accompanying him on the song he had just composed, "I'd Rather Have Jesus." He delighted everyone there with many choice favorites, including "Sweet Little Jesus Boy."

Now that my parents were living in the Philadelphia area, Daddy began his annual custom of buying two season tickets to the Friday afternoon concerts of the Philadelphia Orchestra in the Academy of Music. Mother never went, but Daddy usually did, and he always hoped that I would be able to accompany him. I would have loved to, but classes and later internship and residencies usually prevented it. However, over several years, I was able to hear some wonderful programs with Daddy, first under Stokowski, then under Ormandy. And I was particularly thrilled to hear my friend Jorge Bolet play Rachmaninoff's Third Piano Concerto with the Philadelphia Orchestra. (Bolet, a schoolmate and friend since Stony Brook days, years later succeeded Rudolph Serkin as piano head at Curtis School of Music.) Over the years, Daddy developed quite a friendship with William Kincaid, top flautist in the Philadelphia Orchestra.

Going back in time a little, I want to mention that during my second year at Penn, several of us students approached Dr. Donald Grey Barnhouse, pastor of the Tenth Presbyterian Church in Philadelphia, to ask if he would be willing to teach Bible to some of us medical students once a week, preferably early in the morning before school classes began. To our delight, he said he would, and he offered the use of the Sunday School room next to his church's sanctuary for every Wednesday morning at seven o'clock. Most of the students who attended were from Penn; there were quite a few also from Jefferson Medical College, and several from Temple University.

Dr. Barnhouse taught these classes for many months. When he could no longer continue, Charles Ferguson Ball took over as teacher, but the classes continued in the Tenth Church Sunday School room. Dr. Ball was the pastor of the nearby Bethany Collegiate Presbyterian Church and was married to the sister of John Bellingham, my classmate at Stony Brook; he taught this class almost two years. During my last year at Penn, when Dr. Ball could no longer continue teaching us, my father taught this Bible class;

with my Ford I was able to pick him up in Ardmore and reach the Sunday School room at Tenth Church by seven o'clock.

These early morning Bible classes were never very large, but they were regularly attended and were much appreciated by us medical students and the few interns and residents who were able to come.

People have asked me whether attending medical school jeopardized my Christian faith in any way. It is true that a classmate and medical fraternity brother of mine at Penn, who had godly parents and was a strong Christian in high school, seemed to have lost his faith, but this change took place during his college days, not in medical school. But for me, as with many other physicians I know, medical studies only strengthened my faith, because they enabled me to appreciate, as I could never have appreciated otherwise, how "fearfully and wonderfully made" all living creatures are. I came to appreciate how absurd and naive anyone must be to dismiss the necessity of a Creator-God to design and bring about this amazing world we live in. Only a deeply prejudiced mind, blind to reality, could imagine that the life we see every day just happened by itself. I also noticed that those persons who spoke of evolution as a fact were persons quite untrained in biological sciences.

When I finally received my medical degree in West Philadelphia Convention Hall in June 1941, Daddy and Mother were there. To my knowledge, that graduation was the only graduation of any kind by any of us five children that was ever attended by both Daddy and Mother. And then for a graduation present, Daddy took me to Washington, D.C., to visit historic sites before I was to begin my internship.

CHAPTER SEVEN

INTERNSHIP AND MARRIAGE

THE PRESBYTERIAN HOSPITAL IN PHILADELPHIA, near the University of Pennsylvania and later a part of the university, offered a two-year rotating internship, and this is where I began on July 1, 1941. My first service there was in the pathology and laboratory department. One of my duties was to draw blood for the laboratory each morning from all patients throughout the hospital for whom blood tests were ordered. It was when I came to the men's and women's medical wards that I first met Ann Bicksler, who was supervisor over both wards. In most of the hospital, I had to find the patients I was to stick, unless some student nurse volunteered to show me where to go. But whenever I came to the medical wards, Ann would always personally take me around to the patients I was looking for. This saved me the time and effort of having to ask and hunt around for my quarry.

During my two months on that service I came to appreciate not only what a considerate person Ann is, but also what a good supervisor she is, since her wards were always clean and well managed and her patients smiling and cheerful. She was also an attractive young nurse, but so were most of the young nurses at Presbyterian Hospital, which had a reputation for producing attractive, competent, high-quality nurses. It was readily understandable why most of the interns and residents, (myself included), all of whom were required to be unmarried, liked to date Presbyterian Hospital nurses, and they dated them frequently.

Somehow it was not until the middle of January 1942—six months after I came to Presbyterian Hospital and five weeks after Peal Harbor—that I had my first date with Ann. I took her to Fairmount Park, where we were almost locked up in its Horticultural Hall at closing time. And then we went to Philadelphia's Chinatown for the first Chinese food Ann had ever tasted (she liked it). After that, I dated nobody else, and things moved along rapidly.

Ann was the only woman I had ever dated that I always felt completely comfortable and sanguine with. This was remarkable

Ann Bicksler: the nurse I fell in love with and married, 1942.

because her background was so very different from mine. I was a son of missionaries, brought up in strongly Christian communities, and I was world-traveled. Ann was brought up in a small Pennsylvania-Dutch town and in a farming community that had known much of the economic deprivations of the Great Depression and in a family that was not particularly religious. Yet I soon recognized her as being highly motivated, responsible, and well-organized, and with good common sense—a born leader with the unique faculty of enabling others to work happily with her—and she was honest and unpretentious. Best of all, she seemed to enjoy my company as much as I enjoyed hers, and soon we were deeply in love. The clincher to our love was the fact that, knowing from the beginning that I was committed to the mission field, Ann accepted this commitment for herself and never tried to dissuade me from it. Over our succeeding years together, she was to become an effective, exemplary missionary in her own right.

On March 8 we were engaged, and on July 11, 1942, we were married in the Church-of-the-Covenant of Bala-Cynwyd, where I had been organist for four years. Daddy and our minister Dr. Bieber jointly conducted our marriage ceremony, and Fred Stark (the man I had succeeded at Bala-Cynwyd) played the organ for us. Bunny was Ann's matron of honor, and Ann's brother Lester gave her away. The only other relatives Ann had at the wedding were her stepmother and her grandmother Hannah Brightbill, a woman who used to keep praying, when Ann was a young girl, that Ann would marry a minister or a missionary (Ann had protested at the time that that was impossible). At the wedding, Hannah Brightbill sat on the front seat of the church, a very satisfied, I-told-you-so expression on her face; she lived just long enough to see her prayers answered affirmatively.

With the war on, the two-year internship was shortened to one year. Near the end I applied to take the Pennsylvania State medical examination for licensure, but was told I could not take it because I could not produce my birth certificate to prove I was an American citizen (mine was somewhere in Washington in the State

Department). How about my American passport? No, that wouldn't do. How about my original commission as a lieutenant in the U.S. Army? No, that wouldn't do, either. Well, did I have a certificate of voting registration? Fortunately I was able to get one—the one I had gotten by walking into the fire station in Lansdowne and signing my name. So on that basis, I was permitted to take the state board examination.

Ann and I were married July 11, 1942, and we set out on our two-week honeymoon in our 1935 two-door Ford sedan. Gasoline rationing was already in effect east of the Susquehanna River, and A ration coupons were not being issued for such purposes as honeymooning trips. So our strategy had to be to make a beeline to where gas rationing was not yet in effect, namely, western North Carolina. It so happened that Helen and Gordon and their five children were living then in Montreat, in western North Carolina, and Bunny, who had come by train to be Ann's matron of honor, was also living with her three boys in the same house with Helen and Gordon (Bunny's husband Ted, who had returned alone to China, was already a prisoner of the Japanese in the Philippines).

Daddy and Mother had not yet visited their children and grandchildren in Montreat, but wanted to. Traveling in wartime having its inconveniences, it seemed like a wonderful idea to everyone for us to load all five of us into our car and head directly for Montreat. With our combined A ration coupons we could make it through Pennsylvania and Virginia, both being in ration zones at that time; rationing had not yet reached western North Carolina.

We were packed like sardines, including much baggage, but we survived the trip fine. Earlier, Daddy had sent a news item to the *Mainline Times of Philadelphia* announcing our wedding. Unfortunately, he had included in his report the spicy information that "the groom's parents and the groom's sister were to accompany the wedding couple on their honeymoon in beautiful western North Carolina." Later, when Ann and I returned to Philadelphia, great were the whoops and guffaws our friends greeted us with, sparked by the *Mainline Times* report.

After our initial welcome by eight exuberant little nephews and nieces in Montreat, Ann and I did spend most of our two weeks together alone, as honeymooners should, in the mountains west of Asheville. Returning to Philadelphia was not so easy, since the ration zones kept creeping westward. We barely managed to make it back to Philadelphia by following some backroads through West Virginia.

CHAPTER EIGHT

WORLD WAR II YEARS IN U.S. ARMY: CHINA-BURMA-INDIA THEATER

O N AUGUST 1, I REPORTED TO CARLYLE BARRACKS as a first lieutenant in the Army Medical Corps. By September 1, I was assigned to the Eleventh Armored Division just being formed in Camp Polk (now Fort Polk) in Louisiana. Here I was appointed a company commander in its Armored Medical Battalion. Every medical officer there had to be able to drive every kind of vehicle in the division, that is, from a motorcycle to a half-track—excluding a tank. I liked that, for I have always loved to operate anything that has a motor.

But I missed Ann, who had gone back to nursing in the Presbyterian Hospital. The tiny nearby village of Leesville, Louisiana, had no place to accommodate my bride. But a month later, a kind captain and a lieutenant, who had been able to find a small apartment for themselves and their wives, took pity on me and invited Ann and me to squeeze in with them. Ann quickly joined me, but our life together there was short-lived, for within a month I received orders from Washington instructing me to report to San Francisco *alone* within a week. There were ten other medical officers named on those orders, all first lieutenants, three of whom had Chinese names and two more with names I recognized as missionaries' sons brought up in China. One, Frances C. Tucker, I had known well since childhood. From that list I deduced that my destination must be China.

It was a tearful Ann I said good-bye to on the station platform in Asheville, North Carolina. Bunny, who had heard nothing at all from or about Ted in almost a year, was magnificent at bucking Ann up before Ann returned to Philadelphia to resume her life as a nursing supervisor.

In San Francisco, security required us all to say nothing to anybody about anything. We medical officers were each issued a .45 Colt automatic pistol and a 30-calibre carbine, knowing that the Japanese had never signed the Geneva Convention guaranteeing immunity to medical personnel. One lieutenant colonel (not a medical officer) foolishly phoned his wife to say that he was sailing overseas the next day; he was immediately arrested and court-martialed. I wanted to phone Ann and tell her that I loved her and missed her, but to do so I had to wait twelve-and-a-half hours until my call could go through. Finally, with each of us on the line, acoustics were so bad that she could not understand me and I could not make out anything she was trying to say; then our time was up. That was to be our last conversation for the next two-and-a-half years.

Our ship, the luxury liner *Ile de France*, now converted into a troop transport, sailed from San Francisco on December 7, 1942, exactly one year after Pearl Harbor. There were ten thousand troops on board, quartered mostly in the freight holds. The eleven medical officers listed in my orders were part of a contingent of three hundred army officers destined for combat training and liaison duty with the Chinese Army. All this came to light as soon as we put out to sea. Frank Tucker and I shared a single small cabin with four other officers.

Chinese language study for all three hundred officers began immediately and was very ably conducted by a professional linguist from Yale University who himself had begun learning Chinese only two weeks before. Soon the three hundred officers were divided into eleven smaller classes, each one to be taught by one of us medical officers. With textbooks provided us, I had to learn fast. We soon noticed that the higher an officer's rank, the less inclined he was to learn Chinese; the several brigadier generals didn't try at all.

Our voyage, which took six weeks, was the only voyage the *Ile de France* ever made on the Pacific Ocean. It cruised at twenty-two knots, which for short periods could be increased to twenty-four knots. Japanese submarines, then very active in the Pacific, were reputed to reach only twenty-one knots. Radar was new, and a British radar team was on board, but a crucial piece of radar equipment never reached our ship in time; so the radar team was superfluous. To give us some protection, a dirigible accompanied us overhead for the first two days at sea, then left.

We had to refuel in Pearl Harbor, for this ship, built for Atlantic runs only, had a limited fuel and water capacity. Then we headed south and crossed the equator, and we disembarked for one day only in Wellington, New Zealand, on Christmas Day. We then sailed south of Australia, then northward to Bombay, where we three hundred officers left the ship in mid-January 1943. The ten thousand troops on board continued on to Karachi and beyond.

Throughout those six weeks at sea, everyone had to maintain strict blackout. South of the equator was stifling hot and windless. No air-conditioning existed for anybody, least of all for the ten thousand troops in the holds. Each night a different unit would come on deck to sleep in fresh air. But when faced with going back down again to make room for the next unit to come up on deck, three separate units during our voyage refused to go below again and mutinied; so we had prolonged court-martials on board. Such was life at sea while we three hundred officers were trying to learn Chinese.

After disembarking in Bombay, all the officers took a train to the Ramgarh Training Center in Bihar state, northwest of Calcutta and not far from Ranchi. This huge military camp had earlier housed Axis prisoners-of-war, mostly Italians. There were still graffiti to be seen on some walls, such as *Ora Pro Nobis* and other expressions of disconsolation. Now it was the location of the Chinese Army in India.

After the Chinese Army in Burma became totally cut off from China early in the war and then was decimated by starvation, giant leeches, tropical ulcers, malignant malaria, dysentery, and every conceivable form of jungle rot during their desperate struggle to escape into India, the few surviving soldiers were brought to Ramgarh and there became the nucleus of a military training center for Chinese Army officers and other cadre to be flown across the Hump into India for special training. The courses given were conducted by the Chinese Training Combat Command of the U.S. Army within the China-Burma-India theater, then commanded by General Joseph C. Stilwell, better known as Vinegar Joe.

When our three-hundred-officer contingent arrived by train into Camp Ramgarh, General Stilwell was there in person to meet us. Without mincing matters, he told us that first day, "If any of you men are thinking of getting home in the foreseeable future, forget it. You are here and you will *stay* here until this war is won." At that point, my self-pity leaped to new heights, for I had lived with my bride a total of only six weeks when those army orders sent me overseas. Up to then, the allies had been on the run and were losing the war everywhere. Rommel's defeat in North Africa was still in the future. Among ourselves we tried to give some rational guesses as to how long it would be before the war would be over and we could return home. The guesses ranged anywhere from ten years to twenty years or more. Stilwell did not raise our morale during that welcoming speech.

Living conditions were not the worst. But within a week of our arrival, a hundred officers were down and out with acute amoebic dysentery. We traced the trouble to our food handlers. The cooks in the officers' mess were Muslims and were soon exonerated by stool tests: besides, only hot cooked food was being served. But several of the waiters, who were Hindus, demonstrated pathogenic amoebae. But why such a rapid onset, affecting a third of us? Every dinner began with a soup served in large shallow soup dishes, quite lukewarm by the time it reached the dinner table. We noticed that, to get a firmer grip, the waiters would plant a thumb inside the dish well below the water-line. We learned that the latrine used by the Hindu waiters had no toilet paper; in fact, they would not have used toilet paper even if provided, since every good Hindu has been trained to use his *left* thumbnail for wiping himself after stool; fingers of the *right* hand were used for eating. But with a busy officers' mess like ours, a waiter had to use *both* hands. The solution employed was to provide water, soap, and a basin immediately outside the food-handlers' latrine and to post an enlisted man beside this to compel hand washing after each visit.

There were other indigenous practices to be reckoned with, sometimes with troublesome and mystifying results. Personal laundry was done by the dhobi, a man who took your soiled clothing and linen, dunked it in a nearby stream, then flailed a broad rock or concrete slab with your dripping khaki pants or shirt or whatever, then spread them on the bank to dry. Such treatment aged one's clothing prematurely, which was understandable. Most of the officers soon developed a peculiar itching skin rash, peculiar in that it occurred only at the nape of the neck or somewhere along the waistline. It looked and felt like a poison ivy dermatitis, and its burning and itching was infuriating. No powder or calamine lotion seemed to help, and it was at its worst after a new change of clothes. Could this be a new form of athlete's foot or the result of local chiggers or scabies? Some observant officer noticed that the location of skin eruption coincided with laundry marks on his shirt collars and undershorts. Sure enough! The dhobies had no laundry ink, but were using the juice of a certain local plant capable of making a mark that could survive several washings. One might think that this discovery would immediately stop this practice and the misery it brought, but unlearning an old method is often more difficult than learning a new one, and so this particular misery died only slowly. Also, within a week or two of our arrival, athlete's foot became epidemic (I had to spend a whole week on a bed in the station hospital to control my own case of athlete's foot), and it was stemmed only after socks were boiled.

There were more serious health problems. For example, malaria, including the dreaded malignant malaria caused by the

Plasmodium falciparum protozoa, was rife throughout most of Southeast Asia and the Indian subcontinent, including Ramgarh. Atabrine (quinacrine) had not yet appeared, and Aralen (chloraquine) was even farther in the future. Quinine was available, but was in very short supply because the Japanese had complete control of Java, where most of the world's cinchona plants were grown. Prophylaxis was not possible, even for Chinese and American personnel in Ramgarh, who had not yet developed immunity to malaria and were therefore especially vulnerable. I recall two strapping soldiers in Ramgarh from North China, who began feeling ill at 2:00 P.M.; by 5:00 P.M. they were sick enough to be rushed to the hospital; by 6:00 P.M. they were unconscious, and by 10:00 P.M. they were dead. This made quite an impression on me. Fortunately, the female *anopheles* mosquito does not bite during the daytime, but once sundown arrived, we rolled down sleeves, buttoned up collars, applied insect repellent liberally, and continued a perpetual slapping motion that resembled Saint Vitus's dance until safely bedded down behind a mosquito bar. This was to be my nightly routine for the next two-and-a-half years.

Almost everyone in Ramgarh, Chinese and American, had enough food. But at one time a Chinese engineering battalion had about 150 men hospitalized for beriberi, both the wet and the dry types, caused by Vitamin B1 deficiency, and resulting in a number of deaths. No other military unit had this problem. Why? Three of us medical officers were told to find out, and the explanation was not hard to find. The only food issued to the Chinese military units in Ramgarh was salt and unpolished rice. Each quartermaster would requisition once a month from the British what he estimated his unit would need for the coming month, and he always got as much as he requisitioned. The quartermaster of this particular battalion, not wanting to be caught short, had for many months requisitioned far more than his unit could use. His available storage space became filled with rice, and he finally became persuaded that he would indeed receive whatever amount he asked. What to do now with the enormous supply on hand? He would requisition no more until he had used up what he already had, which had been sitting there for almost a year, now damp and somewhat moldy from the previous drenching monsoons and kept super-hot under a sun-drenched metal roof. The reddish-brown pericarp surrounding each grain of unpolished rice had completely deteriorated, and with it vanished all the vitamins that make unpolished rice a wholesome, almost complete food rich in Vitamin B. Hence the beriberi, which is exceedingly serious and life threatening when it occurs. Fortunately, we seldom see it today, even among the severely undernourished.

The commanding officer of the military hospital in Ramgarh was Dr. Gordon Seagrave, the famous "Burma Surgeon" and former Baptist medical missionary. His entire nursing staff was the Burmese nurses he had trained in his mission hospital in Namkham, Burma—they were not really Burmese at all, but Christian tribeswomen largely from the Karen and Shan and Kachin tribes of northern Burma. Dr. Seagrave and his nurses had fled from the Japanese the year before, along with the Chinese Army troops surviving the escape from Burma who now made up the military cadre in Ramgarh. That exodus from Burma to India over treacherous jungle mountains had decimated countless Chinese troops through hunger, disease, and other horrors peculiar to that area such as Naga ulcers (a malignant form of jungle rot following leech attachments). Seagrave's books *Wastebasket Surgery*, *Burma Surgeon*, and *Burma Surgeon Returns* make fascinating reading today.

In addition to conduction training for Chinese medical officers flown over the Hump from China into Ramgarh, I was also assigned to be in charge of one of the wards in Gordon Seagrave's station hospital. My head nurse was a Kachin princess by the name of Lee Pang-Lu. She and the other nurses were most proficient and worked best when they were under extreme pressure; in fact, they enjoyed working hard, because it kept them from worrying and having nightmares about their families left behind in Burma.

With this hospital connection I was able to learn firsthand about such things as malaria, dengue, kala-azar, amoebiasis, schistosomiasis, tropical sprue, tropical ulcer, and Weil's disease, as well as the beriberi I have already mentioned. Only later on, on the other side of the Hump, would I encounter also typhus and the plague. Tuberculosis (TB) was seen everywhere, but we were quite helpless to do much about it, since the day of chemotherapy had not yet dawned; in desperation and for lack of anything better for TB, we even tried giving an expensive (and worthless) extract of the root of an African plant called *Umkwalo-abo*.

India was at that time under the British. For various historic reasons, including the Opium War, the Chinese regarded Great Britain as their enemy with almost the same emotional intensity as they regarded Japan. Hence, Americans frequently had to act as buffers and middlemen between British and Chinese authorities to prevent a potential shooting outbreak. For example, when it was decided to send a battalion of Chinese troops from Ramgarh to go over the Hump to China in the spring of 1943, I was ordered to accompany them and be their train commander as far as Assam. This was because I spoke English and Chinese and was an American. I was with this battalion for five days and nights as our train headed for Calcutta, then rolled northward until we all boarded a river steamer and rode up the wide Bramaputra River into Assam. Fortunately, all went well; there were no hostile confrontations. I returned to Ramgarh by air from Assam to Delhi, then by train to Ramgarh; on the way I had a clear view of Mount Everest with a snowy plume blowing eastward off its peak, and I also saw the Taj Mahal from the air, its dome covered under a wooden camouflaged shell to deny to the Japanese air force its usefulness as a landmark.

Of great personal concern to me was the health of my brother Francis (Laddie) in Central China. He had almost died from typhoid fever—the Chinese-made typhoid vaccine he had been receiving had the potency of water. Weakened by the typhoid, he had fallen victim to tuberculosis and had spent months at strict bed rest in their mission hospital while Japanese planes made daily bombing raids over the city. He and his family needed to be evacuated from China. But how? I am convinced that it was only by God's providential intervention that I was able to arrange a rescue flight by the Fourteenth Air Force (of General Chenault's Flying Tigers fame), which evacuated the whole family to Calcutta. I was able to meet them in Calcutta and put them up in the Lee Memorial Home for awhile, then see them off by train to Bombay. On arrival in Black Mountain, North Carolina, Laddie was admitted to the Western Carolina State Sanatorium and made a steady and full recovery. It was my concern for him that stirred my own strong desire to become involved with tuberculosis professionally.

After saying good-bye to Laddie and his family in Calcutta's Howrah Station, I wondered how I was going to get back to Ramgarh. Someone directed me to a railroad engine that was going to Ramgarh right away. I found it and was its sole passenger. With a sweep of his arm, its Scottish-Indian engineer invited me to come up into the cab with him, rather than ride in the caboose. I was happy to do so. It was a nice clear day.

The line we rode that day was all single-track, and trains could pass only at railroad stations where there was a siding. For some reason we seemed to be given the right-of-way, for we seldom stopped and frequently steamed through a station where a full train was waiting for us to come through so that it could use the track we had come on.

On one long stretch through open farmland between stations, the engineer suddenly pulled his whistle cord and held it down. At the same time he began slowing down. I couldn't imagine why, because the track ahead looked clear as far as I could see. Then I saw people running toward the track from everywhere, and I noticed that each person seemed to have some kind of produce in his hand. By now the engine was almost crawling. To my surprise the engineer began reaching down and scooping up little bundles of cabbage or corn or beans or whatever the people by the tracks were pushing toward him—all this with much shouting back and forth. Occasionally, some big item like some eggs, and at one time a live chicken, was lifted into the engine cab. Often, if there seemed to be some hesitance to deliver, the engineer would open his throttle and the engine would begin accelerating with loud chug-chugging, and the people on the ground would immediately give in, and he would then close his throttle and slow down, and more produce would enter the cab.

I wondered what the farmers were getting back for all this bounty that was filling the cab, until I looked to the rear and saw the fireman standing on the coal tender busily shoveling coal off the tender onto the ground below. Once, while we were crossing a river, he kept on shoveling the coal, for which the engineer gave him a tongue lashing—coal in the river did nobody any good.

Anyway, without understanding the animated jabbering that I heard during those fascinating twenty minutes of railroad bartering, I got some insight into the give-and-take life of British India. The engineer was a perfect host to me and with a friendly grin offered me a just-acquired tangerine and a stalk of sugar cane to chew on. Before we arrived at the next station, all the produce collected in the cab had been tucked away out of sight. As we puffed into that next station, standing there on the other track was a long troop train loaded with soldiers waiting to enter the single-track we had just been on. Later that day we arrived in Ramgarh. I shall never forget that unique ride.

Throughout my eight-month stay in Ramgarh, I do not remember meeting any Chinese military man who was a Christian. Yet early on, several Chinese officers in the medical unit I was associated with requested that I teach them English and, amazingly, wanted me to use the Bible as a textbook. Although I knew their knowledge of English was pitifully weak, I am glad I decided to go along with them. There were plenty of copies of the Gospel of John available in English, and we got a lot of these together to use. We met once a week, and as time went on, more and more men kept joining, including also Chinese non-commissioned officers, until we had a regular attendance of between twenty and thirty.

I regret that I didn't move along faster in our study because by the time orders came directing our unit to return to China, I still had the crucial last three chapters of John to cover. The class suggested that they meet every other day to get through, then

新生命食堂

NEW LIFE REFRESHMENT

The Chinese Army officers who "completed" the Gospel of John with me in Ramgarh, India, 1943.

finally every day, and this is what we did, completing the Gospel of John the evening before they were to move out of Ramgarh.

Heaven only knows what was accomplished by reading the Gospel of John in English and giving simple explanations in slow, easy English to Chinese military men over the several months this was done. All I know is that attention was rapt, that somehow the gospel narrative penetrated despite language limitations (many intelligent questions were asked), and that during the last class we had, few eyes were dry. Throughout this whole experience I had felt strangely helped.

Prior to the coming of the monsoons I had used the Harley-Davidson motorcycle assigned to me; I found it indispensable to get around the large camp. But with the coming of torrential monsoon rains, I was able to exchange it for a jeep (which was made by Ford). Little could be done during the heavy rains, and Hump traffic was reduced to a trickle.

But as soon as the monsoon rains eased up enough to resume flights over the Hump, Fran Tucker and I were given orders to go into China. Crossing the Hump together in bucket seats of a C-47 (the military name for a DC-3), we were disappointed to be enshrouded in dense clouds throughout the entire flight—we wanted to see some scenery. Little did we realize that the Japanese Zeros were out hunting in force and that on that very day had downed three transport planes crossing the Hump that had become visible to them.

As soon as Fran and I had reached Kunming (the China end of the Hump flight), we set out in a truck down the Burma Road. That first ride took us west to Tali, where there was a large lake some twenty-five miles long and several miles wide. We were sent there to conduct what was euphemistically called a refresher school for Chinese Army medical officers. I say euphemistically because the medical training these men had already had was virtually nil and we were to refresh them on matters they had never heard of before. What medical training they had previously had amounted to little more than sitting in a large hall with about five hundred other students and listening to lecture after lecture given often in Polish or some other language they didn't know. So we had to train groups of medical officers in very basic subjects and in very simple language. We ran this school in Tali for about three months.

Tali, which is on the Burma Road, is beautiful country, but war conditions made for primitive living. Across the lake was a mission hospital run by an elderly Canadian woman doctor who was cheerfully putting up with agonizing privations to serve the people who came to her for medical help available nowhere else. One day I watched in amazement as an attendant held a Coleman gasoline lantern aloft to shed light on an incarcerated hernia this woman was correcting under open-drop ether anesthesia! I believe in guardian angels, and I knew this undaunted saint must have, too. The only alternative would have been for her to say, "I can't help you. Go home and die there." This she had refused to consider.

In Tali we learned that most airplanes would aim for Lake Tali to get their bearings. For some reason the sky over the lake was always clear. And since it was so easy to get thrown one hundred miles off course in a very few minutes by fast air currents, and almost everywhere else was clouded over, American planes and Japanese planes would both head for Lake Tali. We soon learned to distinguish which was which by the sound of their engines, day or night. If we heard a Japanese plane we would immediately get into our slit trenches; if it was an American plane, we stayed put.

While there in Tali, something took place which was embarrassing for me; it was a painful lesson which had to be learned and for which I have ever since been profoundly grateful to God. I am a slow learner of the great lessons of life, and it is only by repetition and persistence on the part of a patient and gracious heavenly Father that I have learned anything at all worth learning. This particular lesson seemed to have come to a head while in Tali. Let me explain.

For years I had enjoyed success and recognition, especially in high school and in college. I was valedictorian when I graduated from Stony Brook School. At Davidson College I had earned Phi Beta Kappa while a junior and had graduated *summa cum laude* and been awarded the Algernon Sydney Sullivan Award at commencement in recognition of student leadership roles that effectively contributed to a swelled ego. I had done well in advanced ROTC and was proud of my army officer commission. Therefore, when I was called into extended active army duty after my internship as a first lieutenant in the Army Medical Corps in August 1942, and was made immediately a company commander in the Armored Medial Battalion of the new Eleventh Armored Division, a position which called for a major, I expected quick promotion. Just as I was about to be made a captain, I was given orders from Washington sending me immediately to the China-Burma-India theater. The policy in the CBI theater, I learned with chagrin on arriving there, was that a first lieutenant must be in the theater for eighteen months before becoming eligible for promotion. As a Christian, I should not have been obsessed with such matters as promotion; but I was. The resulting frustration of being held back as a lieutenant as the months wore on—not getting a fair shake, not being as officially appreciated as I thought I should be—must have made me more of a pill than I realized. And I became inclined to let others do the volunteering for tasks, less inclined to "pitch in" myself. This seemed to be my best way of showing that I felt abused and sorry for myself.

In Tali there were five of us Army medical officers conducting the school I have mentioned. The most senior among us was Paul Hansen, a full colonel and a very fine physician whom everybody liked. Foodwise, we had to live off the land (being guests of the Chinese Army), and about all that seemed available locally were sweet potatoes, bean sprouts, and Chinese cabbage (all healthy foods). Several of the officers used to take it on themselves to go rummaging in the little food shops in Tali in search of some tastier fare to gladden our mess with. I was not one of them.

One evening I was complaining, "Why can't we have something to eat besides cabbage and sweet potatoes?" Colonel Hansen, usually congenial and even-tempered, exploded, "Scott, I'm getting sick and tired of you whining and telling others what they can do. Why don't *you* go on the street and look for some of these things yourself? If you'd help, we'd all be happier."

I was stunned, and my ears must have turned beet red. Colonel Hansen was absolutely right and said what needed to be said, and I knew it. Though shamed and embarrassed at the time, I have been everlastingly grateful to him for this reprimand. The next morning Colonel Hansen was his usual friendly self to me, as he was to everybody. He will always be one of my heroes and the man I believe God sent into my life at that particular time. Soon after that, I was promoted to captain and eventually to major. My colleague and close friend Fran Tucker became a major before I did, and eventually a lieutenant colonel; he fully deserved that recognition, even though he never took ROTC. Somehow the experiences in life that teach me the most are experiences that make me wince when I think about them. In this case, I had let myself become ridiculously like a first lieutenant we knew in Ramgarh who, because he had been a first lieutenant longer than any other first lieutenant on the post, asserted his supposed superiority by insisting that every other first lieutenant salute him whenever he was spoken to. Obviously, the servant-mind of Christ was still foreign to my nature.

After about three months of conducting this refresher course in Tali, the school was disbanded, and each of us U.S. Army medical officers was assigned to a different Chinese military unit as its liaison medical officer. My assignment was to the headquarters of the Chinese Second Army, which then was covering about six thousand square miles and was located well south of the Burma Road in a rugged mountainous territory near the Laotian and Burmese borders between the Mekong and Salween Rivers. This Second Army consisted of three divisions; its headquarters was in Shunning. For some reason its commanding general, a Lt. General Wang, took a liking to me and insisted that I accompany him wherever he went, and I ate all my meals with him and his staff. Here I was, a mere captain, at his table with nobody else lower than a full colonel. But all of his top commanding officers came from the part of North China where I was brought up, and we all spoke the same dialect, which helped a great deal.

In the spring of 1944, General Wang gave me permission to visit all the division and regimental headquarters in his command, which could be done only by foot along lonely mountain trails— up and down, up and down—with a Chinese sergeant as my aide and a donkey to carry my gear and my food (mostly C rations and K rations). This trip took me exactly six weeks. Along one trail I saw the remains of a peasant whom Kawa tribesmen, who were headhunters, had decapitated the day before. Incidentally, I always carried my .45 and my carbine (manufactured by the Underwood typewriter people) with me; these had early on been issued to all American medical officers, since the Japanese had never respected Geneva conventions (as I mentioned earlier).

As I was approaching the Thirty-third Division, the last of the three division headquarters I was to visit, I was greeted by a sight I can never forget. Stumbling zombie-like along the road leading to their encampment were hundreds of sick and weary recruits arriving as infantry replacements. Many would have to squat every hundred yards or so because of bloody diarrhea. Others, supported by a buddy on either side, would amble along unconscious from cerebral malaria. I saw many such persons, since malignant malaria was rife throughout all that area, and I knew that before the day was over they would all be dead. I learned that these recruits had started out on foot, twenty thousand strong, from Central China some three months before. They had followed back trails to avoid the Japanese, who controlled all the major transportation routes. For food along the way they had been issued one month's supply of rice, which they carried in a narrow stockinette worn like a bandoleer. By the time these recruits reached the Thirty-third Division in the south-west corner of China, the twenty thousand had dwindled to about five thousand men. These were untrained, sick, malnourished, homesick, and quite unable to fight or even think. But they were still alive; the other fifteen thousand had perished along the way—for various reasons, they could not have deserted.

In June 1944, shortly after I got back to the Second Army Headquarters in Shunning, the Salween Campaign began. Its purpose was to reclaim the use of the Burma Road, which the Japanese controlled from the Salween River westward. The idea was to connect the China stretch of the Burma Road with the Ledo Road, an entirely new road which the U.S. Army Engineers were then laying from Ledo, Assam, in northeast India, across northern Burma toward Wanding, the point where the Burma Road crossed the Chinese border. This meant driving the Japanese out of southern Yunnan and northern Burma, all of this being rugged mountainous terrain.

Leaving Shunning, all of us walked some fifteen to twenty miles each day along jungle trails, since there were no roads. Food was supposed to be air dropped to us, but within a week the monsoon rains began pelting down, and that meant no air drops were possible for the next six weeks. So all we had to eat were potatoes grown by local peasants. Ironically, when the rains finally slackened enough to permit the first C-47 (DC-3) to appear, what came out of the sky was powdered milk, powdered eggs, and powdered potatoes—but they tasted so good! While the heavy rains were coming, I remember crossing a swollen river on logs tied together into rafts, holding onto the halters of our pack cows, which had to swim across. On the other side was a steep hill. Now, a cow's back is not shaped to hold a saddle, and I remember seeing our field radio slide off the back of a pack cow as it struggled up the hill; the radio tumbled and bounced all the way back down the slope almost to the water's edge. Miraculously, the radio still worked afterwards.

During that campaign, the enemy was not so much the Japanese as it was the terrain, the weather, and disease, particularly dysentery and malaria—I mean the malignant kind of malaria. Some strains of malignant malaria are more frightening than others; I saw whole villages wiped out by it. Incidentally, malaria and tuberculosis are still the leading infectious-disease killers in the world today—far ahead of all other infectious diseases combined. Of course, we encountered other diseases as well.

During the Salween Campaign I developed amoebic hepatitis and in September had to be evacuated to the Ninety-fifth Station Hospital in Kunming with a swollen liver—I weighed only 130 pounds.

I will not easily forget my two weeks as an inpatient in the Ninety-fifth Station Hospital and being on the receiving end of autocratic medical care with no options allowed. For example, no patient could be discharged before getting a dental clearance (a wise policy, since dental emergencies anywhere in the China theater could be dealt with only in this one hospital). To obtain my dental clearance, I faced a dental major who took one look at my mouth and within one hour had removed all three of my remaining wisdom teeth. The army engineer captain in the bed next to mine had been admitted for a fractured forearm. But he languished for weeks in the hospital, even after his fractures had healed, because to get his dental clearance, all his teeth were pulled out and he had to wait weeks for his dentures to arrive from the army hospital in Calcutta.

But a bright hour came to me when Congressman Walter H. Judd, a good friend of my parents who was visiting China, looked me up in the hospital and gladdened my spirits with news from home, having recently seen my parents and my wife, Ann, in Philadelphia. Before World War II Dr. Judd was a medical missionary in North China. During the war he was a U.S. representative from Minnesota, after having alerted our nation before Pearl Harbor, eloquently and effectively, as to what Japan was about to do to us.

"I have just come from talking with General Stilwell," he told me, "and in a few minutes I'm due to see Claire Chenault. But I wanted to see you before I return to Washington." I was dumbfounded and elated. What a man—humble, gracious, a real dynamo. Long before Pearl Harbor occurred, I had heard him more than once address large crowds and electrify them for a full hour or more with his rapid-fire description of what the Japanese were up to. It was this impassioned wake-up call that put this great physician-statesman into Congress when America needed him the most.

As late as September 1944, the place where the Burma Road crosses the Salween River was still under Japanese control. At that point the Salween runs through a very narrow gorge with steep mountains on either side. The Burma Road makes many hairpin turns as it winds down the eastern slope to the river to where there had once been a bridge, and then winds up again on the other side, back and forth through many hairpin turns before it reaches the top. A Japanese fortification astride the road on the western slope directly overlooked about twelve miles of the Burma Road as it zigzagged down to the river and up again on the other side. This fortification was able, through its strategically located artillery and machine guns, to deny any use of the road. This small Japanese unit of less than fifty men was so strongly entrenched that it took over a month to inactivate it, and that was finally done only after an eighty-yard-long tunnel was dug under it in order to plant a big charge of explosives directly under the fortification and blow it sky high. We learned early in the war that the Japanese never surrendered easily.

When I was discharged in October from the Ninety-fifth Station Hospital, I was reassigned to the staff of a platoon of the U.S. Army Twenty-first Field Hospital, which was to care for casualties from the Chinese Sixth Group Army. Our hospital platoon was now able to drive down the Burma Road, now liberated, and cross the Salween on a pontoon bridge. It took about two hours to drive from ridge to ridge, that is, down into the Salween gorge and up again, passing the ruins of the fortifications I have mentioned. Along this stretch were many hundreds of old wrecked vehicles shoved off the edge of the road; these were mostly trucks and military vehicles in use before the Japanese closed off the Burma Road two years earlier.

We continued down the road almost to the China-Burma border and then set up our field hospital platoon alongside the Burma Road. Immediately Chinese casualties began arriving from the front. Whenever a six-by-six Army truck drew near, we knew that wounded were coming when we heard screams as the truck bumped across potholes.

Transportation from the front was so difficult that it was usually five days to a week from the moment a soldier was wounded and given first aid to the moment he arrived at our field hospital. That meant that those with severe wounds had already died before they reached us and those still alive had wounds that were already infected. Many arrived with gangrenous limbs that we had to amputate. It was heartbreaking to see the awful loss of life and limb caused simply by delay. Incidentally, General Stilwell had at the beginning made the policy that no American women would nurse Chinese soldiers. Hence, all nursing was done by our enlisted men; the women nurses had been left behind in India.

By January 1945, there was enough lull in the shooting war to permit several of us medical officers to take a five-mile walk down the Burma Road to Wanding on the China-Burma border. It was a pleasant, sunny January day. As we were resting in Wanding before starting back, suddenly a convoy of jeeps and weapons-carriers breezed into the village from Burma. I recognized several officers from Ramgarh, India, days in this convoy. To our surprise and delight, we were seeing and greeting the very first vehicles to arrive in China from India along the new Ledo Road, and we were the first Americans to welcome them from the China end. What a coincidence!

The construction of the Ledo Road from India across northern Burma had begun in December 1942; this was to connect with the Burma Road as it entered China. The main mission of the U.S. and Chinese Army efforts in the China-Burma-India theater was to reestablish land communication between China and the outside world. This Ledo Road—all of 478 miles long and soon to be renamed the Stilwell Road—was now open for traffic at long last. The great irony is that within two months the British were able to recapture Rangoon from the Japanese and to reestablish the original Burma Road connections. By August, the entire war was over. This meant that the Ledo and Burma Roads were no longer of strategic importance and were soon to sink into disrepair and disuse.

The Army began its first rotation policy for China in early 1945. And since I had already been overseas with the Chinese Army for over two years, I was one of the first to be returned home. My foot locker weighed about seventy pounds, but since my postal address in China was a New York A.P.O., I had to pay only the parcel post rate between New York and Philadelphia, which was $1.60. Flown from China, it arrived home before I did. My own journey by air had to be in stages: from Kunming to Calcutta to Karachi to Cairo to Casablanca, then across the Atlantic in a C-54 to Bermuda and Miami, arriving on Easter Sunday.

I had been cut off from any contact with Ann for so long— except only by v-mail letters—that it was not until several hours after reaching Miami that I suddenly realized I could now actually telephone Ann and tell her I was back in the states.

Ann quickly joined me in Coral Gables. Then after a brief checkup in Walter Reed Hospital near Washington and a one-week stay in Asheville's fabulous Grove Park Inn (at that time run by the

Army for officers' R and R), I was assigned for duty briefly at
Camp Atterbury (Indiana), then at Camp Indiantown Gap (near
Ann's hometown of Lebanon, Pennsylvania).

My duty at Indiantown Gap was to see each army unit arriving
for separation and inspect every soldier for one thing and for one
thing only: scabies. Each unit would assemble in a large hall in
groups of fifty to one hundred men lined in a circle. Each man
would drop his gear, strip to the buff, and stand with fingers
outstretched, palms down, as I walked down the line. Those found
with scabies would be processed before being demobilized. One
observation impressed me much: soldiers arriving from the
European theater were well fed, animated, and loudly talkative;
those arriving from the Pacific were gaunt, yellow-skinned (from
Atabrine), subdued, and silent.

Around Christmas, after my two months at Indiantown Gap, I
was deactivated. (An officer is deactivated; an enlisted man is
discharged.) Ann and I began to take up living where we had left
off three years before.

As I look back at the war years, I realize that, compared with
my brother-in-law, Ted Stevenson, I had had it easy. While Ted was
returning to Canton in December 1941, his ship arrived in Manila
the day the Japanese attacked Pearl Harbor. Manila fell to the
Japanese that same day, and for the next three long years Ted was
guest of the emperor in one or another of the Japanese prison
camps in the Philippines. In February 1945, when MacArthur's
forces finally rescued the prisoners cooped up in the Santo Tomas
Prison camp, they found Ted locked up in solitary confinement
and weighing 128 pounds. As the lone physician in the camp, Ted
had been required to fill out all death certificates. On many of
these certificates Ted wrote "malnutrition" as the cause of death.
The camp authorities, displeased at such an alleged insult to their
emperor, wanted him to write "natural causes." Ted refused to
alter the truth. That was why he was penned up in solitary
confinement and his rations further reduced.

TIME magazine reported that the most abusive bully in that
camp was critically wounded by gunfire during the surprise

rescue by the Americans and that Ted, just released and very gaunt and weak, operated on him in an effort to save his life, but failed to pull him through. Ted is that kind of person.

Throughout all those prison years as a civilian internee, not a single letter or Red Cross relief parcel sent by Bunny to Ted ever reached him, and no message sent by Ted to Bunny ever reached her. Many months went by in which Bunny had no idea as to whether Ted was dead or alive. The Japanese had never signed the Geneva Convention, and they gave little heed to International Red Cross appeals.

CHAPTER NINE

RESIDENCIES AND V.A. HOSPITAL DAYS

MY WORLD WAR II EXPERIENCES IN CHINA MADE me want to become a surgeon. Financial help from the G.I. Bill of Rights made this possible. The Graduate School of Medicine of the University of Pennsylvania gave an outstanding one-year course in surgery, chaired for many years by another close friend of my parents, Dr. Walter Estelle Lee. Dr. Lee was retiring that year, but I had once dated his daughter Jean while I was in medical school, and I was accepted for that class of some seventy graduate students, most of whom had just completed active military service.

Meanwhile, Ann and I had been fortunate to find a nice second-floor apartment in Hamilton Court on Chestnut Street in West Philadelphia near the Presbyterian Hospital, where Ann was supervising student nurses. When my surgery classes began in September 1946, Ann was expecting our firstborn, Kenneth Jr., who was born October 27 in Presbyterian Hospital. Dr. Ford Miller, gruff and bluntly outspoken, would never have permitted me or any other outsider in the delivery room, even though I was a physician and father of the child. The nearest I could have come to the scene of action was to have paced up and down in the waiting room outside the glass window of the newborn nursery. This I refused to do, to Ann's disappointment, but returned to our apartment and then came back to see her and little Kenny when officially permitted to do so during visiting hours.

Dr. Miller was someone with a dim view of ministers, because they usually expected him to offer them the fifty percent discount extended to clergy at Presbyterian Hospital, and he never darkened a church door. But sometime later, when our friends Dr. Bob and Edna Lamont, expecting their first child (this was before they moved to Pittsburgh), asked Ann and me to recommend an obstetrician, we suggested Dr. Ford Miller, warning them that he was an agnostic. But they chose him and insisted on paying his full fee, and so he became Edna's obstetrician. They named the little boy born to them Kenneth, but he was so malformed that he died after a few days. The strong beauty of Bob and Edna's Christian faith in the face of this bitter disappointment so overwhelmed Dr. Miller that Bob was able to lead him to Christ—an unlikely convert, but a genuine conversion and truly a miracle. In 1950, Dr. Miller delivered our second son, Charles.

The surgery class I entered was divided into four groups, and for the purpose of communication and coordinating schedules, each group selected its own representative. I was our group's representative, and eventually I represented the entire class. I mention this because this was a responsibility I voluntarily accepted, in sharp contrast to the selfish reluctance to chip in for others I had exhibited in Tali only two years before. I like to feel that I was beginning to learn something of the Christian way of servanthood. What I did needed to be done by someone, and I found I enjoyed doing it, namely, being somewhat of a factotum in order to help our curriculum proceed smoothly. I was genuinely surprised when at the end of the course my classmates presented me with a bit of personalized jewelry with an engraved expression of their appreciation.

The new chairman of the Surgery Department of the Graduate School of Medicine was Dr. William Bates, a great-great-nephew of

Katherine Lee Bates, author of the hymn "America the Beautiful." After the class in surgery was over, Dr. Bates took me on as his surgical resident in the Graduate Hospital of the University of Pennsylvania for the next two years. In those days, choice residencies paid you nothing other than your bed and food and laundry; but the G.I. Bill helped wonderfully to see us through, along with the money we had saved during our years of forced separation. This residency in general surgery was especially valuable to me in many ways. For instance, it was the Graduate Hospital policy that acute fracture cases were to be handled by the general surgeons, not the orthopods—to the consternation of the orthopedic surgery residents.

It was during these two years of residency in general surgery that I got involved with the student-run free clinics held weekly either in the Eighth Street Wayside Mission or the Twelfth Street Rescue Mission. When several medical students in the University of Pennsylvania wanted to start doing free clinic work in some Philadelphia rescue missions, the County Medical Society would not permit this unless a sponsor with a license to practice medicine in Pennsylvania was present at each clinic to take responsibility for it. I well remember then-medical students David Baker, Newt Spencer, and Birch Rambo asking me to be their sponsor and I agreed. Those clinics became very popular. Dr. Isidor S. Ravdin, chairman of surgery at Penn once dropped in one evening to see one of those clinics in operation and commended the students for what they were doing. Around then, similar student-run clinics were begun in Chicago, eventually giving birth to what today is the Christian Medical and Dental Society.

In 1949, Dr. Robert P. Glover, the son of Dr. Robert H. Glover (director of the China Inland Mission for North America), invited me to be his resident in thoracic surgery in Philadelphia's Episcopal Hospital, and I accepted. This time I would get fifty dollars a month plus bed and food and laundry. Bob Glover's wife had been the roommate of my sister Bunny's at Wilson College. Bob was Dr. Charles P. Bailey's partner, and both men were pioneers in the new specialty of thoracic surgery. In fact, Charlie Bailey was the first in the world to perform surgery on a heart valve, this being a procedure known as mitral commissurotomy.

Bailey and Glover were professors of thoracic surgery in Hahnemann Medical College in Philadelphia, but they always tried their newest operations first in Episcopal Hospital before doing them in Hahnemann Hospital. Both men were affable and a delight to work with, and I treasure my year with them. (Neither man is living today.) Charlie was skilled technically, fast and flawless—every motion counted. He was also fearless, so Bob often had to tether his eagerness. I worked with them both and I know.

For example, when Hahnemann decided to begin its department of thoracic surgery and sought a surgeon to chair it, the choice of applicants narrowed down to Charlie Bailey. To make sure that he was the man they wanted, the selection committee asked him to perform a pneumonectomy for them. (A pneumonectomy removes an entire lung on one side; removal of only part of a lung, such as a lobectomy, is technically more difficult to do and began to be done only later, after pneumonectomies became more common.) Bailey successfully removed the lung, using the crude tourniquet method used by pioneers then. To clinch their choice, they asked him to do another pneumonectomy the following week, and again they watched from the bleachers of the operating theater while Bailey did his second pneumonectomy. This, too, was successful, and he was appointed professor and chair of thoracic surgery. Bailey never told them that not only had he never done a pneumonectomy before, but also that he had never seen one before.

Many surgical colleagues called Bailey a "wild man." The Philadelphia County Medical Society frowned on him because he inaugurated an annual ball every November for ex-patients, that is, specifically for those persons on whom he or Bob had done a mitral commissurotomy—the Medical Society felt that the publicity from these balls was blatant advertising.

It is interesting to me to note that, with few exceptions, every pioneer thoracic surgeon, including Bailey and Glover, had active tuberculosis himself at some time; this seemed to be the strong motivation for doing something surgical with a diseased lung. In its early days, thoracic surgery, made possible because of modern anesthesia equipment and techniques, was therefore aimed mainly at tuberculosis. My own interest in thoracic surgery came because of my interest in tuberculosis, and that interest came, as I have already mentioned, because of my own brother's close brush with death from tuberculosis in China during the Japanese war.

Happily for me, my residency training with Bailey and Glover and their associate Tom O'Neill came during the transition years from old-time anti-TB measures (such as thoracoplasty, phrenemphraxis, pneumothorax, pneumoperitoneum, pneumonolysis, etc.) to more modern surgical measures such as pneumonectomy, lobectomy, segmental resection, etc., so that I had the benefit of good training in both the old and the new. I never was interested in pursuing cardiovascular surgery, my concern being more for the control of tuberculosis and allied problems.

My first three months of this residency program (during the summer months of 1949) was, therefore, spent in the huge 1600-patient Pennsylvania State Sanatorium Number One in Mont Alto, southwest of Harrisburg. Ann and little Ken Jr. were with me then. Streptomycin had just been discovered to be effective against TB bacilli—the first ever in the history of mankind—but its use had to be limited then to preparation for curative surgery, since TB bacilli would quickly become resistant to it.

During that stay in Mont Alto, I became exercised over the contents of a U.S. State Department white paper, just released, which told the world that the United States would not intervene if North Korea should invade South Korea. General Albert Wedemeyer, whom I had come to respect greatly, having served under him in China after he had replaced General Stilwell, strongly warned that such a statement by the United States was a clear invitation to the North Koreans to go ahead and invade South Korea. For those warnings he was moved out of the way by making him commander of the Presidio in San Francisco, a sort of caretaker job. I soon found myself invited to make speeches about the white paper three or four times each week in Lions, Kiwanis, and Rotary clubs in nearby towns in Pennsylvania and Maryland. Little did I realize then that such an invasion would indeed take place in less than a year.

During the spring of 1950, Charlie Bailey, already successful in relieving mitral stenosis, first through finger commissurotomy, then later through instrumental (guilotine) commissurotomy, wanted to try relieving aortic stenosis (narrowing of the aortic valve by scarring, usually rheumatic in origin) on a human patient, having worked the plan out on animals. Our first patient was a lovely twenty-one-year-old bride so severely handicapped by rheumatic narrowing of her aortic valve that the least physical effort or excitement made her unconscious, and death was inevitable if nothing was done.

So that she would not know when surgery might actually take place (lest she become anxious or excited), I would go to her bedside everyday and inject a small amount of Pentothal in her vein. Then when the real day came for surgery—to her it would be like any other time—as soon as she was asleep, the anesthesiologist and other crew members rushed to her bedside, bore her to the operating room, and Charlie went to work. But cutting her thickened, scarred aortic valve only caused a rushing backflow of blood into her heart that was incompatible with life, and she died on the table. Charlie was heartbroken, for he was really a compassionate man. I was his first assistant during this operation. I was saddened, too. However, there could have been no other option, for this occurred well before the clinical use of heart-lung machines had been developed and therefore before bypass open-heart surgery was possible. I think that experience forever laid to rest for me any desire to take up cardiovascular surgery.

The North Koreans invaded South Korea on Sunday, June 25, 1950. Assured that the U.S. would not intervene, and counting on the expected rainy season to give them good cloud coverage, they made no plans for possible air interference against them, nor would they use air power themselves. It was a great surprise to them, then, when President Truman sent American military might against them.

Ann and I were originally scheduled to go to Korea as missionaries that summer. Fortunately, we hadn't yet started. Bob Glover, who had a surgical contract with the VA hospital in Coatesville, about a hundred miles west of Philadelphia, immediately telephoned the VA hospital, and that very day—the day after the North Korean invasion—I was appointed resident surgeon in the Coatesville VA hospital.

That week Ann, Ken Jr., Charles (just three months old), and I left our Philadelphia apartment and moved into institutional housing on the VA hospital grounds. We had just run out of the money Ann and I had saved while I was in the army overseas. Now I was beginning to have a salary as an employee of the VA hospital, and our housing was given free.

My duties in Coatesville were not arduous, for although there were thousands of patients in this hospital and it had about a thousand employees, it was a neuropsychiatric hospital. Most of its physician staff were psychiatrists. I was responsible only for the surgical needs of patients and staff, but had experienced backup consultants in every surgical category to call in when needed. Some of my activities seemed somewhat outlandish by virtue of the kind of patients we had, such as retrieving toothbrushes swallowed by a schizophrenic. But most things were straightforward. Best of all, I had enough time on my hands to study in the well-equipped medical library in preparation for my upcoming Board of Surgery examinations. (If we had gone to Korea as had been planned, before completing my Board examinations, I might never have completed them.)

During my years as surgical resident in Philadelphia, Ann and I had kept our membership in the Church-of-the-Covenant in Bala-Cynwyd, and we always attended there whenever we could. They elected me as a ruling elder and then took official action to support us when we were to go overseas as missionaries. We then became the first Presbyterian missionaries this church had ever undertaken to support—they later undertook the support of other missionaries as well.

While on the session, I was a member of the Pulpit and Search Committee, whose responsibility it was to find a new pastor to replace Dr. Bieber when he retired. Until a new pastor was found, we were fortunate to have as pulpit supply for many months a dynamic Canadian journalist-turned-preacher by the name of Charles Templeton. He had recently become a Christian and had begun preaching in a Nazarene church in Toronto. Feeling the need for formal theological training, he had applied to Princeton Seminary and was accepted there—he was the first student Princeton Seminary had ever accepted without a college degree. Professor Andrew Blackwood had for many years preached one or two Sundays in our Bala-Cynwyd church every summer and had recommended Chuck Templeton to us as our interim minister while Chuck was still a student. So for many months Chuck and his wife (a former Mexican torch singer) would commute from Princeton to Bala-Cynwyd every Sunday, weekdays being spent in classes. Within a month, our church became so crowded that people had to come early to get a seat. We had never before seen our sanctuary so full. Chuck was spellbinding.

Soon afterward, we heard that Billy Graham, just becoming nationally known, invited Chuck Templeton to be an associate evangelist with him. And then Chuck Templeton dropped out of sight. Years later we were saddened to learn that this brilliant and powerful speaker had renounced his Christian faith and left the church, believing, apparently, that our Christian tenets are all a hoax.

Our Bala-Cynwyd search committee was successful. I had the proud honor of introducing Dr. Howard W. Oursler to our congregation when he gave his first sermon at Bala-Cynwyd. Dr. Oursler, a cousin of Bishop Fulton Oursler, had accompanied Dr. Donald Grey Barnhouse around the world in the mid-thirties and had visited Daddy and Mother in our home in Tsinan, China. A more gracious, loving, Christlike pastor one could not find; he is now in heaven.

When Ann and the boys and I moved to Coatesville, we commuted to our Bala-Cynwyd church each Sunday, because I was still on its session. I became secretary of the Foreign Missions Committee of the Philadelphia Presbytery and in 1951 was elected by the Presbytery to be one of its two commissioners to the Presbyterian General Assembly meeting that year in Cincinnati.

Daddy and I went together to that General Assembly. His pastor in Ardmore, Alan McLachlin Frew, was the other commissioner from the Philadelphia Presbytery. Dr. Frew became the chairman of General Assembly's Standing Committee on Foreign Missions, and I was its secretary. This meant that I had to stay up all one night to write the committee report in time to be read the next morning. That committee report had to embody what the executives of the Board of Foreign Missions had presented to our standing committee the preceding day. I felt awkward at the presentation, because these same executives were going to be my top-most bosses as a missionary several months later.

In many ways those eighteen months in Coatesville were a godsend. We had a nice home for our two growing small sons, including a year of nursery school for young Ken, culminating in a graduation ceremony complete with cap and gown, the little kids singing with hand motions their graduation piece, "Itsy Bitsy Spider Climbed Up the Water Spout." More importantly, I was able to complete my Board of Surgery examinations, both written and oral. The Board was generous to me: knowing I was soon to go overseas, they waived the usual requirement of a full year's wait between the written and the oral tests; they let me take the orals much earlier than usual. I reported to Johns Hopkins Hospital for this, just one month before we were to leave Coatesville.

There is one more way in which our eighteen months in Coatesville was a godsend to me, and this way was directly related to the kind of patients I was caring for there. Some of those patients were psychopaths who would gladly have maimed me or anyone else if given the chance and who therefore had to be housed in a maximum-security building. Instead of simply fearing them or resenting their hostility or retaliating against them—as I might have done in earlier years—I came to accept the fact that they acted as they did because they were sick people, and therefore any affronts to me could not be taken personally. It was then that I came to accept them as human beings with burdens needing relief. Thus I found it was easy to be kind to them, and amazingly some of them responded to kindness.

I also came to appreciate the fact that only a thin, vague line divides the mentally normal from the mentally abnormal and that both were created in the image of God. Therefore I find myself taking pleasure in helping all whenever I can. Somehow it took this experience with psychiatric patients in Coatesville to deepen my respect and sense of responsibility for all patients. What a happy conditioning this was for a young surgeon about to begin his life as a missionary overseas!

CHAPTER TEN

EN ROUTE TO KOREA— LIFE IN TOKYO

OUR FAMILY LEFT COATESVILLE IN EARLY 1952 FOR Yale University's School of Oriental Studies, where I was enrolled for four months of Korean language study. My two classmates were Maryknoll sisters, and our tutor was Dr. Chun Sung-Chun, who a few months later became the Minister for Public Information in President Syngman Rhee's Cabinet.

The big problem we faced was finding a place to live. On my exploratory trip to Yale in January, I was able to find only a winter-ized beachhouse in Woodmont, a summer village along Long Island Sound not far from New Haven. The tenants wanted to leave this cottage right away because all the family had suffered incessant colds and sinus infections ever since they came there. I was willing to assume the balance of their lease, because nothing else opened up. Sure enough, as soon as our family moved in, we too began having continuous colds and sinusitis. So we were glad to get away from there for the Easter weekend and visit Laddie and his family in Montrose, Pennsylvania. When we returned to

Woodmont and opened the door of our rented cottage, a blast of hot air almost drove us away. The temperature indoors was around 160 degrees; the rectal thermometer in the closed cabinet of our usually frigid bathroom upstairs on the north side of the cottage registered its maximum of 110 degrees. Apparently the thermostat of the single gas space heater in the central room downstairs had gotten stuck, perhaps by some dust in the gas line, and wouldn't shut off. If we had arrived a little later than we did, everything would surely have gone up in flames. The blessing from this was that all bacteria and molds in the cottage got thoroughly cooked, and we all enjoyed perfect health thereafter.

In July our family drove west to catch a cargoliner (a freighter with a few cabins for passengers) sailing from Oakland to Japan. But a West Coast strike delayed departure by six weeks. The Korean War—officially called a police action by our government, not a war—was already two years old. Our cargoliner, the *President Garfield*, was so loaded that it listed most uncomfortably to port at first, but straightened out eventually as the fuel tanks on port side were emptied. During the two weeks of our voyage, we skirted a typhoon. Our small boys, loving to watch the huge swells, had to be kept on leashes the whole time we were outside our little cabin, since this ship had no railings, only a single chain. The only safe thing that held their interest was a large shipment of California sea lions being sent to Tokyo's Ueno Zoo; we watched these animals by the hour.

When our ship finally docked in Yokohama, nobody was there to meet us. The ship quickly emptied itself of passengers and crew, and we wondered what to do next in this strange new world. When Stan Wilson, also headed for Korea, eventually arrived at the pier, Ann was so relieved to see a familiar face that she rushed down the gangplank and threw her arms around him in a now-historic embrace.

All Korea missionaries, new as well as old, had to live in Tokyo then, since no families were yet permitted in Korea. One practical reason for this was that the U.S. armed forces had commandeered whatever Korean missionary residences were within United Nations

En route to Japan, 1952. Ann with Ken and Charles.

lines and were still habitable. In Tokyo, our family was given the use of the large third-story apartment in the National YMCA Building in the center of the city not far from the Imperial Palace. In a small room next to our apartment lived Dr. Emil Brunner by himself (his wife had not yet joined him in Tokyo). On more than one occasion this gracious, highly-honored theologian acted as our babysitter when some evening engagement took Ann and me away, such as for our Korea missionaries' weekly prayer meeting.

I stayed in Tokyo only that first winter and spring, trying to learn the Korean language. I also acted as house physician to all the many Korea missionaries stranded in Tokyo, and I also undertook to fill out the Japanese income tax forms for all these same missionaries and submit them to the appropriate local tax offices, of which there were many, all of them hidden away in some narrow back alley of that sprawling metropolis. I must have done this for about ten families.

On Sunday afternoons many English-speaking Protestant foreigners attended worship in the Tokyo Union Church, which had its own full-time minister. Early on, I was requested to be their organist, and I continued to play there as long as I was in Tokyo. During that first year in Tokyo, Marian Anderson came to Japan, and through a personal friend of hers in that congregation, arrangements were made for her to sing at our regular worship service in the Tokyo Union Church. My elation knew no bounds when I learned that I would be accompanying her on the organ. Her music score was delivered to me several days beforehand.

I was at church very early that Sunday and had her accompaniment and the organ registrations well under control when a telephone call came saying that Miss Anderson was fighting a cold and, in view of her concert the next evening, her attending physician had instructed her to keep to her room that day; so please, would we accept Miss Anderson's apologies for not being in Tokyo Union Church that afternoon. My reaction was overwhelming disappointment. I had keenly anticipated meeting this great artist, and the thought of personally accompanying the one and only Marian Anderson had sustained me on cloud nine for some days. Now my euphoria collapsed, and I felt terribly let down. The church service we were now about to hold suddenly became bleak, because there would be no Marian Anderson; no one special would be there now.

No one special? Why, this was God's house, and we were about to come together into His presence to worship *Him*, and He had assured us that where two or three are met in His name, He is there! No one special! After all, who could be more important? Marian Anderson or our triune God? Suddenly I felt ashamed of myself for reacting as I had. But as soon as my initial blush of embarrassment began abating and I had regained enough presence of mind to ask His forgiveness, I experienced a surge of excitement and adoration that outlasted any thrill I would have had if Marian Anderson had actually come that afternoon. And ever since then, whenever I enter a sanctuary to worship, no matter how inadequate the pulpit message or the music or what-have-you, I expect to meet God there. And I am elated, because this is His house and I am in His presence.

In December of that year, two important Americans passed through Tokyo on their way to Korea to spend Christmas with American troops there. One was General Dwight D. Eisenhower, president-elect of the United States, to be sworn into office the next month. The other was Billy Graham.

Before proceeding to Korea, Billy Graham gave a dinner for all the Korea missionaries living in Tokyo. About twenty-five of us were there. After we had eaten, Billy spoke to us as we sat at the single C-shaped table. He read from Isaiah 42 (NIV). I do not remember everything he said, but shall never forget his emphasis on verse 8, which reads, "I am the LORD; that is my name! I will not give my glory to another. . . ." I can still see and hear him as he reached his long arm upward and looked up toward the ceiling and said with great firmness, "The moment that I, Billy Graham, reach up and touch the glory that belongs to God, I am *finished*! When I grasp at what is God's alone, He can no longer use me." My spine still tingles whenever I recall that moment, for it revealed why God has been able to prosper Billy's amazing ministry over so many years.

I cherish that memory because it gave me a vivid warning I cannot easily forget. The world has seen too many talented Christian leaders go down the drain because they couldn't handle success; their fame and power went to their heads and ruined them.

In Tokyo those days, a popular spot for Americans, both military and civilian, was the U.S. Army Chapel Center, located in what was called Pershing Heights. The center was popular because eminent speakers from around the world were invited to preach there, and its large auditorium was always filled. While our family was living in Tokyo, we learned that Dr. Harold Ockenga was going to speak at the Army Chapel Center, and Ann and I were able to get there and squeeze into the last two empty seats.

We were eager to hear Dr. Ockenga because of his brief, potential family relationship with my sister Bunny some years before. At that time Dr. Ockenga, then a bachelor, was completing his ministry in Pittsburgh as assistant pastor under Dr. Clarence E. Macartney in the First Presbyterian Church. Dr. Macartney, also a bachelor (and a close friend of my father's) had told Dr. Ockenga that my father had one daughter still unmarried, and he recommended that Ockenga try to woo her. So while Bunny was still a student in college, Dr. Ockenga arrived one day at Wilson College, presented her with a bouquet of flowers, and asked her to be his wife, stating that Dr. Macartney had highly recommended her and that in his list of twenty-five qualifications for a wife, Bunny scored very high. Bunny told him that she was highly honored by what he was asking, but replied, "I've only met you today and don't really know you. I want to know you much better before I could give you an answer." She didn't hear from him again for several weeks; then he called by telephone from Toronto and again asked her if she would marry him. I am not sure whether any further communication took place. All I know is that after Bunny graduated, Ted Stevenson came along, swept her off her feet, and within four months had married her and sailed away with her to China to be missionaries in Canton.

I would not have mentioned these details if it wasn't for what Dr. Ockenga said in his sermon that night in the Army Chapel Center in Tokyo. It was a powerful sermon about falling in love with Jesus Christ. At one point, he used a personal illustration and said, "How do you know you have found the woman you are looking for to be your wife? Do you sit down and make a list of twenty-five characteristics you want in your wife and then score each potential spouse against that list? Is that how you know? Of course not! Why, when I first saw my wife—it was in a library— my heart flipped and I fell in love with her and I said to myself, 'That's the person I'm going to marry.' And we have been in love ever since. When you're in love, you know it!"

That evening, the audience was listening to the sermon too intently to notice Ann and me nudge each other at that point. When we greeted Dr. Ockenga at the door afterwards, we identified ourselves only as Presbyterian missionaries on our way to

Korea. For me, what I heard showed me how a great man of God, as Ockenga surely was, with all his enormous talent and energy and solid commitment to Christ, will always continue to learn and grow all his life. I was privileged to hear him again at the Intervarsity Student Missionary Convention in Urbana, Illinois, in 1957, where Billy Graham also spoke.

Sometime during the spring of 1953 Ann and I were permitted a short look-see visit to Korea, while friends looked after our two young boys. Korea was still at war because of frustrating blocks to reaching a truce agreement. Chief of these blocks was the issue of allowing each prisoner of war to choose whether to return to his own country or to stay behind with the enemy. The United Nations Command insisted that prisoners be given that choice. The Communists were adamant against it because early on, it became apparent that tens of thousands of Communist POWs, both North Korean and Chinese, were going to refuse to be repatriated, many rioting over the matter and signing with their blood their demand to stay in the free world. This embarrassing loss of face for the Communists was too much for them, and so the truce was delayed for more than a year on this issue alone. Eventually the Communists had to give in. The result was that some thirty-seven thousand Chinese POWs refused repatriation; they were later taken to Taiwan, most of them having become Christians while in prison camp. Among the North Korean POWs, we heard that there were at least seventy-five thousand who refused repatriation, of whom tens of thousands became Christians, largely through missionary-cum-chaplain Harold Voelkel's ministry and that of his colleagues in the POW camps. Several hundred of these ex-POWs later became Christian pastors.

The Seoul that Ann and I saw on that first visit to Korea was a ghost city, flattened to the ground mostly by artillery pounding. Seoul had changed hands four times during the war. Only a few buildings were left intact, one of which was the Young Nak Presbyterian Church, around which everything was razed to the ground. Seoul's population then was a mere fifteen thousand; today it is close to fifteen million. I had originally been assigned to

Severance Hospital and Medical School, located in front of the main Seoul railroad station. But Severance was now a destroyed shell; its faculty and staff had evacuated to the offshore island of Koje-Do and was trying to function there. (It was also on Koje-Do that most of the famous prisoner of war camps were located, for both Chinese and Korean POWs.)

As Ann and I looked over the devastation the war had left in Seoul, it was obvious that the only meaningful assignment for me during the coming months must be to the Presbyterian Hospital in Taegu, for this was the only hospital that still remained of all the eight which our Presbyterian Mission once had in Korea before World War II, and it badly needed help now. Severance and Seoul would have to wait. We returned to Tokyo in a daze.

After a delightful spring, summer came. Tokyo can be very hot and humid in summer. So our small family took a four-week vacation in a missionary resort north of Sendai at Takayama Beach, where swimming was great. Our next-door neighbor there was Esther Rhoads, the sister of Dr. Jonathan E. Rhoads, the University of Pennsylvania's famous surgeon and medical educator. Esther Rhoads was the Quaker missionary who tutored the Crown Prince Akihito, now the Emperor of Japan. Elizabeth Vining had gained much publicity for her one year of tutoring the Crown Prince, but Esther Rhoads did most of his tutoring over many years, and without fanfare. Our vacation was all too short.

Tokyo was a fascinating city in which to live, but I was eager, as soon as possible, to get to Korea and work where war had already caused terrible suffering and disruption. So I left Ann and our two boys as soon as we had returned to Tokyo from Takayama, and I proceeded to Taegu alone.

CHAPTER ELEVEN

TAEGU YEARS

EARLIER IN THE KOREAN WAR, THE BATTLEFRONT had come within five miles of Taegu and bordered the city to its north and west, becoming the point of what was referred to as the Pusan perimeter, the Communists at that time controlling everything north and west of Taegu. At one crucial time, when Taegu was expected to fall to the Communists and all military and police personnel had vacated the city for a full twenty-four-hour period, enemy intelligence failed—miraculously, it seems—to know that the Communists could have walked into the city and taken it unopposed. That twenty-four hours marked a turning point in the Korean War and enabled the K-2 airbase outside Taegu to continue to be the busiest airfield in the world for several more months to come, with deadly effectiveness.

When I arrived in Taegu in September 1953, General Earl Partridge, the commanding general of the U.S. Fifth Air Force, still occupied the mission house in Taegu that had been assigned to our family. In fact, all our mission compound buildings were then occupied by Fifth Air Force personnel except for the one house that at one time had been commandeered by the U.S. ambassador and was now returned to the missionaries. I lived in that house, as did also Ray and Mariella Provost and Earl and Ada Woodberry.

Earl Woodberry had been brought up in North China and had already served as a missionary in Tsinan, where I was brought up. When I came to Taegu, Earl was under contract with the U.S. Army to serve as the chaplain to the Chinese prisoners of war. Because he had a superb command of the Chinese language and understood the Chinese mind, he became the human instrument par excellence that God used to persuade thirty-seven thousand Chinese POWs to become Christians and to refuse to be returned to Communist China. (It was this refusal that embarrassed the Chinese Communists to no end and contributed to a full year's delay in reaching a peace accord at Pan Mun Jom, as I have already mentioned.)

The Presbyterian Hospital in Taegu, to which I was now assigned as its superintendent and surgeon, had been built up to become a most commendable hospital by Dr. Archibald G. Fletcher Sr., the father of my good friend Archie Fletcher Jr., a former schoolmate in the Pyengyang Foreign School and later to become director of the Miraj Medical Center in India. In Dr. Fletcher Sr.'s time, this Taegu hospital had been responsible, humanly speaking, for beginning over a hundred new churches in that province of Korea, of which about seventy-five had survived the lean years of Japanese oppression and the chaos following World War II—a truly remarkable example of spiritual fruit bearing.

When I first toured this hospital and saw how dilapidated it had become, I was appalled by the fact that there was no running water at all; water was delivered in buckets from an open well. Electricity came erratically for an average of six or seven hours in a twenty-four-hour period, and there was no backup electrical source at all. A fire during World War II had so charred the supporting girders and joists that the laboratory floor, which was directly over the kitchen, had sunk six to eight inches and was being held up mainly by friction against the walls. On the main stairway between the first and third floors (there was no elevator) the Japanese had sawed out three out of every four iron balusters in their desperate need for

An elderly patient in our hospital in Taegu.

iron, leaving an unstable handrail and gaping holes through which even an adult could fall. The nursing students had only old Army squad tents to live in—boiling hot in summer and freezing in winter, and they leaked whenever it rained.

My first operation (I was the only surgeon there) was an emergency one: an abdominal catastrophe in a man brought to the hospital at sundown. We telephoned the city electrical authorities to please let us have electricity for this emergency surgery. They obliged us by promising electricity for one hour only. The case turned out to be a hopeless peritonitis from a ruptured amoebic abscess of the liver. Just as we were to begin sewing up the incision, the hour was up, the lights went out, the suction machine stopped, and a flashlight helped us finish what little we could do for this dying man. The anesthesia for this procedure had had to be open-drop ether administered by a young intern. Such was my debut to missionary surgery.

When my family was finally permitted to join me in Taegu the following spring (1954), we all had to live together in the one house with the Provosts, the Woodberrys, and also with the newly-arrived Bob Rice family with their four small boys. It was a bit crowded. We noticed that General Partridge was by then away from his house most of the time. So one day, several weeks later, we were alerted by our Korean gardener that the Air Force sentry was off at lunch. We quickly moved our family possessions into the general's house—our house really—and we stayed there for the next two years, exercising our full squatters' rights, without opposition, taking advantage of a technicality.

The technicality was that by September 1950, U.S. military lawyers had realized that it had been unlawful for the U.S. armed forces to commandeer our American mission property, since the U.S. was not at war in Korea—the U.S. was engaged only in a police action. However, South Korea was at war with North Korea. So the charade was consummated by which the South Korean Army seized American mission property and turned it over to the U.S. armed forces for their use. But when fighting finally ceased, it was unclear as to who should hand mission property back to the missionaries— the Korean Army or the U.S. armed forces—and how? The only solution for such a quandary before it got any more complicated was for us to walk into our house and inhabit it. And it took us only one hour and twenty minutes to do it.

Before long, other property began returning to our mission, and within a few months, all of it—residences, school buildings, Bible Institute—was back, but requiring considerable repairs and renovations.

The hospital kept me busy, for it was crammed full all the time. Because the Kyung Puk University Hospital in Taegu was not yet functioning, all accident and all surgery cases in most of that area seemed to come to our hospital, and I was the only surgeon available that first year. I well remember our first Christmas Eve in Taegu when a bus ran off the bridge into the river between the city and K-2 airfield. They brought all the surviving casualties to our hospital. I marveled that though there were dozens of fractures, there was not a single *compound* fracture—the bus had been too tightly packed with people to permit the free-play flailing of limbs that causes *compound* fractures.

But our hospital services were not limited to our hospital premises. For example, during the summer of 1954, as a result of the heavy rains, a Korean village of over sixty houses became partly flooded and then was suddenly covered by a landslide. Our hospital, in response to an appeal for help from the chief of police, sent within an hour a volunteer team of three Korean doctors, five nurses, and a hospital chaplain. During the thirty-mile trip to this village, this team had to abandon the hospital jeep in a swollen stream and continue on foot the remaining seven miles, often wading (or battling) through swift, muddy streams that sometimes came up to the chests of the little Korean nurses and almost swept them away. This party was the first to reach the buried village, and it immediately began to dig out bodies and survivors under a torrential rain. They gave first aid treatment and then, with the help of village survivors, started back to the hospital with fifteen litter cases, the worst of the wounded. Incidentally, all fifteen of these made a full recovery. Of great interest to us was the fact that the only house to completely escape destruction belonged to the only Christian family in this village. Also, this village had long resisted any entrance of the gospel—rather unusual in Korea. It was thrilling to see this resistance vanish. Those taken to our hospital heard the Good News in the hospital and received Christ openly, and soon there was a church in that village. This was one way the hospital was able to plant 120 churches over the years, 14 of them just in the short time we lived in Taegu.

It took me a year to become familiar with workings and problems of our Presbyterian Hospital in Taegu, the only hospital our mission had remaining in Korea at that time. During our first year there, it operated on a budget of $125,000 almost ninety percent of which came from patients' fees. Private patients paid $1.60 a day, semi-private $1.20, and ward patients 80 cents. An appendectomy cost the patient $8.00, a gastrectomy $10.00 to $20.00, and a pneumonectomy $30.00, if the patient paid his bill in full (as a private patient). And yet a mediocre hotel in Taegu then cost a Korean $2.00 to $3.00 a night, not including food. Even at that, patients often had to sell a farm or house or business just to pay hospital expenses. To meet operating expenses, we had to trim salaries so that a chief-of-services, for instance, got as total compensation for his full-time professional services about $50.00 a month—a Korean physician in private practice then easily made ten to twenty times this amount. Only the loyalty and Christian spirit of service on the part of our Korean staff kept them with us, and we thanked God for every one of them.

Throughout our first term overseas, I was the only physician for all our Presbyterian missionaries in Korea as well as for missionaries of other missions who had no doctor. So when Dr. Peter K. Emmons of our Presbyterian Board in New York told my parents that I was "the most outstanding doctor we have in Korea today," he was not stretching the truth to make them feel good, because I was then the *only* doctor our board had in Korea. Many consultations had to be made over the U.S. Army telephone system I was a party to (the only system then that was workable). Whatever missionaries needed hospital care, including deliveries, had to be boarded either in our home or in the Provost's home (Mariella is as excellent a nurse as Ann), since our hospital was too crowded to provide bed space for an occasional foreigner. The hospital had only large, open wards, and extra beds often had to extend into the hallways; besides, with no running water, it was difficult to keep things properly clean. So our bedrooms became delivery rooms for American babies, as when our own daughter Betsy was born.

As soon as hostilities simmered down, the U.S. armed forces sensibly applied their efforts and resources to helping the Korean civilians, and we soon became familiar with such acronyms as KMAG and KCAC and other helping hands. We were able to obtain badly-needed cement and lumber and hospital equipment through these agencies. When K-2 airbase dismantled a hangar, it not only gave it to us, but it also delivered it to us, and out of its steel parts we constructed a beautiful stone-surfaced chapel/auditorium for the hospital. Before we left Korea on furlough in 1957, we had also completed a concrete-block nurses' dormitory and a large outpatient building (there had been none before that), which was connected to the hospital building and now housed the laboratory. We also established a working water system.

Dr. Bob Pierce, head of World Vision, gave us the money to build a pediatric annex to our hospital and was there to dedicate it; he also provided and supported a nurse to be in charge—Kathy Cowan from Belfast. We needed such a facility because orphanages

A worship service inside the chapel/auditorium built from an airplane hangar donated to our hospital by the K-2 Air Base, Taegu.

were sprouting up all around us and abandoned mixed-blood babies were constantly being left on doorsteps. Almost every patient admitted to this children's hospital was an orphan and needed medical care obtainable nowhere else. One newborn baby left at our front door had had much of his scalp chewed away by rats by the time he was picked up and rescued; he eventually made a good recovery. Two of our young orphan patients became two of the eight mixed-blood children Harry and Bertha Holt adopted into their own family. (One of these two weighed only eight pounds when she was first brought to us at eight months of age.)

It seemed that the war brought more problems and suffering to children than to anyone else, perhaps because we saw and treated so very many children crippled by burns and explosions and other accidents related to the war. For example, a napalm bomb has two detonators, one on each end; when it lands and is set off by one detonator, often the other detonator is thrown free unexploded and then is apt to be discovered months later by some young boy who plays with it, hammers it with a stone, and burns himself from the resulting explosion. I saw at least a dozen such casualties, including a ten-year-old boy who lost both his eyes and both his hands.

Burns afflicting boys and girls of all ages seemed to be particularly common because so many of these youngsters were brought to our hospital with crippling scar contractions that usually follow old third-degree burns and resulting, for instance, in a child's being unable to close his eyelids or in having his lower lip fastened to his chest, or both. Extensive fires were common in the many crowded refugee settlements. One reason: because military gasoline was plentiful and kerosene was scarce, some unscrupulous fuel dealers would often stretch limited kerosene supplies by adding gasoline, with predictable results. So very soon I found that a growing part of my surgical efforts was trying to correct burn-scar contractions, which meant making skin grafts. By mixing ether with some latex cement we found in the market, I was able to use the old Padgett dermatome I had brought to Korea with me.

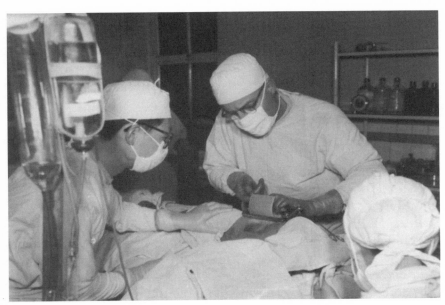

Skin grafting in Taegu, 1955.

Soon after I first came to Taegu, a young factoryhand was brought to us by his employer after sustaining a third-degree burn of his entire upper back while at work. By the time we first saw him, his back was raw and he was very anemic. Now for a skin graft to take, any patient with marked anemia has to have one or more blood transfusions. But nobody in Taegu had ever given blood; such a thing was unheard of then and was considered life-threatening. This man's blood type happened to be the same as mine; so I gave him a pint of my blood, with the hope that others would follow my example and help break the fear of donating blood. I was able then to successfully graft him.

The mother of this young burn patient was most interesting to me. She was not a Christian and would have preferred her son to have gone to the local snake-medicine shop. When the staff told her that the American superintendent had given his own blood for her son, instead of being grateful, she eyed me with increased suspicion, reasoning that I must have done something very wrong for her son and so had given my blood as a cover-up. She watched me ever so closely to try to discover what my mistake could have been, especially since we were now caring for her son free of charge. Eventually, as he healed and gained weight, she became all smiles and was most grateful. As a sequel, other staff personnel began donating blood when needed—and word of the safety of donating blood began to spread through the city.

I remember when a man brought his eight-year-old grandson to us several days after a viper had bitten the boy's leg. (Incidentally, the only poisonous snake in Korea is the viper, but there are many of them.) The leg and foot were black from gangrene, and I told the grandfather that the leg was dead and had to be cut off. Koreans fear mutilations, and the old man took the boy back home. One week later the two returned. This time the two bones of the boy's leg were bare and clean as a whistle; maggots had done a perfect job of debridement, removing every trace of dead tissue. The old man was now convinced, and he consented to having the leg removed.

Dr. Reuben Archer Torrey Jr., at our Amputee Rehabilitation Center and limb shop in Taegu, with two double-arm amputees. Cho Kwang-Woo, our amputee instructor, is at the right.

From the time of our arrival in Taegu, amputees were to be seen everywhere—not only casualties from the war, but casualties from everyday life. But nothing had been done in Korea for amputees until Dr. Reuben Archer Torrey Jr., himself an amputee, came to Korea as a Presbyterian missionary just before we did. Dr. Torrey, son of the famous evangelist R. A. Torrey, and his family had been our next-door neighbor in Tsinan, China. He was also the minister who conducted Betty and John Stam's wedding ceremony in Tsinan in 1933, the year before their deaths. He lost his right arm near the shoulder in a truck accident in China during World War II. When he and his wife Janet came to Korea and established an amputee rehabilitation center in Taejon, he soon helped us open a branch in our hospital in Taegu.

The boy bitten by the viper was one of the first amputees to have a prosthesis made in our limb ship and then be trained to walk. His main problem was that, being a growing boy, we had to make a new and larger limb almost every year. Which was just as well, because he was such an active kid, a one-time prosthesis wouldn't have lasted much longer, anyway.

Cho Kwang-Woo was the bilateral arm amputee who headed amputee training at our hospital. He had lost both hands when he grabbed a live high-tension wire many months earlier. Cho astounded us by learning to do, quickly and deftly, almost anything with his hooks. He was an enthusiastic instructor and a good one, but I always worried a little whenever he went barreling pell-mell on his bicycle through the crowded streets of Taegu. In Korean society, anyone with a missing limb almost automatically becomes unmarriageable. So it was with a great sense of achievement that Cho was able to woo and win a bride. Ann and I were present at their wedding in our new hospital chapel. The bride walked down the aisle poker-faced, not because she was

Cho Kwang-Woo and his bride at their wedding in Taegu, 1956.

indifferent or reluctant, but because Korean brides believe that if they crack a smile, their first child will be a girl, and they all want a boy. This couple was really very happy.

———————

Four miles west of Taegu was the Ae Rak Won, the Presbyterian leprosarium with about 1,400 residents at the time we lived in Taegu. Adjoining the Ae Rak Won was an orphanage for untainted children of leprosy patients, children who had had close contact with leprosy but had so far shown no evidence of having the disease themselves. They had been removed from all leprosy patients, including their own leprous parents (if still living), in the hopes that they would remain free of disease. So they were, in effect, orphans, because in those days it was thought that "once a leper, always a leper." Today, of course, such Draconian measures are not always necessary.

Ann undertook to help a number of orphanages around Taegu. The Ae Rak Won Home for Untainted Children was one of them. This meant her bringing relief food from Church World Service— powdered milk, canned meat, cornmeal, vegetable oil, etc. Many American service personnel received relief packages through the army post office mail and would turn them over to Ann to distribute to orphanages she knew were dependable and were being properly run. Christmastime was always an exciting time for distributing relief clothing, toys, and other gifts. The kids in the Ae Rak Won home always seemed to be exceptionally exuberant and appreciative at such times, bringing us all much joy.

I was officially the superintendent of the Ae Rak Won itself, in addition to my hospital responsibilities, though the colony functioned efficiently with its own leadership and regulations. Men and women lived separately; the women made the food preparations for everybody. The center of the colony was the large church, which always had some people in it day and night and was always packed during daily worship services. And I soon learned why.

There were many in Korea with leprosy, and these were particularly attracted to the Christian faith. When we were there, it was

In the Ae Rak Won Leprosy Center, Taegu, 1954. The patient on the left memorized all the New Testament and much of the Old Testament after becoming blind.

estimated that at least ninety-five percent of the whole leprosy population was Christian. After all, it was the Christians who first had shown concern for them and helped them and treated them like people; others had shunned and banished them, sometimes violently. But the thing that seemed to grip their hearts the most—and this was told to me time after time—was the gospel record of how Jesus dealt with lepers, particularly the statement that Jesus reached out his hand and *touched* them. Nobody they had known would ever touch a leper.

One man I will never forget. He had been in the Ae Rak Won for thirteen years. He was not a Christian when he arrived, but became a Christian and at the same time lost his eyesight (through leprosy) soon after his admission. Since then, in his blind state, he had memorized all the New Testament and much of the Old Testament. Though his face and hands showed all the stigmata of advanced leprosy, he had a radiant smile that made him truly beautiful and a benediction to all who knew him.

For many years the only medicine used for leprosy was chaul-moogra oil, which was painful to inject and was essentially worthless. Then in the mid-forties, Dapsone, a sulfone drug, appeared, and by the time we came to Korea was being issued by the Korean government to all leprosy colonies for treatment. While we were in Taegu, Dr. Robert Cochrane, the acknowledged world authority on leprosy, was invited from Vellore, India, by the Korean government to visit and advise its Ministry of Health on national leprosy policy. Leprosy was then a political as well as a public-health problem in Korea, where a full fourth of government funds for public health was being spent for leprosy alone. I toured a number of centers with Dr. Cochrane and learned much from him. He stayed in our home in Taegu and even preached the Easter sermon during the English-language worship service held in our living room.

We were delighted that the Korean government heeded the radical policy changes Dr. Cochrane recommended and thus thwarted forever the strong political pressure to have all lepers banished to vacant offshore islands for life, a pressure due to an out-of-sight-out-of-mind mentality that had great popular appeal at the time. In all fairness, though, it must be said that public revulsion of lepers was not entirely without cause, when all too many of them would make a handy income by dressing in hideous rags and bursting into a shop or house, causing its frightened occupants to fling good money at them to induce them to leave.

But since those days, leprosy management and outlook in Korea has changed dramatically for the better. Patients are getting cured, and the restorative surgical measures pioneered by Dr. Paul Brand in India are being carried out in a number of Christian leprosy rehabilitation centers. The most difficult of hurdles to be overcome has always been to get society to accept cured or arrested and non-infectious expatients back into their communities; we are finally seeing some progress in this matter. What impresses me most is that worldwide, and notably in Korea, it has always been the Christians who have led the way to giving practical help and kindness and hope to our human brothers and sisters who happen to have leprosy. (Most people today refer to it as Hansen's disease.)

One wrong impression I had during my first year in Taegu was that mental illness didn't seem to exist among Koreans, for I had seen no evidence of it. That was surprising to me, considering the enormous stress among their people in recent years. However, during our second year, our hospital chaplain invited me to accompany him to an abandoned, roofless Japanese icehouse far outside the city of Taegu. This was on a Sunday morning in January. The sky was clear, but a cold north wind chilled me quickly as soon as I stopped walking briskly. The chaplain led me to a large tent to the lee of the icehouse, which helped serve as a windbreak; the sides of the tent were secured to the ground to keep out the winter wind. As we approached the tent, I could hear voices singing a Christian hymn.

As we entered the tent and my eyes began adjusting to the dark inside, there being no windows, I must have seen thirty to forty men and women of all ages sitting on the ground and filling the tent so completely that those nearby had to bunch up more closely to make a spot for the chaplain and me to sit. The only heat in that tent was body heat.

As my eyes became a little more accustomed to the dark, I saw friendly faces looking at us, but I could also see that most of these people were mentally impaired. At the far end of the tent a kindly man arose and welcomed us—obviously in charge. "I am Elder Park," he said, "and these are all my family." After introducing us to those gathered there, he began singing another hymn, and most everyone joined him. This was followed by his telling a story Jesus had once told, and amazingly the audience was fairly quiet and attentive as he spoke.

After this simple worship service, I began talking with a tall young man there who was able to converse quite well in English and who spoke intelligently and rationally as he told me his unusual story. For a long period of time, he said, his mind had been controlled by alien forces he was powerless to withstand. People said he was a madman and they chained him for months to the foot of a lonely mountain exposed to the weather. To prove his story he showed me the heavy scars on both his wrists where he was chained. I do not recall whether it was Elder Park or some other Christian who came to where he was chained and prayed over him in Jesus' name, but the result was his complete deliverance from whatever forces had bound him. In any case, here he was, a smiling Christian, to me as normal as anyone. Elder Park had taken him under his wing and was giving him food and shelter, along with the dozens of others in his family, because with his history and reputation of having been a madman, he was still without a job to support himself.

To me, Elder Park is one of those unsung Korean Christian heroes, of whom I was to meet many. He sacrificed a comfortable life to give himself to serving the poor and helpless and, yes, the outcast; for Koreans, I learned that day, were so ashamed to have a mentally handicapped member in their family that they would either lock that person up in a back room where he or she would be invisible, or they would throw that member out on the street to wander, where starvation and exposure to the weather would eventually eliminate that person. Thus a mentally handicapped or deranged person was ostracized, cast out, put out of sight, and ultimately died of neglect. And here this humble Christian, Elder Park, was seeking out this kind of people and caring for them as his own family, virtually becoming an outcast with them. I had learned more about mental patients in Korea in those two hours than I had learned in all the preceding years.

At the hospital, several suicide attempts came to my attention. I remember one young woman, Lee Pong-Mi, twenty years old when I first saw her and in a rather emaciated state. Some months before, she had been the bride in a traditional family-arranged marriage. I learned that on the night of her wedding, the groom, inebriated and violently ugly at the time, threw her out on the street and bolted the gate. She was so distressed and humiliated that she tried to take her own life by swallowing either glacial acetic acid or caustic soda—I could never find out which, since both corrosive chemicals were commonly swallowed in those days among young Koreans as the means to end it all. If enough is swallowed, the shock and disintegration of the digestive tract from either agent brings a very painful and early death. But often these chemicals may cause only a severe burn of the esophagus, which over a period of weeks heals by scarring; and over the next few months those scars contract until the esophagus becomes narrower and narrower allowing less and less food or even liquids to pass through. This is what happened to Pong Mi, and she was slowly drying up and starving to death.

When we admitted her into the hospital, we made a permanent opening from her stomach directly to the skin of her abdomen so that she could be tube-fed through this opening. She quickly responded to the nourishment we were now able to give her by tube, and soon she became a beautiful woman. More striking than her new beauty was the change in her whole personality and outlook on life which came about when she became a Christian in the hospital and acquired a hope and cheerfulness and a desire to live that enhanced her natural beauty and made her a truly lovely woman. She left the hospital a new person, but still dependent on a rubber catheter to feed herself through the hole in her abdomen (called professionally a gastrostomy). Because there was nothing more that we could offer her in Taegu with our limited facilities at that time, I never expected to see her again. Nor did I realize then that some years later, during our life in Seoul, I would be seeing many such patients whose esophagus had closed down following corrosive burn contractures, including herself. (We will hear more of Pong Mi later on in my story.)

When we lived in Taegu, roads between cities were horrendous—dirt-surfaced and mostly one-lane, with many bridges washed out. Thick dust kicked up when dry, thick mud demanded four-wheel traction when wet, quite unlike the smooth-paved super-highways in Korea today.

The main highway between Taegu and Pusan then crossed the wide Nakdong River on the one-way track of the mainline railroad bridge, requiring one to stop, look, and listen carefully before venturing on it. At one point this highway used an old abandoned, one-way railroad tunnel a mile long through a mountain, the roadbed of which was dirt and mud, with water dripping through the rock wall. Military guards at each end of the tunnel communicated by telephone to control the alternating one-way traffic. Going south on a trip I made to Pusan, I drove a Jeep 4-wheel-drive station wagon we were delivering there. Coming back north that same day, I was driving a brand-new three-quarter-ton Ford pick-up truck belonging to our colleague Ray Provost in Taegu. This vehicle was quite low-slung and did not have 4-wheel drive. My companion on this trip was Dr. Torrey's amputee-program director from Taejon, a Korean man who himself was an amputee. As we approached the southern end of the tunnel at dusk, the guards informed us that during the day certain depressed spots within the tunnel had filled with water up to three feet deep and had made the tunnel impassable. What could we do now? We asked, "Is there some other way we can go?" "Yes," they said. "If you go back about six miles, you will come to a side road on the left. Follow that, and it will take you over the mountain. The road is little-used and is much longer, but it will connect you to the highway on the other side of the mountain."

By the time we found the bypass, it had become dark. We climbed and climbed and our lights revealed a narrow road with many hairpin turns, sheer wall on the right, and sheer drop on the left. Eventually we reached the top and started the winding descent. Almost near the bottom, I noticed that the steering wheel seemed loose and wobbly, so I came to a full stop and lifted the steering wheel right off the steering post! Apparently the nut on the post was so loose that the frequent turnings had unscrewed it off. In the dark it took us some time to find the nut on the cab floor, but we eventually found it, replaced the steering wheel, and

Dr. Bob Pierce and his daughter in Taegu, 1954. World Vision built the Children's Hospital wing to our Presbyterian Hospital.

screwed the nut back on as finger-tight as possible. Then with grateful relief, we bowed in prayer as my Korean companion offered one of the most fervent thanksgivings I have ever heard.

A year later, when I borrowed this same pick-up truck to take Ann and our two boys for a short trip, we got stuck in a wide river we were trying to ford as we were returning home. This was also at night, and nobody was in sight. Our son Ken, barely nine, wailed, "Oh, why did we ever leave Philadelphia?" Eventually, a Korean Army six-by-six GMC truck appeared and pulled us out of the river. We never borrowed Ray's truck again.

As many American servicemen will remember, only about fifteen percent of the Korean peninsula is flat, arable land. With many mountains and narrow valleys, flooding can happen quickly. We will never forget one particular sign which reflects American G.I. humor and was erected alongside a valley highway and stood about six feet above the road surface. The sign read, "IF THIS SIGN IS UNDER WATER, ROAD IS IMPASSABLE—Courtesy, 82nd Eng. Bn."

In Taegu we were privileged to have many notable visitors come our way. We were glad to have them come, for, rather than be an imposition on us, busy as we were, they were a source of inspiration and encouragement to us. I well remember when both Dr. Louis Evans Sr. (then pastor of the Hollywood Presbyterian

Church) and Dr. Richard Halverson (later Senate chaplain in Washington) were guests in our home at the same time. Ann and I never laughed harder in our lives than when these two distinguished men of God regaled each other around the dining table one evening with anecdotes that kept escalating in hilarity and one-upmanship; our split sides were still sore the next morning. Soon after that, Louis Evans Jr. came to Taegu—this was before he married Colleen Townsend. Together with another young man and two young women, these four young folks came to Korea with high hopes of using their summer vacation time to help Koreans rebuild villages shattered by the war. Out in the country, they ate what the villagers ate, but unfortunately an outbreak of dysentery incapacitated all four of them, and they had to return to America much sooner than they had planned.

Dr. Donald Grey Barnhouse and his second wife Margaret were also guests in our Taegu home. While on the staff of Philadelphia's

Left to right: Princeton Seminary classmates Harold Voelkel, Dr. Han Kyung-Chik, Gordon Mahy, and Fran Kinsler, Taegu, 1956.

Dr. E. Stanley Jones in our garden in Taegu, 1956.

Presbyterian Hospital, Ann had nursed Dr. Barnhouse's first wife throughout her terminal illness with cancer, and I had known their family when their children were growing up. It didn't take much persuasion to line up Dr. Barnhouse to preach to our small missionary group when we met in our living room for our Sunday afternoon worship together. The next week I was to hear him preach in the famous Young Nak Presbyterian Church in Seoul. Not long after that, during our first furlough in America, I was privileged to hear him address some fifteen thousand students attending the Fifth Student Missionary Convention in Urbana, Illinois (1957). Only four short years later, this energetic and powerful Bible preacher would be gone—in Heaven with his master.

Dr. E. Stanley Jones also visited us in Taegu, as did many others I could mention. All visitors were deeply impressed with the Korean Christians, perhaps because these Korean brothers and sisters managed to put us westerners to shame by the buoyant joy and loving enthusiasm of their Christian faith. I marveled at the ease with which I could identify a Korean as being a Christian simply by looking into his or her face, and many visitors would make this same observation and remark on it.

One prominent minister from America visiting in Taegu—I won't name him—asked a local Korean minister who spoke English, "How many persons come to your prayer meetings?"

"Oh, about three hundred," the Korean pastor replied.

"That's wonderful," the American visitor said; "I have about that number come to my Wednesday-night prayer meetings, too."

"Oh, excuse me; I misunderstood you," the Korean pastor said. "I thought you were asking about the daily prayer meetings we have at five o'clock every morning."

That reminds me of another visiting American minister, invited to bring the Sunday message in a rural church not far from Taegu. He began his remarks, incredibly, with the statement, "I want to preach this morning on three Ps—patience, perseverance, and praise."

The Korean pastor, interpreting for him, very wisely responded in Korean, "The distinguished visitor from America wishes to bring warm greetings from his congregation to you Christian brothers and sisters this morning." The people smiled and nodded in appreciation as he spoke, causing the visitor to turn to the interpreting minister and comment to him, "My, but you have an intelligent congregation."

Incredible as it may sound to us westerners, many, if not most, Korean churches would not consider an applicant for baptism and membership until that applicant had brought at least two other Koreans to Christ and then had passed an oral examination given after six months of Bible instruction. And we observed that the practical, daily lives of Korean Christians were consistent with their Christian profession, thereby proving the genuineness of their faith. We found them loving and generous, gladly giving of themselves and their possessions until it hurt.

We also noticed that they avoided questionable and selfish practices, sometimes for reasons that might never occur to us sophisticated westerners. For example, Korean Christians would not smoke, even though non-Christians all around them were smoking. Why? Not primarily because smoking was an expensive habit and was harmful—the American Surgeon General Luther Terry had not yet announced the first warning on cigarettes. Their primary reason ran like this: Nobody would ever dream of smoking in the presence of the Korean emperor; such disrespect and boorishness would be unthinkable. And is not our God much greater than the Korean emperor? And are we not constantly in God's presence? Incidentally, I have often wondered how we in the West can happily sing, "His eye is on the sparrow, and I know He watches me," and yet somehow fail to connect that with what we are *doing*.

Compared to the heart-warming Korean Christians we were privileged to know, the dreary dog-eat-dog practices of the non-Christians stood out in bold contrast. Burglary was rampant, for instance, so that no house, Korean or foreign, dared be unattended at any time even though securely locked up. Even then, houses were broken into, including our own, as happened in Taegu twice while we were asleep, and valuables were taken. The second time was accompanied by a bit of wry comedy: Our two boys had gotten a Monopoly set for Christmas and were playing the game so avidly that they sometimes left the set spread out on the card table in the living room overnight. The burglar, thinking the Monopoly money was MPC (military payment certificates), made off with all the Monopoly money. Our boys were heartbroken the next morning. We immediately wrote to Parker Brothers, detailing our misfortune and requesting that some money be sent by airmail. Parker Brothers quickly sent us the money *free* and enclosed a good-humored covering letter.

Our sons Ken and Charles were old enough for schooling and were excellently taught by our next-door neighbor Helen Campbell, Arch Campbell's good wife. The Campbells served in Korea from 1916 to 1960, beginning in Kangkei, where I had spent my last Christmas vacation in Korea while a student in Pyongyang.

On the Korean national holiday, March 1, 1956, our daughter Betsy was born. We named her Elisabeth Alden Scott, the name my sister Betty had. I delivered her in our bedroom at home, Mariella

Sam Moffett weds Eileen Flowers in Seoul, 1956. Left to right: Rev. Chun Pil-Soon, Sally Voelkel, Ed Kilbourne, Delle Moffett, Horace Underwood, Eileen, Fran Kinsler, Sam, and Howard Moffett.

Provost assisting me, just as I had delivered Mariella's boys in her bedroom at home, Ann assisting me. A friend of mine from World War II days, an ordnance colonel whom I had known in Ramgahr, India, was visiting our home that day and brought us a crate of oranges (a real delicacy in Korea in those days). We reminisced and continued chatting in our living room even after I informed him that my wife Ann was in labor upstairs. Only when Ann made an urgent call for me and I informed the colonel that I was the one who had to deliver her did he catch the hint; within five minutes he was gone from the house. Ann and I had told our Korean friends that we were hoping for a girl, since we already had two boys. But when Betsy arrived, our Korean friends, true to Korean thinking, never congratulated us but went about as if someone had died. That in no way diminished our own great joy when Betsy joined the family.

Throughout our first term in Korea, I was the only physician in our Presbyterian Mission doing any doctoring in Korea. During those years in Taegu we were able to acquire a good staff of Korean physicians in our Tong San Presbyterian Hospital. These colleagues included another general surgeon besides myself, Dr. Lee Chul, whose wife, also a physician, became our ophthalmologist; she was also the daughter of the then president of Kyung Puk University in Taegu, Dr. Koh Byung Kan, a Christian surgeon who later became the president of Yonsei University in Seoul when we came to live there.

It was during our term in Taegu that Severance Union Medical College (the first medical college established in Korea) was united with the Chosen Christian College in Seoul to become Yonsei University, where I was to serve after our furlough. Meanwhile, before and during that merger, I served on the Board of Directors of Severance Union Medical College and Hospital, and it was during one of those board meetings in Seoul that I first met Dr. Paul S. Rhoads. Dr. Rhoads had just arrived in Korea with his wife Hester as an expert consultant to help Severance, almost completely destroyed by the war, get back on its feet.

Dr. Rhoads was a member of the Presbyterian Board of Foreign Missions in New York (later called the Commission on Ecumenical Mission and Relations). He was also professor and chairman of the Department of Internal Medicine at Northwestern University

Dr. Paul S. Rhoads and his wife, Hester, in our home in Taegu, 1956. In time, Dr. Rhoads, as one of the Ludhiana "Three Wise Men," would be responsible for our going to India.

The Wilsons and Scotts leaving Seoul for their first furlough, June 1957. Left to right: Stan, Jimmy, Marian, Jack, Ken holding Betsy, myself, Ann, and Charles.

School of Medicine in Evanston, Illinois, and for many years was editor-in-chief of the *Annals of Internal Medicine*. I invited Dr. and Mrs. Rhoads to come visit Taegu for two or three days, since our hospital there was now the only one remaining of the eight Presbyterian hospitals active in Korea before World War II. Dr. Rhoads (known as Dusty to his friends) and his wife graciously accepted my invitation and visited with Ann and me for three days. At the time, little could I even guess that their stay in Taegu would be directly responsible for our going to Ludhiana, India, a few years later.

CHAPTER TWELVE

FIRST FURLOUGH

OUR FIRST FURLOUGH BEGAN IN THE SUMMER OF 1957, and our family lived that year in the Payne Hall missionary apartments on Alexander Street next to the seminary. Our boys attended public schools there in Princeton, New Jersey. Poor Charles, whom Helen Campbell had already started doing third-grade work in Taegu, was forced, because of his age, to enter the second grade; he was in real agony over the lack of challenge, but survived.

Daddy and Mother were living in Ardmore, near Philadelphia; so we were able to see them fairly often. Bunny and Ted were living in Tenafly, New Jersey, across the Hudson River from Ted's office in Manhattan, where he was serving as the medical secretary of the Board of Foreign Missions. As medical secretary, Ted probably visited more mission hospitals in more countries than any other Presbyterian, past or present. That fall, Ted was on his way to visit Korea and had his ticket confirmed for a Pan American flight from San Francisco. I happened to be with Bunny in their Tenafly home the day his flight left San Francisco. While we were in the kitchen washing the supper dishes, Bunny turned the radio on for the evening news, and we heard the anchorman say, "Pan American Flight Number (whatever it was), which left San Francisco early today for Honolulu and Tokyo, is reported overdue and is presumed to be lost in the Pacific."

"Why, that's the plane Ted is on!" Bunny cried out. I was shocked, too, and tried to console her. About an hour later, the telephone rang. Ted was on the other end, calling from San Francisco. He said that, unaccountably, his Korean visa had been held up and had made him miss the plane he was booked on. The visa was delivered to him just after the plane had left, and he now had a reservation on a plane flying the next day. The lost plane simply disappeared, the newspapers reported. I know that the world doesn't believe in providential circumstances, but I certainly do—I have seen so many throughout my own life.

During that first furlough year, people in America were eager to hear about Korea, the war being still fresh in their memories, and I soon found myself quite inundated with invitations to speak in churches about Korea and the Korean Christians. I guess I must have spoken every Sunday morning from some pulpit and to some group somewhere at least two hundred times over that nine-month period, mostly in Pennsylvania and New Jersey, including the pre-assembly meetings of the General Assembly in Pittsburgh when the old Presbyterian Church in the U.S.A. merged with the old United Presbyterian Church to become the United Presbyterian Church in the U.S.A. I enjoyed telling people about those fascinating and lovable Korean Christians, because everything about them seemed to suggest that we were seeing in them the Acts of the Apostles and the witness of the first-century Christian church repeated before our eyes.

It was during that furlough year that the young Korean Christian student Oh In-Ho was savagely kicked and thrashed to death one night in West Philadelphia by some juveniles as he was dropping a letter home into a street-corner mailbox; these kids were angry because he had so little money in his wallet. When Oh's body was buried in the Pine Street Presbyterian Church's

With my parents in Chautauqua, New York, August 1958. This was the last time we were to see my father.

graveyard in central Philadelphia, Mayor Dilsworth was among the many who attended and sobbed openly. Judge Griffiths, the Christian judge who presided at the boys' trial, told me how Oh's family in Korea, instead of being bitter and vengeful, wrote to him pleading that the hoodlums be forgiven, and they even sent money from Korea specifically to help rehabilitate those boys, reasoning that anybody who could do what those boys did must surely need Christ in their lives.

That year (1957–1958) was also the furlough year for our Korea colleagues Stan and Marion Wilson, who lived in the apartment next to us. A terrible tragedy occurred near the end of our furlough year when little Jimmy Wilson, Betsy's close playmate who was born in the same bedroom in Taegu where Betsy was born, was accidentally struck in the head by a playground swing and died that night in the hospital. To Ann and me, this was as though our own child had fallen.

CHAPTER THIRTEEN

SEOUL YEARS

F OR OUR SECOND FIVE-YEAR TERM IN KOREA, WE were assigned to Seoul, where we were originally headed before the Korean War broke. During that war, Severance Union Medical College and Hospital had had to evacuate to offshore Koje Island, where there were also major United Nations prisoner of war camps. Its buildings in Seoul, located as they were across the plaza from the main railroad station, had been almost destroyed during the war and remained inoperable until the U.S. Fifth Air Force offered to reconstruct the buildings at no expense to Severance if they (the Air Force) could use them as a hospital for their civilian employees; then when the Air Force no longer needed the hospital, they would be returned to Severance. But when the main hospital building had been reconstructed enough to put it into operation, the Air Force decided they would not need to use these facilities after all. So when we returned to Korea in 1958 after our furlough, I was appointed Professor of Surgery in the Severance Union Medical College, which had just united with Chosen Christian College to form the newly-named

Yonsei University. The university's teaching hospital was still called Severance Hospital and it was here that I spent all my days.

There were five western physicians on the faculty of this newly-named Yonsei University College of Medicine:

1. Ian Robb of Nova Scotia, supported by the United Church of Canada, was professor and chairman of the Department of Anesthesiology. Ian and I had attended school together in Pyongyang as kids.
2. Ernest Weiss, a former missionary to China supported by the United Methodist Church, was a surgeon, but was soon spending most of his time and efforts chairing the important Building Committee.
3. Roberta Rice, a Board-certified, Mayo Clinic-trained surgeon, was also supported by the United Methodist Church.
4. Courtland Robinson, Board-certified in obstetrics and gynecology, was supported by the United Presbyterian Church in the U.S.A. His wife Sally is the daughter of the late Episcopalian Rector Sam Shoemaker and the granddaughter of the late Senator H. Alexander Smith, President Dwight Eisenhower's close friend. (I mention this because when Eisenhower visited Korea, he invited Court and Sally to have breakfast with him in the U.S. Embassy in Seoul.)
5. I, of course, was also supported by the United Presbyterian Church.

The Chairman of the Department of Surgery at Yonsei was Dr. Min Kwang-Sik, a Korean. The department had two divisions. Dr. Min headed one of them, I the other. In my division was Dr. Hong Pill-Whoon (Phil Hong), an outstanding surgeon trained in Dallas by Dr. Denton Cooley, the surgeon who operated on Governor Tom Connally at the time Connally was shot and President Kennedy was killed. Phil Hong was also Board-certified and later founded the Korea Chapter of the American College of Surgeons. In my division also was a younger surgeon, Dr. Lee Sae-Soon, who had just returned to Korea from a residency in the Children's Hospital of Philadelphia under Dr. C. Everett Koop. Dr. Koop told me years later that Sae-Soon Lee was the best resident he ever had

Left to right: Dr. Min Kwang-Sik (chairman of Surgical Department), Dr. Lee Sae-Soon (former resident of Dr. Koop's in Philadelphia), Dr. C. Everett Koop (before he grew a beard), Dr. Harold Voelkel, Dr. Moon Tae-Joon (chairman of Neurosurgery Department and former neurosurgical resident in Philadelphia).

(Dr. Lee is now an American citizen and is Chief of Surgery in Grace Hospital, Morganton, North Carolina). Phil Hong and his brilliant nurse-wife Julie, though they both spoke English as fluently as any American and later spent several years on the faculty of the University of Hawaii, always remained loyal Koreans. Eventually Phil chaired the Department of Surgery at Yonsei University.

From the beginning, I felt that Phil Hong was a better surgeon-teacher-administrator than I, so that even though he was officially an assistant professor and I a professor, I insisted that he run our division as its head. I have always been glad that I did that; it seemed only right.

The old Severance Hospital across the street from Seoul's main railroad station was patched up enough for us to use it for the next

Commencement at Yonsei University. Here the graduating class of the College of Medicine, with hands upraised, are repeating the Hippocratic Oath.

Severance Hospital when Ann and I first saw it in 1953.

General Maxwell Taylor, seen at right, during dedication of the Eighth U.S. Army Memorial Chest Hospital (the new Severance Hospital). At left is Dr. Ernest Weiss, who chaired the building committee.

four years. General Maxwell Taylor, commanding general of the Eighth U.S. Army in Korea after the truce had been signed at Pan Mun Jom, providentially decided that the most fitting memorial to the Americans who had perished in the Korean War should be, not some elegant monument to look at, but a hospital in Seoul that would be useful to the Korean people, this to be built with funds and building supplies donated by the U.S. Army. This hospital, his staff decided, was to be constructed as a major part of Yonsei University on its campus, along with a rebuilt College of Medicine and College of Nursing, and it was to be named the Eighth U.S. Army Memorial Chest Hospital. I was on its building committee throughout the three years of its planning and construction; this consumed many hours of our time each week and entailed many vexing questions such as which of several official money-exchange rates was applicable for our use. But progress was made, and during two days of August 1962, all inpatients and activities in the old Severance Hospital were transferred to the new complex on the Yonsei University campus. Whew!

The Eighth U.S. Army Band at dedication ceremony of our new hospital on the Yonsei University campus.

But before that wonderful day arrived, we were to endure four full years of relying on downtown's patched-up buildings. Although both Phil Hong and I did thoracic surgery, I was never interested in taking up cardiac surgery, but Phil Hong was, and was good at it. I remember the day Phil was doing a mitral commissurotomy and the electricity went off just as he had gotten his index finger into the left atrium. Holding the purse-string tight around his finger, Phil had to wait a full eight minutes in darkness and without suction while the maintenance men wrestled with the stand-by generator which was powered by an old temperamental army GMC truck engine. Finally, after an agonizing wait with his finger in the patient's beating heart, the emergency electricity came on and Phil was able successfully to complete his surgery. I also remember when the mayor of Seoul was rushed to our hospital with a stone in his ureter and in great pain, and the only bed available in the whole hospital was an army cot in the pediatric Quonset-hut annex. No wonder we looked forward to using the new buildings going up on the Yonsei University campus.

Those first four years in the old hospital were busy for me as a surgeon. Almost immediately I became swamped with patients with old burn-scar contractions, there being no plastic surgeons at all in Korea to whom these neglected burn victims could be referred. I did my best and learned a lot. Soon people were sending me other kinds of patients requiring plastic surgery, such as children with cleft lip, and we made good progress because of the excellent anesthesia available for our needs.

While we were still in Taegu, Dr. Ernest Struthers of Canada began a pilot program for tuberculosis whereby the disease could, for the first time in Korea, be treated on an ambulatory basis. A survey showed that almost two percent of the population of Korea had clinically active, infectious tuberculosis. The public health problem that this situation posed was so overwhelming to the government that it did virtually nothing except maintain a pitiful thirty-two beds in a small sanatorium which was usually half empty, since the populace quickly learned that anyone going there soon died. Dr. Struthers, who had been a professor of medicine in Cheeloo University Medical College in Jinan (Tsinan), Shandong, China, and had been my pediatrician when I was a youngster living in that city, got Church World Service to sponsor and support his pilot project. Since he was now getting along in years and would soon be retiring, he prevailed on me, as soon as we returned to Korea in 1958, to direct the program he had established, now known as the Korea Church World Service Tuberculosis Control Project. I was glad to do this because there was a tremendous need in Korea to do what this program was doing effectively and economically, and nobody else was doing it at the time. Soon we were treating fifteen thousand active tuberculosis patients in seventeen TB clinics throughout South Korea, five of which were in Seoul itself.

Basically, each clinic had a physician and nursing staff, including visiting nurses and social workers, and an X-ray unit. Patients came and were treated on an ambulatory basis, a concept previously unknown in Korea but now made possible with the discovery after World War II of effective drugs to treat TB. Those patients too ill to come to the clinic were visited by a nurse, and those patients suitable for lung surgery were admitted into our Severance Hospital (later to be the Eighth U.S. Army Memorial Chest Hospital), usually for resection of a lobe of a lung or occasionally of a whole lung. Appropriate anti-TB drugs were supplied to every patient and their use carefully monitored for proper compliance. Although drugs were given virtually free, something, no matter how small, was deliberately charged to all patients according to their means because of the general belief in Korea that if medicines and advice cost nothing, they couldn't be very good and so were not worth taking; and a little something paid by patients also did much to preserve their self-respect.

Of course, there were those who were destitute. And where a patient needed food to recover strength and healing, rice and other food was given by the clinic. And where a family was crowded together with an infectious patient in a small *hakaban* (a hovel usually made of cardboard, scrap wood, and straightened-out beer cans—and following the war there were many of these), a small lean-to structure was then provided by the clinic to separate the patient from exposure to others, particularly to small children. The importance of an ambitious home-visiting program, which meant training specific personnel to evaluate and instruct and assist patients and their families, early became obvious if tuberculosis was ever to become controlled, and this feature of the Korea Church World Service (KCWS) Tuberculosis Control Project was the secret of its success.

In fact, the success of this ambulatory program became so obvious that I was invited to be the sole advisor to the Korean government's Minister of Health on tuberculosis matters. And before our second term in Korea had ended, the Korean government adopted, in considerable detail, the policies of the KCWS Tuberculosis Control Project for its own management of tuberculosis in Korea. This was most gratifying to us who had often seen, right after the Korean War, desperate TB patients buying expensive drugs on their own at medicine shops only on the advice of store clerks, there being then no other recourse for their disease. And when their symptoms improved after several weeks, they would stop buying more drugs—no wonder we encountered multi-drug-resistant tuberculosis as far back as 1960! But the development of this ambulatory program, proven to be both effective and economical, was due, humanly speaking, to the vision and initiative of this wise and quiet-spoken Canadian physician, Dr. Ernest Struthers. In a greater sense, however, it was all God's doing, for the time for it was ripe and the Koreans were receptive to it.

There were triumphs and surprises and also disappointments. I remember one poor woman who lived in a *hakaban* with three small children. Her husband had died of tuberculosis and she herself had one lung completely destroyed by TB, but the other lung was, amazingly, quite free of the disease, and all three children were quite well. Our main TB clinic in Seoul started her on appropriate anti-TB drugs, but it was agreed at our regular weekly TB conference that if she were to experience a cure, her destroyed lung must be removed. Tuberculosis patients requiring lung surgery were always admitted to our service in Severance Hospital, and she became my patient.

But this woman happened to have the rarest blood type of all—type AB, Rh negative—and we dared not undertake major lung surgery without having three pints of her kind of blood on hand. (Any kind of Rh-negative blood is most rare among Orientals.) In this situation we appealed to the U.S. Army Twenty-fifth Field Hospital's blood bank near Seoul for help, and they promised to do what they could. But we had to wait six weeks before they were finally able to get together two pints of AB-Rh negative blood and one pint of O-Rh negative blood. So we went ahead. I did the pneumonectomy and the woman did well and made a good recovery. We were all happy that this patient's three children could look forward now to having their own mother stay well and take care of them.

Now the city of Seoul is divided by the broad Han River flowing through it, and in those days there were only two bridges across it, one for the railroad and the other for everything else. Ferry service was in much demand. About two years after this woman's surgery, a certain ferry crossing the Han River was so crowded that it capsized, leaving very few survivors. This woman was on board and was among those who perished. We think her children perished with her, but we really had no way of knowing for sure.

We had our share of trying times with the Tuberculosis Control Project, such as when we received a shipment of X-ray film from our New York supplier for which we paid seventy-five thousand dollars, only to discover that ninety-five percent of the shipment was spoiled by radiation. The company in New York told us there must be something wrong with our X-ray machine or our X-ray technique, or our storage facilities or our developing chemicals must be to blame. After months of sleuthing on our part, we proved that our equipment and technique were not at fault and that radiation damage could not have taken place during ocean transport, because another order of film in the same ship's hold, we learned, was undamaged. A year later it was proved and reluctantly conceded that our seventy-five thousand dollars worth of X-ray film was already spoiled before it left the supply company in New York. Our seventy-five thousand dollars was ultimately reimbursed. Nobody was ever sued. How could a mere missionary in faraway Korea ever prove that a prestigious firm in New York City had knowingly shipped him bad film? But the time and energy wasted trying to sort this problem out and to get our clinics supplied with film from alternative sources didn't seem quite fair.

I mention this incident as one example of why servants of Christ overseas must be "wise as serpents and harmless as doves" (Matt. 10:16 KJV). There are, unfortunately, those who feel they are free to pass off something shoddy on people simply because they are faraway in some third-world country and will be helpless to fight back and perhaps might not even know the difference. Fortunately, the world is full of honest, good-hearted generous folks, and many of them are found in the most unlikely places. We are happy to encounter them every day.

Generally, our frustrations were few and our experiences with patients and colleagues were highly rewarding in the joy that was ours at seeing people in real trouble come through successfully to enjoy a full and happy life, enhanced very frequently by their having found a life-changing Christian faith while in the hospital.

I can never forget, for example, Yang Nam-Hee, a country woman who before her admission into Severance Hospital had never met a Christian. Her husband was a policeman who had a terrible temper, and from what I could gather, she must have had a terrible temper, too. These two had found it increasingly hard to get along together, especially after he had become interested in another woman. One day, Nam Hee's husband tried to poison her, but failed. Then he led her up onto a lonely mountain and tried to push her off a cliff. Failing in this, as she was running away from him, he drew his service pistol and shot her. And while she lay wounded on the ground, he pulled out of his pocket a small bottle of gasoline he had brought for the purpose, threw the gasoline into her face and lit it. Then he left.

Somehow Yang Nam-Hee survived. Her husband was imprisoned. Her face and neck and hands healed with thick, angry-red scar contractions which attached her mouth and face down onto her chest. People who saw her ran away from her in fright. Several months later, Nam Hee heard of our hospital and came to us for help. Through a series of plastic operations I was able to do quite a great deal for her. But dramatic as the transformation of her appearance was, even more dramatic was the transformation in Nam Hee's personality; for in the hospital she heard the Good News of God's love for her and received Christ into her life almost immediately. No longer was she hard and bitter and vengeful. Instead, through the residual scars on her face there shone the radiance of a transformed heart. She even offered to go visit her husband in prison and tell him that she forgave him. And in Asia, where it is a matter of personal honor never to forget a wrong but only to seek redress, I am convinced that such a forgiving spirit has to be attributed to God's miracle of grace. You can imagine the big lump that came in my throat when, many months later as we were getting ready to leave for our second furlough, this woman came more than a hundred miles to say good-bye.

I am a general surgeon, and I relish a variety of surgical challenges. In Seoul I encountered a new one—a new one I had not expected to have. It was peculiar to Korea, it seemed , and was too serious to ignore. A wag, referring to overeating, once said, "Many a man has gone to his sarcophagus by what he let go down his esophagus." But I am here referring to something more painful and lethal than overeating, and that was the deliberate ingestion of caustic soda or glacial acetic acid as a way to end it all. All too often death does not come quickly; often it takes months of slow starvation and dehydration, when the chemically-burned esophagus, trying to heal from the initial damage, steadily shrinks by scarring until the passage of even liquids through it is blocked. I hinted at this situation when I told about Lee Pong-Mi coming to us in Taegu, the young lady who was thrown out onto the street on her wedding night by a drunken groom and then tried to end her life in the wake of this humiliation.

Phil Hong and I were distressed that not a single surgeon in Seoul (or anywhere else in Korea, so far as we knew) was addressing the plight of those who tried suicide and failed, especially those young people who really didn't want to die after all. They had become dejected, perhaps, after failing a crucial school examination, or had missed getting appointed to a job position they had set their heart on, or they had been jilted by the person they had thought was their one-and-only in life. These corrosive chemicals I mentioned were in common household use and so were readily available—so readily available that small children were frequently burned by them. It was only later on that more sophisticated methods of ending it all came into more general use, such as ingesting large quantities of Atabrine (the malarial suppressant once used by the U.S. Army) and later on still, heavy doses of barbiturates.

Somehow, these distressed young people all seemed to be coming to us. They were not sick or diseased, only starving. The first thing we had to do for them was to make a semi-permanent opening from their stomach through their abdominal wall to the outside in order to feed them liquids and nourishment. If the esophagus was still open and healing was well on the way, we would try, very gradually and gently, to dilate the esophagus, if we could. This method often worked successfully with small children.

But much more commonly, especially with older children and younger adults, we had to bypass the destroyed esophagus altogether by bringing a long loop of bowel up through the right chest cavity and connecting it to the esophagus above the area of stricture, or sometimes even to the throat (if the entire esophagus was destroyed). At a later operation, this loop of bowel could then be connected to the stomach, allowing food and liquids to reach the stomach from the throat through this transposed loop of bowel, bypassing the esophagus.

This is major surgery and is exceedingly tricky to do, because the blood supply to the transposed loop of bowel in the chest cannot be jeopardized at any time, or the loop will die and then have to be removed surgically at great risk to the patient. And the danger of jeopardizing this blood supply increases greatly the higher into the chest the loop has to be brought. In America such an operation has been done usually for cancer of the esophagus, and the ultimate prognosis then is always poor. But our patients were young and had no diseases, and so if their surgery was successful, they would be cured for life.

In the five years we worked together, Phil Hong and I between us did a total of forty-one such operations. This was one procedure we dared not entrust our assistants to do—it was too hazardous. The integrity of the blood supply to that transposed loop of bowel is absolutely crucial. For me, this particular operation was always the most daunting of any I ever did, and it could never have been attempted without the superb anesthesia administered to these patients by Ian Robb and his anesthesiologist colleagues. I am also convinced that our pause for the *keedo* (prayer) that we always offered out loud together before making the first incisions accounted for the good success we enjoyed with almost every patient we operated on—as if some hand not our own were guiding ours.

I was particularly conscious of God's help and encouragement when one day Lee Pong-Mi, the young woman I tried to help in Taegu, appeared in our Severance Hospital clinic and asked to see me. For many months she had fed herself through her gastrostomy (the opening in her abdomen) and now she had heard that I was in Seoul doing the operation I have just described. Her sister came with her. I admitted Pong Mi and operated on her, and everything went well even though I had to bring a loop of bowel all the way into her neck and attach it to her throat ("anastomosis to the right recessus piriformis" is the way the operative notes put it at the time the second stage was done).

After about ten days of healing, when I thought it would be safe to try to swallow something, we tried a small sip of water. About a half-minute later, a look of disappointment in her eyes told me that the water hadn't gone down, and she spat it out. The next day, Pong Mi's sister brought her a banana—a rare delicacy in Korea in those days and something she was fond of tasting in her mouth. Expecting to have to spit the banana out after savoring it, she was pleasantly surprised when she realized that the bite she had taken had disappeared! They called me in great excitement, and I found her ecstatic. From then on she could swallow normally and was discharged after closing her gastrostomy—a truly happy young woman.

In Korea, once patients' problems have been taken care of, that is usually the last one sees of them. I often longed to know what happened to many on whom I had spent hours and sometimes months to get them back on their feet. For instance, I wanted to know how Lee Pong-Mi had made out, but she had gone back to Taegu, and I was in Seoul.

For some years Severance Hospital had a contract with the U.S. Consulate in Seoul to take and read the chest X-ray films made of Koreans applying for visas to enter the U.S.A. Such X-rays were strictly required of all Koreans seeking American visas because of the high incidence of tuberculosis among Koreans. In fact, only in Korea are visa portraits incorporated into the chest X-ray film itself to prevent surrogates from posing for visa X-rays. I often helped read those X-rays.

One day, one of my colleagues asked me to see a peculiar visa X-ray film which he couldn't figure out. A quick look at it and the portrait and the name revealed the subject to be no other than Lee

Pong-Mi, who, some two years after I had last seen her, was now applying for a visa to California with her G.I. husband. The peculiar appearance in the right chest was due to the loop of bowel we had put there. We arranged for Pong Mi to have a barium-swallow study and to film it to prove this was the case and not something horrendous, and I have those films today. She got her visa, and I earnestly hope that she has kept her Christian faith and is today a happy American citizen.

For our first two years in Seoul we lived in two different houses, each one belonging to some other family while they were away on furlough. Our Presbyterian Mission appropriated fifteen thousand dollars for us to build our own home, and friends in America provided an additional ten thousand dollars. So on August 3, 1960, our family moved across the city and began living in our newly-built home on the Yonsei University campus. All windows, plumbing, heating, and electrical supplies and other hardware came from Montgomery Ward, including our roof made of aluminum sheets.

This move was most welcome because it meant we were now living within easy walking distance of the children's school. Our neighbors next door were Jim and Berta Laney, Methodist missionaries, and their kids. Jim had astounded everyone by mastering Korean so rapidly that within six months of starting language study he was making commencement addresses in Korean and was now in constant demand for speaking at all kinds of public events. Later he was to become dean of Emory University's Divinity School, then chancellor of the entire university. In 1993 he was appointed U.S. Ambassador to Korea.

The first house guests we ever had in our new home on the Yonsei campus were Ralph and Ruth Blocksma from Michigan, former missionaries to Pakistan. Ralph, an eminent plastic surgeon, spent that week with us performing difficult reconstructive operations on patients we had lined up for him, using these patients as teaching cases and by his skill and enthusiasm making us all want to be plastic surgeons but knowing we would never be in his league. Ralph was always generous with his time and talents helping people all around the world at his own expense. Several

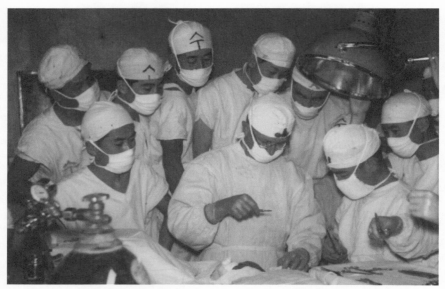

Dr. Ralph Blocksma demonstrating a new reconstructive operation in our new hospital at Yonsei University.

years later, he and Ruth would again be our guests in Ludhiana, India, again doing remarkable plastic surgery on poor patients at his own expense.

Then we had a surprise visit by Dr. Walter H. Judd, U.S. congressman from Minnesota, who had lunch with us in our new home.

Another guest in our new home was Dr. C. Everett Koop, then professor and chief of pediatric surgery in the Children's Hospital of the University of Pennsylvania in Philadelphia, who gave two memorable lectures in our Yonsei University College of Medicine. He also had an interview with the President of Korea in the "Blue House"—both he and the President were Presbyterian elders in their own churches.

Soon after Chick Koop was with us, another professor and chief of pediatric surgery came, this time from the Children's Hospital of the University of Pittsburgh—Bill Kiesewetter and his wife Grace

(Bill had trained under Chick Koop). Bill and Grace had already visited us several years before in Taegu. At that time I had asked Bill to speak at our Taegu Hospital's morning chapel service and had asked Dr. Lee Chul, our newly-arrived surgeon then, to interpret for Bill. I remember Bill's opening his message with the statement, "Man's extremity is God's opportunity." Lee Chul, being a surgeon used to referring to one's arms and legs as extremities, immediately sized up the coming message to be something like "God has no hands but our hands His will to perform"—but unfortunately not the message Bill had in mind. I had enough knowledge of the Korean language to sense that, with each successive sentence, a collision was inevitable—before speaker and interpreter would have to sort it out together and get going again.

When Bill gave his illustrated lecture at Yonsei, no interpreter was needed, for our medical students and teaching staff all knew English fairly well. Bill and I had been contemporaries in Davidson College and in the University of Pennsylvania's School of Medicine, and he was one of our ushers when Ann and I were married. Both Bill and Grace were our close friends over many years—they are no longer living today.

Our living on the Yonsei University campus was a great boon for Ann, because when we returned to Korea in 1958, she was appointed director of Korea Church World Service's Crippled Children's Center, which was then being built on the Yonsei University campus. To reach that new center, which opened in late 1958, she would have to travel clear across the city of Seoul from where we were then living. But when we moved to Yonsei, this center was only a short walk from our new home.

Polio was common in Korea. A young Methodist missionary had recently died of bulbar polio in Seoul, and there were thousands of children in Korea paralyzed by polio. No program of physical therapy or orthopedic rehabilitation had existed before in Korea, nor had polio immunizations become widespread. Ann was the first director of this new Crippled Children's Center, and she built it up so that it soon became a major showplace for visitors.

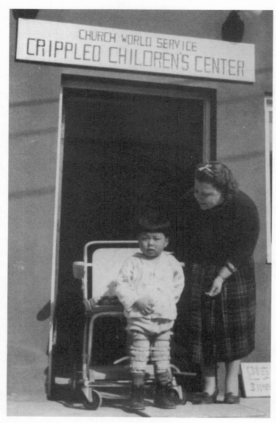

Ann and a patient at entrance to Crippled Children's Center (on Yonsei University campus), which she directed from 1958 to 1963.

This center accommodated forty youngsters between the ages of four and twelve. Most of them were polio victims, but there were always a few victims of burn-scar contractions undergoing multiple-stage plastic surgery. (Ann let me put some of my patients there.) These kids lived there around the clock and even had their own school there. Yonsei University's Department of Orthopedic Surgery provided all the necessary consultations and corrective surgery for the polio patients, and they supervised physical therapy. But it was Ann who hired all the nurses and teachers, the cook and the maintenance personnel, and it was she who made the place hum. Ann has always had the genius of being able to run a tight but happy ship, keep it clean and attractive and efficient; and those she supervises always seem to enjoy working with her. The center was always a cheerful, up-beat place. People found it particularly heart-tugging to see these exuberantly happy kids hopping around in braces or on crutches or whooshing about in wheelchairs. It was no wonder that military and international dignitaries visiting the sights of Seoul were regularly brought to see the Crippled Children's Center on their tour of the city.

I was not surprised, then, when, on May 5, 1962, the fortieth anniversary of Korea's National Children's Day, in Seoul Opera House and in a nationally televised ceremony, Ann was feted as one of the three "National Mothers of the Year for 1962," she being the first non-Korean ever to be so honored. At this ceremony Ann was presented with a gold ring by the wife of the President of Korea, Park Chung-Hee, while a dozen cameras flashed. The nearest that I, Ann's husband, could get to see all this was at the back of the fifth balcony, standing room only.

When Penny DeFore, the daughter of movie and television star Don DeFore, came to Korea to help Korea's kids, she worked every day in the Crippled Children's Center. When her parents came to visit Penny, we were privileged to have them in our new home. The kids at the center loved her, and she loved them, as she so beautifully describes in her book, *With All My Love.*

It was impossible to live in Korea in those days without somehow getting involved, directly or indirectly, with political developments in the nation. During the fall of 1959, as the nation prepared for national elections, the only serious candidate to run for president against aging Syngman Rhee seemed to be Chung Do-Won, who himself was well along in years and also had health problems. In fact, when it was decided by his physicians that Chung needed to have some stomach surgery and could not wait until after elections to have it done, the question arose as to who should do the surgery and where. The professional consultants called to a secret meeting to discuss this question consisted of five leading Korean physicians, mostly surgeons, and three Americans—George Rue

Penny DeFore, holding Betsy, and her parents, Mr. and Mrs. Don DeFore, in our home at Yonsei University. Penny spent many months assisting Ann in the Crippled Children's Center.

(Syngman Rhee's personal physician), Roberta Rice, and myself. This meeting took place at night in a remote spot with tight security, and we were asked to say nothing about the meeting to anyone.

In a nutshell, the Korean surgeons assured us that they were confident they could do the necessary surgery in Seoul, and they were excellent surgeons, to be sure. But Dr. Rue, who knew Mr. Chung personally, pointed out that Mr. Chung had some real arteriosclerotic problems which could make him a prime candidate for serious post-operative complications. "What would you do," he asked, "if you should raise the patient's sheet after your successful surgery and discover an ivory-white, pulseless lower extremity? Do you have immediate access to the special equipment and drugs to deal with such a crisis?" The Korean surgeons admitted that their facilities were not prepared for such emergencies. Then Dr. Rue, a

Seventh-Day Adventist and the seniormost medical missionary in Korea, reminded the group that if any serious complication should happen to Mr. Chung while hospitalized in Korea, the Korean public would immediately charge foul play, and the police would never be able to quell the riots that would follow. All of us there knew the political air to be electrically charged already because of almost universal resentment against the corruption and police brutalities so prevalent under the Rhee regime.

Eventually, all of us consultants that evening agreed that, to win the trust of the Korean people, who had faith in the U.S. government, Mr. Chung should be flown by U.S. military transport to Walter Reed Hospital in Washington and operated there. The next morning, all five of Seoul's newspapers gave a full report of our "secret meeting," including the names of everyone there and who said what. Chung Do-Won was flown to Washington, was operated on in Walter Reed Hospital, and died there before the day was over. When nobody blamed his death on foul play, we all breathed a sigh of relief that a probable blood bath had been averted.

What this meant was that President Syngman Rhee was now completely unopposed in his bid for reelection. Unfortunately, the prospect of a shoo-in for Rhee in early 1960 only emboldened his corrupt and high-handed, lower-echelon politicians (President Rhee, in his eighties, was kept unaware of what was going on in his country). When police needlessly stepped up their intimidation and brutality to make the elections appear more decisive, students all over Korea erupted in what became known as the Student Revolution, and the police did not hesitate to shoot them down.

A major slaughter took place in the wide plaza between Severance Hospital, which was still in the old buildings downtown, and the main railroad station. We organized six surgical teams, all operating simultaneously as the wounded were brought in to us, while outside our windows gunfire continued unabated for hours. We knew that each gunshot we heard probably meant another casualty for us to take care of. Phil Hong took the chest wounds, and I took those wounds where both the chest and the abdomen had been penetrated.

As night fell, the shooting stopped. Some twenty-one or twenty-two dead bodies lay stacked in the ground-floor corridor of the hospital near the main entrance. Our six surgical teams continued operating until around 5:00 A.M. the next morning. Getting home that morning, I was without transportation, so walked the forty minutes it took to get there—we were then living near Seoul's East Gate. As I got near home, I could see the East Gate Prison going up in flames.

That night, about midnight, Ann woke me up. Flames were leaping outside our bedroom window. A house very near ours was engulfed in an inferno. Usually, whenever a fire breaks out in Korea, fire engines respond quickly, with much noise from bells, sirens, and shouting. This time there was only silence except for the crackling of the flames. The burning house belonged to one of the most hated men in Rhee's regime, a man blatantly corrupt and mean as a crocodile. Obviously, nobody was coming to his help.

The result of the Student Revolution was that Rhee's administration collapsed, and every cabinet member and most persons holding top administrative positions ended up in prison, including my former language teacher at Yale, Dr. Chun Sung-Chun, Rhee's minister for public information. In the new national elections, which were notably honest and fair, our friend Dr. George Paik, Yonsei University's president, was elected vice president of the Republic of Korea. Unfortunately, with their sudden

President L. George Paik at a Yonsei University convocation, Seoul, before he became vice president of the Republic of Korea.

and complete release from the repressions they had long endured, the Korean people, especially the students, felt that the freedom they now enjoyed meant they could now do whatever they wanted, and they began to express themselves without restraint. The result was near anarchy, with a "demo" (originally meaning true democracy, but soon meaning a confrontational demonstration) constantly rocking the land and preventing the newly-elected administration from ruling effectively. Communist agents from North Korea took full advantage of this free-wheeling permissiveness and greatly expanded their mischief making, sometimes not too covertly.

For example, during the fall of 1960, Yonsei University students rallied for a demo and ended up vandalizing the Underwoods' residence on the campus and also the home of the Board Chairman, Dr. Sauer. Afterwards, the students came to realize that the inflammatory student who was passionately egging them on was nobody anyone had ever seen before—a real non-student. And while all this vandalism was going on, Radio Pyongyang in North Korea was reporting what was going on at Yonsei University, including the attack on two American residences. The remarkable thing is that Radio Pyongyang was broadcasting this information in detail twenty minutes *before* the event ever began! Make your own conclusions.

The military coup which occurred one year after the Student Revolution put an end to the chaos attending the year of democracy and so was accepted by most people with a sigh of relief. There were no more demos and no more student shenanigans. In fact, there were no more public gatherings of any kind; no more than five persons were allowed to converge publicly at any one time. A friend of ours from Reading, Pennsylvania, Joseph Abey, had just been installed president of Rotary International in Tokyo and wanted to visit rotarians in Korea with his wife. They flew to Seoul, only to find that all public meetings had been canceled by the military government. Abey phoned me from their hotel, and Ann and I brought them to our Yonsei home. The next day they and the Seoul Rotary Club officers met together in our home for an impromptu "secret" Rotary Club meeting. I was not a rotarian at the time, but I had been invited to many Rotary meetings in Seoul, probably because I was the only one there able to play the Korean national anthem on their piano.

One of our Presbyterian Mission colleagues, Otto DeCamp, had started an excellent Christian radio network in Korea. Station HLKY was listened to more than any other radio station, not only because of its superb programming, but also because its news reporting had the reputation of being factual and undistorted, in contrast to government-operated stations. In 1961 the Korean director of HLKY had to undergo a portacaval shunt operation. This is a difficult and hazardous procedure because of its location and the possibility of massive bleeding, but this director's life depended on its being done. Phil Hong was the surgeon. One big problem lay in the rarity of this man's type of blood.

During the surgery, more blood than they had was needed urgently, and the only immediate source of it was the U.S. Army Twenty-fifth Field Hospital's blood bank; they had it and would provide it. So for the next forty-five minutes, I rode at top speed with police escort, sirens wailing, through Seoul's streets to the blood bank outside the city, then back again to Severance Hospital with the blood. The operation was successful and Director Park did well.

This event became the subject of a featured broadcast by HLKY and was given to illustrate how many kinds of people had cooperated together and so had achieved something everybody could be proud of: a university hospital, a Korean surgeon, the U.S. Army, the Korean government police, and an American missionary.

But this story, broadcast all over Korea, did not go unnoticed by North Korea's propaganda machine, which was always trying to drive a wedge between the Koreans and the Americans and to discredit Christianity. So when Ann made headlines as Mother of the Year in May 1962, because of her work in the Crippled Children's Center, it was not surprising that, two months later, Radio Pyongyang broadcast the following fifteen-minute drama portraying an American missionary and his wife, a Dr. and Mrs. Scott by name:

This missionary couple ran a large orphanage for Korean children, and so they were looked upon as great benefactors. But the truth about them, which the public was not aware of, was that Dr. and Mrs. Scott were keeping all these Korean orphans really as a blood farm. In fact, they drew blood from the children every week on the pretext that they were conducting some valuable research, but actually they were selling that blood at great personal profit to the U.S. Eighth Army. Furthermore, Dr. and Mrs. Scott were so greedy that they would often over-bleed these orphans so that many died. And when that happened, they didn't even bother to bury their poor little bodies, but would callously chuck them over the wall. So now you know the *real* Dr. and Mrs. Scott.

So went the drama.

Ann and I and our children were at Tae Chon Beach when this broadcast from Pyongyang was made in July 1962. Many Koreans recognized it for what it was, but many others became quite infuriated and demanded that the police investigate us. The authorities did, but reported it was false propaganda. However, the drama must have had some intended effect, for it was rebroadcast the following November. We know, because one of Ann's nurses in the Crippled Children's Center happened to hear it. She came to Ann greatly distressed and broke down in tears. So much for Radio Pyongyang.

I mentioned that our family was at the beach that summer of 1962. Most of the missionaries and their families went to Tae Chon Beach during July and the first half of August every summer and enjoyed the same kind of rest and recreation in a loving, friendly community that existed at Sorai Beach in North Korea before World War II. Everybody had a lot of fun at Tae Chon Beach. Swimming in the Yellow Sea was the chief sport and there were lots of beach events. When we returned to Korea from our first furlough we brought with us a Sailfish kit, which we assembled on our living room floor in Seoul and which gave us many hours of great fun in the summer. The Sailfish (made by Alcort in

Connecticut) is a flat-decked pontoon with a sail, centerboard, and rudder. It is small enough so that we could easily carry ours to our cottage when it wasn't in the water.

We also played a lot of tennis and volleyball. During several summers the community put on abbreviated Gilbert and Sullivan performances. Most missionaries in the world, if they are to enjoy any entertainment, have to make it themselves, and they get to be pretty good at it. We had no electricity and no telephones. But we developed a community water system and even had a community bakery. As the years passed, Tae Chon Beach became less isolated, and our last summer there saw a U.S. missile site erected half a mile from our cottages, and a Korean hotel went up a short way down the beach.

During that summer of 1962, James Carroll from Australia came and conducted a week of inspirational community Bible study similar to what Ruth Paxson held at Sorai Beach when I was a boy. I do not remember now what was studied, but I do clearly remember a commitment that Stan Wilson and I made during the final morning meeting. In response to a challenge by Jim Carroll, we two came forward, knelt, and promised before God and everyone assembled that we would give the Lord, not ten percent, but twenty percent of our income as our tithe. This was a promise which, like our marriage vows, I intended to honor. Ever since then I have kept that promise. I keep a double-entry ledger to make sure my commitment is being fulfilled.

The Yonsei University College of Medicine (formerly Severance Union Medical College) had many advantages going for it. The Eighth U.S. Army was providing a new hospital complex on the university campus, and the China Medical Board (the Rockefeller Foundation agency that prior to World War II had supported the Peking Union Medical College) was providing a new medical college building next to the new hospital. These new buildings opened for use in mid-1962. In addition, several eminent American medical educators came to live at Yonsei for many months as expert advisors and consultants to the Medical College throughout our years there. A few of them:

1. Dr. Warfield M. Firor, emeritus professor of surgery at Johns Hopkins, a no-nonsense but warm-hearted, helpful friend. His wife was with him.
2. Dr. John R. Brobeck, chairman of the Department of Physiology at the University of Pennsylvania School of Medicine.
3. Dr. Jean A. Curran, once called "the Dean of Deans" of medical colleges in America. Dr. Curran began his career as a medical missionary in China; Dr. Walter H. Judd served after him in the same hospital in China. Then Dr. Curran founded the Long Island Medical College and was its dean until he moved to Boston. An understanding and hard-working educator and administrator, indefatigable in his retirement, Dr. Curran spent many days with each academic department at Yonsei, assessing their strengths and weaknesses and proffering wise, practical solutions to difficult situations. During his year with us, I was greatly impressed by his level-headed attitude toward leadership and by his skills in interpersonal relationships. Today I recognize that Dr. Curran was God's man for helping prepare me for future responsibilities I then had no inkling of.

Ann and I and our children were very happy in the large and congenial community life we enjoyed in Seoul. The wedding of Sam and Eileen Moffett in 1956, for which I was privileged to play, began the social highlights in Seoul, continuing with the marriage of Stan Topple, Southern Presbyterian orthopedic surgeon, to Mia Amundsen, the Norwegian physician whom Dr. Bob Pierce of World Vision recruited to head his Children's Hospital. Here again I was asked to play for their wedding. There were no pipe or electronic organs in Seoul then, and so it was always a piano I played, as I did at the English-speaking Sunday-afternoon worship services of our Seoul Union Church, which had its own full-time pastor and a talented volunteer choir (under Carol Underwood's leadership).

In Korea we missionaries enjoyed a friendly relationship with both the Eighth U.S. Army personnel and the U.S. Embassy. When the Student Revolution broke, the U.S. ambassador was out of the country, and so the Deputy Chief of Mission, Marshall Green, was in full charge throughout that crisis and earned high praises for his handling of an ominous situation. When telephone and cable communications to the outside world were cut off by the falling Rhee regime, a leading Toronto newspaper reached Marshall Green around 1:00 A.M. on the only line that had not yet been cut. Green, who had just fallen fast asleep after an exhausting day, was able to wake himself up and to give a masterful account of all the important developments of the day and what they meant. And that telephone interview became the only source of Korean news to reach North American newspapers for the next four or five days.

The day after, Marshall Green and his wife invited Ann and me for lunch, because Governor Bob Meyner of New Jersey and his wife Helen were visiting them. Why Ann and me? Well, it happened that Helen Meyner is my brother-in-law Ted Stevenson's niece (her father Bill Stevenson was president of Oberlin University at that time). Also, it happened that Marshall Green's mother and my mother grew up together and were lifelong close friends, and our families had known each other for years. Incidentally, Marshall was in Tokyo with Ambassador Joseph Grew when Pearl Harbor occurred, and it was Marshall who first inspired our son Ken to join the U.S. State Department as a career foreign service officer years later.

Friends in the Eighth U.S. Army persuaded me to take two weeks' active duty as an army reserve officer when the Station Hospital in South Post, Seoul, was going to be without a surgeon for over two weeks. This suited me fine, for I was able then to buy a small electric refrigerator in the PX, which we badly needed. During that short tour, a Mr. Lee, a Korean business man who distributed fuel supplies to the Eighth U.S. Army, came to me in the South Post clinic, having lost about forty pounds because of a serious stomach problem. I was not permitted to operate on him in the Army hospital because he was a Korean civilian, but I made arrangements to operate on him in Severance Hospital. We corrected his problem, and because there was no cancer, he made a rapid and full recovery. Several weeks later, Ann and I were swept off our feet when Mr. Lee invited us to his lavish home for a feast and we learned that he was reputedly the wealthiest person in Korea. He was not a Christian.

During Christmas of 1962—our last in Korea—I took some of our most senior Korean colleagues at Yonsei, including our Yonsei University President Dr. Koh, to Pan Mun Jom for the day. Each of these distinguished physician friends had been brought up in North Korea. It was most ironic that the only way they could visit the demilitarized zone was for an American (myself) to obtain official permission for them from the United Nations Command and then for an American (myself) to take them and chaperone them in the DMZ. My Land Rover happened to be the lead vehicle in the long convoy to Pan Mun Jom that day. It was eerie driving through no-man's-land, silent and without a person in sight, knowing that every square yard outside the one-way dirt road was heavily mined.

That Christmas, the UN Command had set up a Christmas tree at Pan Mun Jom, with lights and decorations, on a bluff overlooking North Korea. The Communists had strenuously objected to this "blatant propaganda" and had demanded it be removed. The UN said, "No, it stays." We learned that the day before we were there, the Communists had forcibly tried to abduct the Christmas tree, and the UN had wrestled it back. When we arrived, two armed MP's had to guard the Christmas tree day and night. Beside it a lighted sign facing north proclaimed "Noel" in half a dozen languages. The men I brought stood silent as they peered toward the north, beyond the "Bridge-of-No-Return," into what had once been their homeland; I saw their eyes brim.

While at Pan Mun Jom we visited the small wood-frame building where North and South have been meeting for the past forty-some years, in the center of which is the long, narrow, green-felt-covered table down the center of which runs a microphone cord which is the dividing line between North and South Korea. At opposite ends of this table were two small flags, one of North Korea and the other of the United Nations. We had known that after long and contentious disputes over the relative heights of the little flagstaffs, it was finally agreed that they should be of the same height. Being curious, I measured the little staffs and noted that the North Korean one was a centimeter taller than the UN one.

The North Koreans also had other subtle signs to indicate that they were better. There were pigeons flying around the cluster of buildings at Pan Mun Jom, brought by the North Koreans and trained to rest only on Communist buildings, never on a UN building. This, of course, was to tell the world that even peace doves recognize and choose those who are for peace.

CHAPTER FOURTEEN

CALL TO INDIA

L IVING IN KOREA WITH OUR MANY MISSIONARY
colleagues supported by many different sending agencies, and especially living and working with our many
Korean Christian colleagues and friends, Ann and I came to love
and appreciate these wonderful people. They were an inspiration
and a joy to us, and we could not have been happier than we were
in Korea. But as the fifth year of our second term in Korea rolled
on, we began to wonder exactly what we would be doing when we
returned to Korea for a third term. Where would we be most
needed?

For example, I had been up to my ears doing plastic and reconstructive surgery simply because there was no one else in Korea,
western or Korean, doing plastic surgery that I knew of. Now there
was a Methodist plastic surgeon just finishing language study, and
two Korean plastic surgeons had just returned from America to
Seoul having completed residencies in reconstructive surgery. And
surgeons like Ron Dietrick in Kwangju, and Paul Crane, and Dave
Seel in Chunju, were already getting into this.

Also, more and more Christian Koreans with professional and administrative expertise and growing responsibility were arriving on the scene. After all, our missionary goals were to do ourselves out of our jobs by raising up nationals to replace us, and we were delighted to see excellent Korean Christians coming into their rightful places of leadership. But what should Ann and I do in the next years?

The answer came like a thunderbolt out of a blue sky, totally unexpected. First came a cablegram from London, followed within a day by one from New York—this was near the end of January 1963—inviting me to come to India to be the director of the Christian Medical College and Hospital in Ludhiana. Ludhiana? I had never heard of Ludhiana. India! I had lived eight months in India during World War II. To be honest, Ann and I had more than once thanked the Lord that we were not missionaries in India.

Soon covering letters arrived, expanding on the cablegram. I had heard of Vellore Christian Medical College in South India. Apparently Ludhiana Christian Medical College (CMC) in Punjab State was somewhat similar to Vellore in that it had started originally as a medical school for training women physicians but was now coeducational. I replied that I could not give an answer to their invitation until Ann and I had had a chance to visit the institution. We wanted to learn for ourselves whether the people in Ludhiana really wanted us or whether this was just the idea of some far-away mission bureaucrats in New York and London. Almost immediately I received a lengthy cablegram from Ludhiana saying that the annual meeting of the governing body of the Christian Medical College and Hospital was convening there in ten days, and they invited both Ann and me to attend the meeting at their expense.

My initial reaction was, "Why me, Lord?' Significantly, my daily Bible reading just then was about Moses at the burning bush, and it gave Moses' many excuses telling God why he was not the man for the job. Then, after God had vaporized every excuse with wonderful promises, Moses finally said, "O Lord, please send someone else to do it." It is no wonder that "then the Lord's anger burned against Moses," and I didn't want that to happen to me. I

On Victoria Island, Hong Kong, en route to India, February 1963. Left to right: Erwin Raetz (of World Vision), Ann, Consul General, and Mrs. Marshall Green in their home. Soon after, Marshall Green became U.S. Ambassador to Indonesia and then to Australia.

knew I wasn't Moses, but the story squarely hit its target as far as what my response to Ludhiana's invitation should be.

The cablegram from Ludhiana arrived on a Friday. The next day, Saturday noon, Ann and I reported to the British Embassy in Seoul with our passports and photos (India had no offices in Korea), and by 2:00 P.M. we had our visas to India.

Our flight to India included almost a day in Hong Kong, where we had lunch with Marshall Green and his wife; Marshall was now U.S. consul general in Hong Kong. Our next stop was in Bangkok, where we stayed a full day with old friends of ours, Marshall and Helen Welles. Marshall, an outstanding missionary surgeon, was in charge of the new large Bangkok Christian Hospital he was building. This stop proved to be most providential, because Marshall had spent three months with the previous director at Ludhiana, Dr. Melvin Casberg, at the time Casberg resigned from his position there. Marshall gave me many valuable insights on both Dr. Casberg and the Ludhiana Christian Medical College. These insights were crucial to our understanding the institution and to helping us with the decisions we would have to make.

Briefly, Mel Casberg, a surgeon brought up in India of American missionary parents, was a brilliant administrator. During World War II he was assistant secretary of defense for medical services and knew President Roosevelt and General Eisenhower personally then. Following World War II he became vice president of the University of Texas for medical affairs. After accepting the call to Ludhiana he was able to implement many commendable and necessary changes in a remarkably short time. But he was impatient for more improvements, all of which required big money. The many Christian supporting agencies responded generously to his requests, but they could not begin to match what he had been used to getting from the U.S. federal government and the state of Texas simply by requesting it. Therefore he felt that the Christian supporting agencies were letting him down and were frustrating his efforts to build up the institution. So he resigned, feeling the future for Ludhiana CMC was hopeless. He apparently had not faced the fact that overseas Christian missions have always operated on a relative shoestring, doing much good with the little they have and trusting God for the results.

By February 1963, Ludhiana CMC had already been without a director for eighteen months. Several good men had been approached and had decided not to touch the job. Meanwhile, interpersonal problems were beginning to disrupt faculty harmony. All this important background information was what Marshall Welles was able to give us on our way to Ludhiana.

When we reached Ludhiana, the governing body meeting was just beginning. Its chairman that year was Allan Norrish from the UK, who was also the director of the Bible Medical and Missionary Fellowship (named "Interserve" in later years). Ann and I were warmly received, and it became obvious that these good people in India really wanted us to come. When one Indian member of the governing body wondered whether I might be a bit young to be director and they asked to know my age, I replied that I was older than President John Kennedy.

From then on, at no time did Ann and I ever doubt that it was God who was leading us to Ludhiana, nor did I ever doubt that He would somehow make up for my own inadequacies as director. The governing body asked me to promise that I would stay on the job a minimum of ten years. I promised that I would, and I kept my promise. They, in turn, extended to me, without strings, full authority over the entire institution, which at that time consisted of the Christian Medical College, the Nursing School, the Brown Memorial Hospital, and the institutional housing being provided for all the faculty, staff, and students. At that time the predominantly Indian faculty and staff were supplemented by western personnel from ten different countries and supported by twenty-six different Christian mission agencies—truly international and interdenominational.

Only after we had been in Ludhiana several days were we able to solve the mystery as to how *my* name ever came up for this responsibility in India. When Mel Casberg abruptly resigned after only two years there and the future of Ludhiana CMC needed top-level guidance, including the search for the next director, a special task force of three eminent medical educators was appointed to study the institution in depth and to come up with specific recommendations. The three men—one American, one Briton, and one Indian—were referred to as "the Three Wise Men" by everyone. One of these three was the American, Dr. Paul S. Rhoads, who with his wife Hester had visited us in Taegu.

After Ann and I returned to Korea, the remaining weeks before our furlough slipped by all too rapidly. Farewell engagements and gifts and the disposal of our household effects, including our Kawai grand piano, occupied a growing portion of our time as our June departure date drew near. Even as we entered the Kimpo International Airport to board our plane, such things as a live chicken and a "string" of eggs (eggs tied in tandem in a straw bundle) were pressed into our hands as we approached the ticket counter (in Korea it would be unthinkably rude to refuse such gifts).

Ann and I will never forget one Korean friend of ours, Cho Il-Jae. Mr. Cho apologized profusely to us because his wife, Lee Hae-Ja, wasn't there to see us off that day—she had given birth to

I led Cho Il-Jae and Lee Hae-Ja in their marriage vows in Seoul on February 6, 1960.

their second son earlier that morning and her doctor forbade her to come to the airport.

These two were special friends of ours. My first contact with either of them was when Lee Hae-Ja, then a graduate student working on her master's degree in chemistry, was found to have active cavitary tuberculosis. That was in 1958, and I had to remove the destroyed upper lobe of her left lung in Severance Hospital to effect a cure. I happened to be on the hospital floor when, during her recovery from surgery, a long-distance telephone call from her fiance, Cho Il-Jae, then in Washington, reached her. I saw a happy woman. Mr. Cho had been sent to America by the Korean government to learn municipal management and did not get back to Korea until a year after Miss Lee had recovered. On his return to Korea, Mr. Cho became the personal aide to the Minister of Reconstruction in the Rhee administration. The two planned to be married in February 1960, and although they were not Christians when I first met them, they wanted me to perform the marriage ceremony. I protested that I was not a minister, but they persisted, assuring me that in Korea anybody can conduct a marriage, and I finally yielded. What troubled me was that in a Christian wedding in Korea, the person officiating must always deliver a sermon, and the sermon, of course, must be given in Korean, and my Korean wasn't that good. Anyway, I wrote out a sermon in English, and a Korean friend translated it into proper Korean for me. The spacious auditorium of the new YWCA building in Seoul was rented for the occasion.

The day came, and I reported to the YWCA Auditorium in my academic gown and hood, the ceremony and sermon written in Korean clutched in my hand—I dared not rely on memory. To my astonishment, the auditorium was filled. The Minister of

Cho Il-Jae and Lee Hae-Ja with little Cho Hyung-June, born in 1961.

Reconstruction, who was the wedding master of ceremonies, had invited about two hundred of his government associates and friends to the occasion. Fortunately, all went well that day.

In less that a month, the Student Revolution exploded, and the Minister of Reconstruction and all of President Rhee's Cabinet and probably a third of those persons at Cho Il-Jae's and Lee Hae-Ja's wedding landed in prison. Mr. Cho was spared incarceration, but for the first two years of their married life, the two knew the stress of hunger and want. I heard that they were attending church, and I did see them briefly after their first boy was born. So I appreciated Mr. Cho's taking the time and effort to see our family off at Kimpo Airport when we left Korea in 1963. We did not think we would ever see these good friends again.

When we left Korea, our most poignant and lasting memories would be of the many unsung Korean Christian heroes we were privileged to have known personally, such as "Dwight Moody" Cho,

Chaplain "Dwight Moody" Cho of Severance Hospital, with his family shortly before he was stricken with terminal cancer.

the beloved head chaplain at Severance Hospital, who died of cancer at the age of thirty-nine, the morning after Christmas 1961. When Mr. Cho first acknowledged Christ years before, his father threw him out of home and family and ordered him never to return—this is what his decision for Christ cost him. Throughout his terminal days with cancer, his only concern was for the seven children he must leave behind, all under fourteen years of age then, and how to feed and educate them. Ann and I helped him personally for some time, but did not know what would happen to them when we left Korea.

I last saw Mr. Cho on Christmas Day, the day before he died, very weak and emaciated, but clear in mind and radiant in faith and eagerly waiting to see his Lord face-to-face. He had summoned to his bedside at home the little neighborhood congregation he had established during his last months before death. There they were, two dozen humble folk, poor as mice, huddled like sardines around Cho's pallet on a floor scarcely eight by twelve feet in total area. All were singing or praying aloud together in the manner which is so natural among Koreans. Mr. Cho asked to be propped up, and then, exerting his last remaining strength, he recited from memory the entire eight through twelve chapters of Romans, expounding as he went along and exhorting with the holy confidence and earnestness of a Saint Paul in chains with heaven appearing through the door. Three weeks before he died, Mr. Cho had seen his own father confess Christ, the last remaining hold-out in his immediate family to become a Christian.

"Dwight Moody" Cho was not an "important" person and would never have made headlines. But he was a good example of the many humble, unsung, unspectacular heroes of faith who have neither the inclination nor the money for self-promotion and who continue to radiate Christ in their lives.

I would remember also Yoo Chung-Nam, the young Christian refugee mother who, when we were living in Taegu, lost her right arm at the shoulder and her right leg while trying to rescue her little boy from an on-rushing train. She was then pregnant with another child and was near term. During her hospitalization in our Taegu hospital, five of the women in her ward who accepted

Yoo Chung-Nam and her son who was born in our hospital in Taegu in 1955 after she lost her right arm and right leg trying (unsuccessfully) to rescue her first child from an on-rushing train. They are seen here when I visited them six years later in Taegu.

Christ while in the hospital testified that the reason they accepted Christ was the radiant triumph of this Christian woman in the face of her great personal tragedy.

I happened to find this former patient of mine some six years later on a visit to Taegu and was able to see her in her single four-by-five-foot room in a back alley, which she kept immaculate. Her husband, not a Christian, had deserted her and married another woman. Because she was too poor to rear the little boy who was born during her hospitalization with us, she had had to let him go live with her aunt in another city. When I saw her again, she was holding a tenuous job—guarding bicycles parked at the Provincial Hospital gate, a job which brought her twenty-five cents for a ten-hour day. She was still triumphant and young in heart, and Christ was obviously very near and dear to her. She attended her church regularly, often the early-morning prayer meetings, too, in a Presbyterian church located a mile from where she lived and worked. To save the five-cent jitney fare each way, she usually walked the entire distance, using the wooden leg we made for her six years before. And she tithed faithfully and cheerfully. I am humbled by the memory of such people, who no doubt are among "the first in the Kingdom of Heaven."

Our son Ken, who had just finished his junior year at Stony Brook School, met our plane in San Francisco. We bought a car, and we all drove east and settled for our furlough year again in Princeton Seminary's Payne Hall apartments built for missionaries. Both our boys, Ken and Charles, attended Stony Brook that fall.

I know that all our supporting churches and friends, accustomed to associating us with Korea, were genuinely perplexed when they began hearing Ann and me talking now about India instead of Korea. I admit that we often felt we had split personalities as we tried to shift focus to a country very different from Korea. It is true that our field of engagement would be unchanged; it would still be Christian medical education and not just some general "medical work." We would still be training nationals to be full-fledged physicians and nurses, pharmacists, X-ray technicians, physical therapists, and laboratory technicians. As the Ludhiana Christian Medical College motto had long expressed it, it was "Christians training hundreds to heal millions." Still, to our American friends and supporters the switch seemed confusing, unfocused—at least initially.

I sensed that whatever lay ahead in India would be an enormous challenge. Ann and I were also not a little wistful at leaving behind in Korea wonderful people we had loved to be with. Moreover, I realized that as the director of this large medical teaching center in India, I would no longer have the time and energy to do what I had loved most to do—surgery and teaching. Yet one thing was abundantly clear: This call to India was God's call. To ignore it would have been to disobey God. By obeying, I could count on His continued blessing and help, though administration has never been my forte.

CHAPTER FIFTEEN

EARLIER YEARS IN LUDHIANA

WE WERE DUE A FULL TWELVE-MONTH furlough. But as the autumn season progressed, disturbing news came from Ludhiana and seemed to worsen as time went on. The chairman of the physiology department, a man who wielded considerable influence in the medical college, was dismissed. I never did fully understand the allegations leading to it, but I did know that this Indian professor was a Hindu, and his dismissal divided the Christian Medical College—its faculty and staff and to a lesser extent its students— into two warring camps. Instead of simmering down, the schism intensified. The cleavage was between the evangelicals, those who wanted greater Christian identity of institutional personnel and programs, and those for whom professional excellence was the main basis for collegiality and policy.

It became clear that I would have to cut my furlough short and leave for India right after Christmas. Before I dared leave America, however, Ann, who had never driven a car before, would have to learn how in a hurry. They say that a husband should never be his wife's driving instructor. But Ann was eager to learn, and she mastered the art quickly on our stick-shift car, and no hackles were ever raised!

As soon as the Inter-Varsity Student Missionary Convention in Urbana, Illinois, (which I attended) was over on New Year's Day, I flew to India with two suitcases packed for both cold and hot weather and arrived in Ludhiana at 3:00 A.M. on the train known as the *Frontier Mail*. It was an unusually cold winter, and it had snowed in Athens, Istanbul, and Beirut as I passed through those cities on my journey. I never felt so cold for so long in my life as I did my first month in Ludhiana—buildings are not heated in the Punjab. I had to wear my ski pajamas day and night. In the Punjab there is no spring; the climate suddenly changes directly from winter to summer in early March. They say you can tell precisely the moment the seasons change, and that is when folks move from sitting on the sunny side of the street to the shady side. Anyway, I was grateful when I finally thawed out.

Those first few months I lived with Guy and Joan Constable's family; they were from the United Kingdom (U.K.). Guy, who was the principal of the Christian Medical College as well as the professor of anatomy, had been acting director of the institution for all the eighteen months since Mel Casberg left, and he had bravely and cheerfully done whatever could be done to hold things together. He welcomed me with obvious relief.

I had learned from Dr. Jean Curran that the head of an institution must represent and look out for the good of everybody in the institution and not side only with those factions he chooses to take sides with, just as the president of the United States is committed to represent and seek the welfare of all Americans, not merely of the party that got him into office. I therefore sought to befriend everyone in the institution and to listen to all who would like to talk with me. I soon realized that everyone deplored the animosity that pervaded the staff and that everyone sincerely wished me success in resolving the issues. Many made suggestions. One colleague, wanting to be helpful, said that the only solution he could see was for me, as the new director, to ask each member of the faculty and senior staff to submit his/her resignation in writing and then for me to accept the resignations of those I thought ought to go and reject the resignations of those who I felt should stay. I did not follow that draconian suggestion, but I thanked that colleague, realizing he had given the matter serious thought and was only trying to be helpful.

First of all, it was clear that all who came to India from abroad to serve in Ludhiana's Christian Medical College were not only highly competent professionally, but they were highly motivated; otherwise they would never have accepted the relatively paltry remuneration that every missionary has learned to expect. Highly-motivated persons, especially those who are skilled professionals, are usually strong-willed. Hence the passion that reigned among the more than a hundred expatriates on the faculty and staff coming from the ten different countries and supported by the twenty-six sending agencies. In addition to these were the many Indian nationals from all regions of India—from Bengal to the Punjab and from Uttar Pradesh to Kerala.

It was obvious that my mandate was not to rule who was right and who was wrong, but to get folks to accept one another, yes, to appreciate and trust one another, and, by God's grace, even to love one another. This, of course, was outside my realm of capability, and I knew it. And here is where God intervened with a series of unexpected visitors whose ministry at meetings they conducted in our institution did much to transform the atmosphere.

The first visitor to come to Ludhiana was the man God used to touch me deeply at Tae Chon Beach in Korea the summer of 1962 less than two years before—James Carroll from Australia. By an unusual coincidence I heard that Jim was on his way to the United Kingdom and I was able to contact him and to persuade him to hold a week of meetings with us, mostly with the expatriate members of our Ludhiana community. His visit came within three weeks of my own arrival.

Right after Jim Carroll left, the second visitor arrived, whose coming was not of my arranging at all, although I authorized the use of our college's assembly hall for his meetings. He was

Sudharkar Menon, the nephew of the Indian Ambassador to the United Nations, Krishna Menon, the man many American television viewers will remember as ranting and swooning to emphasize a point. Like his uncle, Sudharkar Menon was a brilliant intellectual and highly educated, a powerful public speaker with burning, deep-set eyes, and now he was a Christian and had changed his name to Paul Sudharkar.

Sudharkar's story is a fascinating one. In his university days he learned all the Hindu holy literature almost by heart. His deepest longing was to find the perfect guru whom he could follow as his disciple. In his quest he sought the advice of the man most Indians recognized as the greatest authority on Hinduism, Dr. Radhakrishnan, who later became president of India. Dr. Radhakrishnan told Sudharkar, "I know of only one perfect guru. His name is Jesus Christ."

Sudharkar: "Sir, where can I find Him? I want to know."

Dr. Radhakrishnan: "I'm sorry, he lived two thousand years ago."

Sudharkar: "Where can I find out about him? I must know."

Dr. Radhakrishnan: "The only place where you can find out about him is in the Christian 'New Testament.'"

Sudharkar immediately searched through Indian book stores until he found a New Testament, and he started avidly reading it, beginning at the first page of Matthew's Gospel: "The book of the generation of Jesus Christ, the son of David, the son of Abraham. Abraham begat Isaac; and Isaac begat Jacob; and Jacob begat Judas and his brethren; and Judas begat Phares and Zara of Thamar; and Phares begat Esrom. . . ."

Few of us would introduce Christ to a stranger by suggesting such a genealogy, but this list made Sudharkar ecstatic. He read on, and on, fascinated because here was a real person with definite human ancestors, unlike the nebulous Hindu deities and saints with their fuzzy origins. He didn't stop reading until he had read through the entire New Testament, and on the basis of what he read, he committed himself to Jesus Christ. Only afterward was he to meet the first Christian he ever met.

In Ludhiana Paul Sudharkar made a great impression on all of us. His lectures were thrown open to the public. The non-Christians of Ludhiana city packed our college assembly hall night after night. I attended every meeting because he spoke in English, since English is the only language every educated Indian understands. In his lectures he eloquently proved that Jesus Christ is the ideal God-man that the Hindu scriptures have been groping for but can never find. I marveled as I saw tears well up and roll down the faces of many of Ludhiana's intellectuals while Sudharkar was speaking. Most of his audiences were Indian, and most of our own Indian colleagues heard him.

I could already see once-hard feelings begin to soften, and this greatly encouraged me. Also, chapel attendance increased, both at the English-language services in the College chapel, and also at the Hospital chapel services, which were conducted either in Hindustani or in Punjabi, or sometimes in Urdu.

I promised Ann and the children I would be with them for Easter. I arrived in New York on Good Friday only to learn that earlier that day a young woman by the name of Kitty Genovese had been stabbed to death by a stalker who took half an hour to kill her. All this was being watched from their apartment windows by at least thirty-eight persons, none of whom lifted a finger to help; no one even called the police. All thirty-eight spectators gave the same excuse, "I just didn't want to get involved." This event hit me hard. One month later, when I addressed the members of the British Christian Medical Fellowship meeting in Bournemouth, England, I began my speech recounting that incident. In the audience was the Rev. John R. W. Stott, who made some notes and later wanted to quote this incident in one of his books to illustrate a point. As is his practice, Dr. Stott never uses a story without first checking its accuracy in every detail. In this case, when he later asked me to send him documentation, I was able to send him photostatic copies of the *New York Times* and of two national weekly magazines describing this event.

June 1964 was a busy time for our family. We all attended our son Ken's graduation from Stony Brook School. The same day we drove to Kennedy Airport and put our son Charles on a Pan

American flight to New Delhi in time for the new school year then beginning at Woodstock School in the hills; poor Charles would have no summer vacation that year. The rest of us—Ann, Ken, Betsy, and I—then began our more leisurely journey to India. We spent several days in London getting acquainted with some of the many friends who were staunch Ludhiana CMC supporters. We hugely enjoyed the few days we had in Switzerland. In Naples, where we were to embark on the motor ship *Victoria*, we experienced some culture shock, because we never expected to see such a poor, unkempt city as Naples anywhere in Europe. Aboard the *Victoria*, we sailed through the Suez Canal to Bombay.

*Ken and Betsy on our way to
Ludhiana, India, 1964.*

In Bombay we boarded the *Frontier Mail*, the same train that brought me to Ludhiana at 3:00 A.M. back in January. Our family was wondering if anyone would be meeting us at that unearthly hour. Imagine our surprise when we stepped off the train at 3:00 A.M. onto a station platform that was jammed solidly with greeters from the Christian Medical College and Hospital. And even more unexpected, they all began singing the Doxology.

May and June are the hot dry season in India, and in Ludhiana then the temperatures get into the 120s, sometimes as high as 130 degrees. July and August and the first half of September are the hot-wet season, when the monsoons bring one hundred percent humidity; though the temperature then drops slightly, the humidity makes the heat more unbearable than during the hot-dry season. So I took Ann and Ken and Betsy to Mussoorie in the hills where Woodstock School is located and where most missionaries go to escape the heat. Also, Charles was there in Woodstock School, and we had promised we would come see him as soon as possible.

The monsoon rains that summer were unusually heavy, causing much flooding in the Punjab. Many of our medical students and younger medical graduates who were serving as interns and residents in our Brown Memorial Hospital responded to urgent government appeals to help in a massive flood-relief program whereby food and potable water and emergency medical service and supplies were brought by boats to marooned villagers to combat starvation, dysentery, typhoid, and cholera. I was proud of their voluntary response to acute suffering and need.

By the time the flooding had become serious, Ann and Ken and Betsy were back in Ludhiana—I had come back to Ludhiana earlier. Ken wanted to join one of the rescue-boat teams from our college. Unfortunately, while out helping flood victims on a very hot day, Ken became so thirsty that he gave in to accepting a well-meaning Indian woman's proffer of some lemon squash made with unboiled water, with the result that he became violently ill with dysentery and had to be hospitalized for several days. Fortunately, he recovered enough to fly back to America in time for college.

One of the surgeons who joined our teaching and clinical staff in Ludhiana Christian Medical College and Hospital about the

Dr. Narayan Nambudripad (then chairman of Department of Neurosurgery) and Betsy.
Dr. Nambudripad became my immediate successor as director of the Christian Medical
College and Brown Memorial Hospital—the first Indian national to hold this position.

time I came was Dr. Narayan Nambudripad, who opened our
Department of Neurosurgery. The name Nambudripad is well
known all over India. Mr. E. M. S. Nambudripad, a distant cousin,
was the chief minister of the communist state of Kerala in South
India at the time. Also, the Nambudripads of India are a very high-
caste family, considered by all Hindus to be somewhere between a
Brahmin and deity.

Dr. Nambudripad was of that family. He studied medicine and
neurosurgery in the University of Madras and then went to the
United Kingdom to complete his neurosurgical training. While in
Bristol, England, he became a Christian and was baptized. His
father, alarmed that his eldest son should desert the family religion
for Christianity, dispatched two of Dr. Nambudripad's younger
brothers to England to try to change his mind or bring him back to
India immediately. One brother took a pistol with him and vowed
that if Dr. Nambudripad would not recant his new faith forthwith,
he would kill him, firm in the belief that it would be better to bring

his brother back dead than a Christian. But his life was spared. The family met their ship in Bombay and immediately committed Dr. Nambudripad to a mental hospital in Bombay. There he was subjected to repeated electro-shock treatments—thirteen in all—the family was sure he had gone out of his mind. When he was finally discharged, his family disowned him. And even his own wife left him, taking with her their four children.

Through the help of the Vellore Christian Medical College in Madras State, Dr. Nambudripad was directed to us in Ludhiana, and in 1964 his wife and children came to Ludhiana to live with him again. In succeeding months, one by one, beginning with his daughter, who was impressed by the change she saw in her daddy, each one of his immediate family, including his wife, became a Christian. Dr. Nambudripad himself grew more spiritually during the years we lived together than most of us will ever grow in a whole lifetime.

I once asked Dr. Nambudripad what it was that first prompted him to become a Christian. He told me he thought it began with an experience he had soon after his arrival in the United Kingdom that shook him greatly. During his first night on call in the neurosurgical hospital in Edinburgh where he began his residency, the telephone at his bedside woke him, and a nurse at the other end reported that a woman patient of his had a splitting headache and was in great distress. He told the nurse over the phone to give the patient a certain amount of morphine, then he rolled over in bed and went back to sleep. The next morning the patient was dead. Well, that didn't disturb him too much—after all, people do die in hospitals from time to time. But then the neurosurgical chief, the director of the hospital, called him into his office the first thing that day and gave him a dressing down because he had not gotten up during the night to see for himself what the trouble was and attend to his patient personally.

The thing that shook Dr. Nambudripad was that the big chief himself should care enough about an ordinary patient to take the time and trouble to summon him, Dr. Nambudripad, into his office to call him to task. This concern of the chief's was most baffling. Nobody Dr. Nambudripad knew in India would have much concern about an ordinary patient. After all, this woman was not a relative of the director's and she was not a paying patient—what could she mean to the director? Soon he noticed that those doctors and nurses he met who cared most for their patients were *Christian* doctors and nurses. The verbal witness of these Christian colleagues, backed by their lives and their attitudes toward those they served—all of which he watched with increasing interest and a growing desire to be like them and to have what they had—eventually brought him to commit himself to Christ. This was Dr. Nambudripad's background.

During my first year in Ludhiana, as I got to know and appreciate Narayan Nambudripad better, I found him to be a heart-warming, true Christian soul brother, and I early regarded him as the person I would like to see succeed me as director.

As director, I found myself involved with all kinds of mundane things, some of them trivial. For example, the hospital needed repainting inside, and I said so. Throughout the building all ceilings and walls had been painted the same battleship gray, and the paint was scratched and peeling. I wondered why every surface was that color and soon learned that Dr. Casberg had been able to get huge quantities of war-surplus Navy-gray paint for almost nothing and had ordered that it was to be used for everything. I had to smile when the manager told me that the supplies of gray paint were now depleted and that he was having trouble finding enough gray paint on the market—he apparently thought that Dr. Casberg's mandate for gray was forever. I assured him we were free to choose whatever color we wanted, and so we settled on something like mint or seafoam, and soon the hospital became truly attractive.

Our compound was large, and to get around I early bought a bicycle manufactured in Ludhiana. Ludhiana had three bicycle factories and numerous other factories that made bicycle parts. The largest bicycle factory in Ludhiana, which made and assembled all the parts, including the tires, had a daily output of sixteen

Dr. Bill and Grace Kiesewetter in our home in Ludhiana. They had visited us also in Taegu and in Seoul. They had been part of our wedding party.

thousand complete bicycles, the majority of which were being exported to iron curtain countries. So buying an executive bicycle for myself was no big deal, and I used it constantly. I wasn't going to let myself get holed up in an office; I had learned while in military service the value of PR—personal reconnaissance—get out bodily and see things for yourself.

Ann found herself busy from the beginning—not as a nurse, but as a hostess. Almost all visitors—and they were coming and going all the time—seemed to find haven in our home, because Ludhiana had no reputable hotels at that time and ours was the most spacious residence on the compound. Besides, important visitors who were interested enough in the Christian Medical College to come great distances from around the world to see us deserved VIP treatment and expected it. And Ann was a wonderful hostess and was glad to contribute this public-relations service.

Moreover, we were eager, if at all possible, to bring to the facility and senior staff a sense of family cohesion. So from the beginning we scheduled monthly faculty fellowship events in our home (which was always referred to as the director's bungalow) to which all senior faculty and staff and their spouses were invited. The programs varied widely, but the hospitality and refreshments provided by Ann were the standard ingredient that made these events memorable and very popular, and they brought us all together wonderfully. Everyone came, and we would have as many as a hundred persons in our living room at one time. Soon we were acting like a family, and pretty soon we were *feeling* like a family—accepting one another, appreciating one another, even liking one another. Our prayers toward this important goal were being answered, and being answered surprisingly early, for which we thanked God.

We seemed to be entering a period of smooth sailing when suddenly, as the monsoon rains of 1965 were subsiding, war broke out between India and Pakistan. We were only seventy miles from the border between the two countries. Total blackout was imposed immediately, initially when all electricity to the city was cut off, and air-raid sirens wailed every night as enemy aircraft dropped paratroopers and one-thousand-pound bombs within hearing distance, some of them only four miles away.

Ludhiana had never in its history experienced an air raid before, and so I as director had to spell out in detail the specific instructions to be followed by our institutional community in time

Betsy selling white mice at a Brown Memorial Hospital fair, Ludhiana, and attracting great interest, 1965.

of war and then have them distributed. We quickly rehearsed our previously-prepared disaster plan, which mobilized everyone, including our three hundred medical students, for any immediate inrush of more than twenty serious casualties. We dug trenches, blacked out operating and recovery rooms, the blood bank and other strategic areas, taped fixed window panes to reduce splintering, distributed bags of sand to cope with incendiaries, procured standby supplies of water, crucial fuels, plaster of Paris, etc. We painted three giant red crosses on the roof of our hospital, but these of course would have had little effect during night raids.

Within two days we had prepared space in the hospital for a possible 250 casualties by rapidly setting up extra beds and by discharging all those patients who could possibly leave. Why this urgency? Because we were the only large hospital in a city of half a million people, the most populous city in the Punjab and the largest industrial center in the Punjab; and the Punjab was at war.

Of all the major cities near the border, Ludhiana alone escaped any destruction; the casualties brought to us came from nearby villages. We had prepared for the grimmest, but in God's good providence the worst never happened. It became known that Pakistani bombers tried several times to reach the city of Ludhiana but somehow failed to locate it. Why? For one thing, blackout discipline in Ludhiana was excellent. But we also knew that our friends around the world were praying for our safety, and Psalm 91 seemed written precisely for our situation. Our nine-year-old Betsy showed no fear at all, nor did the other staff children.

The members of our institution, student and staff, Indian and western, rallied to the crisis and gave unstintingly of their time and energy with cheerful goodwill and forbearance, despite the background of tension and uncertainty. Peace Corps personnel and the foreign government agencies were ordered at the outset to evacuate the Punjab; other foreign civilians were recommended to do so. But all our staff, Indian and western (with the unofficial blessing of their embassies), remained on duty where they were most needed.

Most touching was the heartfelt appreciation expressed by all in high authority. During the hostilities our hospital was visited by the governor of the Punjab, the chief minister of the Punjab, the minister of health of the central government, the minister of health of the Punjab, the deputy commissioner, the chief medical officer, the superintendent of police, the director-general of the National Cadet Corps, the Maharani of Patiala, and many others. They watched with growing interest the casualties brought to us respond to good care and return to their home villages restored. They were fascinated to see a battered young soldier, who lost his leg, walk on the third day on a temporary prosthesis made for him in our limb and brace shop.

But not all casualties pulled through. A little village girl, her shoulder shattered and her liver protruding outside her body on arrival, encouraged us for several days to think that she was winning her fight against death, only to slip away finally after late complications. Perhaps this was more merciful after all, for the same bomb that injured her had killed her mother and brothers and sister earlier: only her father had survived.

The cease-fire that ended that September's three-week war was most welcome. But no war is without its aftermath. This war left about 140,000 displaced refugees from the hard-fought Chhamb sector who had to live in vast tent villages in the hills of Jammu-Kashmir. Initially they were without medical care of any kind, and in two of these camps they were being struck down hard by typhoid, dysentery, and pneumonia. In response to an appeal by the Indian government through the National Council of Churches of India, all of our interns and house officers volunteered to set up and operate some clinics in the two worst-hit camps, and they continued working in two-week shifts of five or six doctors each until the camps were finally disbanded six months later, when winter was over.

During those six months, forty-eight of our doctors, both men and women, made a total of 62,000 clinic visits, or 430 visits a day, attending to refugee patients. For the first few months they were too busy to stop even for a midday snack. When one of them was asked how he felt being mobbed by patients, he said, "Well, I get quite upset and when I am about to shout at them, one look at them makes my heart well up with sympathy; it is hard to say anything to these people, they have suffered so much."

When our Ludhiana CMC staff found out that winter was closing in on these refugees up in the mountains and that they had only one blanket to eight people, we immediately bought all the blankets we could for them and warm underwear for their children. By Christmas our staff had donated about $2,200 for this purpose, having forgone our usual Christmas parties and exchange of presents to raise this relief money. Church World Service also gave us the cash to buy an additional one thousand blankets for them, and the World Council of Churches assisted us with some funds to help meet the medical expenses of these refugee camps; otherwise we could not have undertaken what we did.

Lal Bahadur Shastri was prime minister during that war with Pakistan. He succeeded Jawaharlal Nehru as prime minister when Nehru died in 1964. I admired Shastri immensely. He was short of stature physically but big of heart, affable, humble, and impeccably honest. I had the high honor once of shaking his hand. That was when he made his one and only visit to Ludhiana as prime minister. About two hundred government officials and leading citizens of Ludhiana District were given invitations to come meet him at the military airfield outside Ludhiana. I was the only non-Indian there. We all stood in a single row around the edge of the airfield, and when Shastri's plane arrived, he walked along the whole line of greeters, shaking hands with each person and speaking with each person. He then enplaned and flew away. We were stunned when, while signing the peace accord with Pakistan in Tashkent in January 1966, following that 1965 war, he suddenly died of a massive heart attack—a great loss to India.

Following Shastri's death, we had to go through the turbulence of Punjabi Suba, or the proposal to divide the Punjab into two main language areas, with threatened fasts-to-the-death and self-immolations, stores closed in protest, looting and rioting, curfews, and clashes with police, etc. But we were able to continue uninterrupted, the only college out of ten in Ludhiana to remain open throughout the unrest. The fact that our students and staff were made up of persons from almost all the Indian states and from twenty-three countries outside of India, living and working together in close harmony, drove home more eloquently than many sermons the Christian answer to peace among men.

While all public life around us was being disrupted, I was amazed, not just that the Christian Medical College and Hospital kept functioning, but that it was moving forward academically. By early 1966 we were approved for training for post-graduate degrees in Internal Medicine and in Pharmacology. In 1965 post-graduate training was approved for anesthesiology and for ophthalmology degrees. Surgery and Pathology had already been approved before then. And for the first time our medical college students broke all Punjab State records when eighty-one percent of those taking the official First Professional Examinations in the 1965–1966 academic year passed.

During July 1966 I was in England, where I had been invited to be one of the speakers at the Second International Congress of Christian Physicians, which met that year in Oxford. They even paid my travel expenses between India and England, and they housed me in Oxford University's New College. New College was so named, they told us, because it was relatively new—it was established in 1490 A.D. My talk was on Christian medical missions. The chief speaker there was D. Martyn Lloyd-Jones, the well-known preacher and Bible expositor who had formerly been a pathologist.

On July 1, on my way to Oxford, I was taken to attend Billy Graham's final meeting in Earls Court in London and was told that Ruth Graham wanted to see me. While sitting beside her, she said she wanted me to meet Dr. Akbar Abdul Haqq, one of Billy Graham's associate evangelists. So there in Earls Court I met Akbar Haqq for the first time and learned that he had been born in our hospital in Ludhiana and knew all about our Christian Medical College. He then made a proposition. He said that he would be holding meetings in India later that year and that the first week of September would be free for him to hold public meetings in our institution if we wished him to come. I immediately jumped at the opportunity, and so we both clinched that week for public meetings in Ludhiana.

By the time September arrived, a huge *shamiana* (tent-like structure) had been erected next to the hospital. Dr. Akbar Haqq stayed in our home with Ann and me during that week of meetings, which had packed attendances every night and made a positive spiritual impact on the whole community. He told us that he had seven young children, but his wife had died of cancer quite recently, and he was deeply concerned as to whether he could continue his present evangelistic ministry which took him away from his children for weeks and months at a time, especially now that his children had lost their mother. We promised we would add our prayers to his for God's guidance in this dilemma.

On the last day of his meetings, while we were having breakfast together, Dr. Haqq asked me, "Do you suppose I could have your permission to take one of your doctors with me?"

"Why, of course," I replied agreeably, not realizing exactly what he had in mind. Ann caught on to what it was about before I did, and we learned then that during the week of his meetings, Akbar Haqq had been conducting a double campaign—the evangelistic campaign which we knew about, and also a successful campaign to woo and win our assistant professor of surgery, Dr. Doris Sohan Lal. He had never met her before that week, but apparently there had been extensive communication between Akbar's family and Doris's family, and Ann and I were among the last to know about it. Anyway, the two were married on November 21 in Jullundur, near Ludhiana, and almost the entire college and hospital attended their wedding. Doris and Akbar's home today is near Minneapolis. We still believe Christian marriages are made in heaven regardless of all the maneuverings and arrangements that we humans make.

October of that same year took me once more out of India, this time to visit Australia for three weeks and New Zealand for one week on a tight deputation schedule for Ludhiana CMC which included almost all the major cities down under—Perth, Adelaide, Melbourne, Sydney, Brisbane, Townsville, Christchurch, Dunedin, and Auckland. (This visit coincided with President Johnson's in both countries.) It was spring there, and a summery Christmas was in the air. This was the first visit a Ludhiana director had ever made to either Australia or New Zealand. As in England in July, people everywhere showed warm interest and gracious hospitality, for our college in Ludhiana had faculty members from both these countries down under, and their support had been generous over the years. My time there was encouraging and invigorating, and my only regret was that Ann could not be there to enjoy it with me.

The caliber of our medical students seemed to be getting better all the time. In 1966, there were 1,537 applicants for the fifty seats in the first-year class. And that year one of our Indian faculty, Dr. Sargit Singh Gill, who was also one of our graduates, returned from two years of advance surgical training in the U.S. under Dr. Michael DeBakey in Houston, Texas. Dr. DeBakey had wanted Dr. Gill to join his staff and had offered him a starting salary fifteen times greater than what we could give him, but Dr. Gill chose to return to us instead.

One of our senior medical students that year gave his heart to Christ, then after winning his Hindu roommate to Christ, volunteered to become a medical missionary to the Northeast Frontier Agency, where the Mizo and Naga tribespeople live and where non-Indians were no longer permitted to come.

In November 1966, the government of India began requiring special entry permits for all commonwealth *missionaries*—other commonwealth personnel had no such restrictions but could continue coming and going ad lib. This brought added concern for the five new staff members we were expecting from the United Kingdom the next few weeks. We were thankful that permits did come through eventually for all five British colleagues, but two ship sailings had to be canceled before their official visas arrived— all part of the growing militant Hindu pressure on the Indian government to exclude Christian missionaries.

Also in November 1966, our new student nurses' home was opened for occupancy by our 150 student nurses. But two-fifths of our Brown Memorial Hospital still remained unbuilt, due to lack of funds; the three-fifths already built was always crowded.

With Mr. Darma Vira, governor of Punjab and Haryana States, at the Christian Medical College Convocation, Ludhiana, March 18, 1967.

Apparent when we first began serving in Ludhiana was how dependent we were on continued support from western Christian sources, if the Christian Medical College and Hospital were to survive. This would be particularly important for funding capital projects. To get this support, we depended on representatives in each of the major countries supporting us who could effectively represent, interpret, and promote our institution in Ludhiana. We will always be most grateful for all those persons who over the years have devotedly served, often full-time, in the Ludhiana offices in London, New York, Toronto, Sydney, Christchurch, and elsewhere. We owe a special debt of gratitude to a couple whom Methodist Bishop J. Waskom Pickett recruited for us soon after we arrived in Ludhiana, namely, the Rev. Charles Reynolds and his wife Maud, formerly Methodist missionaries in Hyderabad, India. Throughout the more than thirty years they directed the Ludhiana

Christian Medical College Board, U.S.A., office in New York City, Charles proved himself an indefatigable go-getter. He has been phenomenally successful in obtaining support for us, both private and governmental, including the first USAID grant from PL-480 funds to be awarded to any Christian project overseas. Charles has for years conducted tours to India and Ludhiana, assisted staff and graduates with personal needs, and has managed countless transfers of funds and equipment. He has traveled everywhere to raise interest and support for CMC. Over the years I have been convinced that without Charles's tireless energy and enthusiasm and his talent for getting big things accomplished with dispatch, our Ludhiana CMC would probably have foundered long ago.

On June 5, 1967, the Six-Day War between Israel and its neighbors began. One might think that that conflict in the Middle East could have no bearing on a nation like India. Not so. When the rumor spread that Israeli planes had bombed Mecca (which they did not), three Christian churches in Srinagar, the capital of Kashmir, went up in flames—mob thinking is not always carefully reasoned. At that moment the Ludhiana Christian Medical College Village Eye Service was making final preparations for an eye camp to be held in a village forty-four miles from Srinagar, the first ever to be held in Kashmir. The obvious question arose: Would it be safe now to hold the eye camp, or should it be canceled?

But Christian concern for others in need is not easily discouraged, and so the eye camp was held as scheduled. Over 2,200 patients came from all parts of Kashmir to be helped, some travelling for weeks on foot. Hindus and Muslims camped elbow to elbow, and along with their eye surgery—mostly cataract surgery—and refractions and other treatments, they heard for the first time the Good News. All this was without incident. It is interesting that the church-burning made newspaper headlines. The eye camp event, not considered newsworthy, was known only to those who were there, that is, to those who performed this service and to those who received it, including the 133 blind who could now see and the hundreds of others rescued from threatened blindness.

Our Brown Memorial Hospital was the fortunate recipient of a complete, modern diagnostic X-ray unit provided through the Presbyterian (U.S.A.) Fifty-Million Fund. This was the kind of equipment we had desperately needed for some years. It was manufactured by General Electric and was shipped to India in thirty-two huge boxes duty-free through the Indo-American Agreement in early 1967. Unfortunately, only thirty boxes were unloaded in Bombay, the other two—the most important and the bulkiest—sailed on to Calcutta at the opposite end of India. When the mistake was discovered, the two boxes were finally place on a returning ship and were to be off-loaded at Bombay. Unfortunately again, the two boxes sailed on and were reported to be in Port Said. In response to frantic messages to Port Said the two boxes were placed on another freighter at Port Said and cleared the Suez Canal just five days before the Six-Day War began, and we eventually received them in Ludhiana. If this had happened one week later, we would probably never have seen this equipment, because the Six-Day War closed the Suez Canal for many months.

An important part of this donated X-ray unit—and the last thing to arrive—was its image intensifier, the element essential today for doing fluoroscopy. But all image intensifiers made for General Electric were made in France then, and no Indo-French Agreement existed. Furthermore, an image intensifier had to be activated at the place it was to be used within ten days of its manufacture in France.

I had to make three trips to New Delhi to visit innumerable governmental offices in order to arrange permits and schedules. I felt that as director, I had to do this myself because so much was at stake; and in India one uses the highest man on the totem pole to try to surmount official inertia, simply because he carries more clout and may succeed where others won't. The customs chief was kind to me and very helpful, I believe in great measure because he had a daughter he was eager to have accepted as a student in our Christian Medical College, and he told me so. I tried to be gracious, but insisted that I could make no promises concerning his daughter. When the image intensifier arrived by air in New Delhi, I personally met it, saw it through customs, took it to Ludhiana and notified the General Electric engineer in Bombay to come to Ludhiana immediately.

Do you want to know what a missionary does? Well, everything under the sun comes under his or her purview, and so you find a missionary doing anything that is "needful" (to use a common Indian expression), whatever it is.

My birthday in 1967 was a special day for our family, but not as we had intended it. I had been detained in my office in the hospital all day until dusk and was eager to get home, because I knew that Ann and Betsy were waiting for me to come home to pop a birthday surprise on me. I jingled the bell on my executive bicycle as I neared the director's bungalow. Betsy heard it and came bounding out the front door to greet me. In the dim light she didn't see the large brown dog lying on the doormat and stepped right on him. He bit her above her ankle, and I could see from his groggy, uncoordinated behavior that he was probably rabid. Rabies is common in India and is always a nightmare. We penned up the dog that night; by morning he was dead.

One of our younger surgeons removed the dog's head and drove with it to the Indian Health Service's Regional Rabies Laboratory about a hundred miles away. That happened to be on Good Friday, which is a national holiday in India; so the laboratory was closed. Easter is also a national holiday, so the Saturday between the two days was a holiday, too. Therefore no examination of the dog's brain could be made until the following Monday. On Tuesday we received a telegram informing us that the dog was indeed rabid.

We, of course, had not waited for confirmation, but had begun anti-rabies vaccination immediately, using the only material then available—fourteen injections of monkey brains, one each day, into Betsy's tummy. The Chief Medical Officer of Ludhiana always insisted on keeping all rabies vaccine in his possession in the Civil Hospital, across the street from our Brown Memorial Hospital, in spite of the fact that electricity interruptions in Ludhiana were frequent and his old-fashioned refrigerator was warm much of the time.

But God was good to us, and Betsy suffered no harm. We have personally seen several tragic deaths in India from rabies, including one of our own interns and also a young American missionary mother of three small children. We have seen rabies in many cats and dogs and even in a donkey. One week after the big brown dog bit Betsy, another large rabid dog appeared at our front door. Don Wysham, our chief cardiologist, brought it down with his shotgun, only to have some of the dog's brain tissue splatter onto his hand, which had a small cut in it; that required Don Wysham to undergo fourteen injections of monkey-brain vaccine! A few months later, we had to destroy our beautiful pet Siamese cat because she had fraternized with a neighbor's rabid cat. So much for rabies.

That same year (1967), near the southern tip of India in the communist state of Kerala, a new Christian hospital was being erected. This hospital was being entirely financed by an Indian Christian who had made a promise to God and was keeping his promise. Mr. Verghese owned a plywood industry that had once hit on hard times and faced bankruptcy. He promised God that if God would rescue his business and cause it to prosper, he would give God nine-tenths of all his income for the rest of his life. Almost overnight his fortune turned and he became the wealthiest man in a community where poverty was rife. Because no medical services were available for many miles, Mr. Verghese felt God wanted him to build and operate a Christian hospital for that populous district and provide free care for its poor.

Building the hospital structure was begun. But staffing a hospital with physicians is always more formidable an undertaking than putting bricks and concrete together, and for this Mr. Verghese appealed to the Christian Medical College and Hospital in Ludhiana for help. Before we knew it, we had lost two husband-and-wife doctor teams from our Ludhiana senior staff—Doctors John and Naomi Vettath and Doctors Samuel and Susie Joseph. All four doctors were graduates of our Christian Medical College and were experienced physicians. All four were assistant professors in our medical center in their respective fields: John in general and thoracic surgery, Naomi in pharmacology, Samuel in internal medicine, and Susie in anesthesiology.

Late in 1967 I made a short visit to see these four doctors, the Vettaths and the Josephs, in their new hospital. It was my one and only visit to Kerala State. I found the hospital was still being built, but was already in full operation and all its available beds were occupied. I also met Mr. Verghese, now white-haired but young in spirit and vigorous in lending a hand making final touches. I found that he had also just built a church; I attended a heart-warming service in it.

Here in this crowded city was a strong Christian witness, backed by an effective humanitarian service in Christ's name, in an Indian state where no foreign missionary was permitted to serve. All of this came into being because an Indian Christian industrialist had kept his promise to God and because a Christian medical teaching center a thousand miles away had trained and provided the very agents he needed for that Christian presence.

The 1967 Christmas pageant in our hospital in Ludhiana, in which a Christian Tibetan student nurse in our School of Nursing played the part of the Virgin Mary.

At the very northernmost part of India was the Dalai Lama of Tibet, who had had to flee from his native land along with his many brothers and sisters when the Chinese Communist Army invaded his country. During my first term in Ludhiana each one of the Dalai Lama's brothers and sisters was, at some time, an in-patient in our Brown Memorial Hospital. The Dalai Lama himself was never in Ludhiana, but our Mobile Eye Service did examine his vision and provided him with the first pair of glasses he ever owned.

Every Christmas a pageant was always presented in our hospital which told the Nativity story. To this day I can vividly recall the 1967 Christmas pageant in which a Tibetan nursing student of ours played the part of the Virgin Mary. I remember that my eyes welled up when I thought of the gospel's rare contacts with Tibetan people, yet here was a lovely young Tibetan woman portraying Jesus' mother with tenderness and grace, because she believed in Jesus.

CHAPTER SIXTEEN

ANOTHER FURLOUGH

OUR FURLOUGH YEAR 1968–1969 GAVE US NO TIME to rest. It began with our attending Charles's graduation from Stony Brook School on Long Island, then rushing south to see our son Ken graduate from Davidson College in North Carolina. At that outdoor commencement event, which was interrupted by a mighty cloudburst before the degrees could be awarded, I was given a doctor of laws honorary degree, as was also my friend Carlton Chapman, class of '36, president of our student body and a Rhodes scholar. It was Carlton, later a physician like myself, with whom I had teamed to give a joint musical recital during my junior year at Davidson—a recital, you remember, which was canceled when Professor Thomas Lingle suddenly died.

Ken Jr., who had taken ROTC at Davidson, immediately went to Germany with the U.S. Army—he had been given the choice of going either to Germany or to Vietnam and predictably chose Germany. Charles entered Princeton University that fall, and Ann and Betsy settled for the year in the Payne Hall missionary apartments in

Princeton. I was making deputation visits most of that furlough year. I found myself in California during all of January and February, 1969—January in San Francisco Bay area and February in the Los Angeles–San Diego area, staying in various peoples' homes as their guest each night, daily talking on medical missions and Ludhiana CMC in particular.

One pleasurable duty I promised to do while in San Francisco was to look up the chief of surgery in the medical center of the University of California at San Francisco and to thank him personally for saving the life of our beloved Ludhiana Professor of Orthopedic Surgery, Dr. Lionel Lobo, an Indian from Goa. Dr. Lobo had rapidly developed kidney failure, and it soon became apparent that dialysis alone could give only temporary reprieve and that only a kidney transplant could save his life. We had found a merchant in Ludhiana whose tissues matched Lionel's and who was willing to go to America to give his kidney to Lionel, whom he greatly revered. In those days it was highly unusual for anyone from overseas to be considered for renal transplant surgery in America even if they could pay for it. The acceptance of Dr. Lobo for this procedure, at minimal expense to him and to us, was therefore a near miracle, and I felt I had to express our deep gratitude personally to the surgeon who did all this for us. When I met him in his office, I found him to be a most friendly and compassionate man and, I was delighted to learn, a truly great African-American hero. Lionel Lobo was at that moment still in California recuperating from his surgery, which had been successful and which enabled him not only to continue as chairman of our department of orthopedic surgery, but also in addition to succeed Dr. Guy Constable as the principal of the Christian Medical College on Dr. Constable's retirement in 1971, becoming the first Indian national ever to head our Christian Medical College. Dr. Lobo, who finally died several years ago, was deeply loved and respected by everybody, not only because of his great abilities and his warm personality, but also because of his unbeatable courage and resilience in the face of the severe hip pain and disability subsequent to his kidney transplant which eventually required hip replacements.

Returning to my winter in California: It was an eye-opener to me, for that was a period of great student upheaval and rebellion, partly as protest against the Vietnam War, partly as hippie revolt against precedents and discipline. The battle cry of youths kicking off moral restraints was, "Do your own thing; if it feels good, do it. And don't trust anyone over thirty." As one student told me, "If I were to study when I didn't feel like it, I'd be a hypocrite." And movie idols were, characteristically, *non*-heroes.

I remember my attending and speaking at a meeting of the San Francisco Presbytery. I was invited to come by its then-moderator, Dr. Cary Weisiger, a Stony Brook School alumnus and the senior pastor of the Menlo Park Presbyterian Church. At that meeting, a young minister, bearded and wearing a T-shirt and sneakers, sat, not in the pews with the other ministers and elders, but by himself in the balcony of the church, his legs dangling out between the balusters—that is how I knew he was wearing sneakers. He interrupted several times the persons who had the floor at that moment. Finally someone asked him, "Why did you ever choose to enter the ministry?" His reply was, "I wanted to find myself." The following Sunday I gave the sermon in Cary Weisiger's church—the only time in my life that I preached at three successive worship services on a single Sunday morning.

While I was in the Los Angeles area, I was privileged to stay overnight in the home of Dr. J. Edwin Orr, a small man physically but a spiritual and intellectual giant, also an acknowledged authority on the history of spiritual awakenings, having been personally involved in some great Christian revival movements himself. I was impressed with his energy and self-discipline and with the prodigious amount of literary output that came from this humble man of God. While his good wife Carol was preparing dinner for us, I had the temerity to ask Dr. Orr if he would be willing to hold some meetings in our Ludhiana Christian Medical College and Hospital the next time he came to India—he was always on the go somewhere in the world. To my delight he said he would be glad to do so, and we made a date for March of the following year for both him and Mrs. Orr.

On May 31, 1969, our son Ken and Norma Dudde were married in the same church where Ann and I were married and where I had been the organist throughout my four years in medical school—the Presbyterian Church-of-the-Covenant of Bala-Cynwyd, Pennsylvania, which was now our chief supporting church. Ken had just returned from Germany on a short leave. Norma, the daughter of a Lutheran minister and former missionary in India, had just graduated from Bryn Mawr College earlier that same year, after completing her studies in three years. Her father performed the wedding ceremony and I was the organist. That same night she and Ken boarded a military plane at JFK Airport in New York which flew them to Frankfurt. What a whirlwind of events for them both within less than a week! Ann and Betsy and I followed them shortly on our way back to India, spending several days with them in Germany. How a young bride could cope so well with all that and then have three new in-law guests thrust on her so soon, and that in a foreign land, is a tribute to her resilience.

CHAPTER SEVENTEEN

REMAINING YEARS IN LUDHIANA

UY CONSTABLE HAD DONE A GOOD JOB AT holding the fort as acting director during our furlough year. I found on our return to Ludhiana that plans were already being developed for celebrating the seventy-fifth anniversary of the founding of the Christian Medical College, which was to take place early in 1970.

All day January 30, the day before the celebrations were to begin, heavy rains drenched everything. And trains and buses to Ludhiana were canceled when violence broke out in neighboring Haryana State. One of the chief guests telephoned that he could not come. Things did not look promising. But January 31 dawned under cloudless skies. The chief guests all arrived after all, including the Union Minister of State for Health and Family Planning, the American Ambassador Kenneth B. Keating, and our former Director/Principal from England, Dr. Eileen R. B. Snow. A large party of Ludhiana friends and former staff members from America and Canada were there, too, brought by Charles Reynolds in a chartered plane from New York. Alumni/Alumnae

Ann with Dr. Eileen R. B. Snow, who had been director and principal of the Christian Medical College and Hospital throughout India's turbulent partition years.

and guests came from all over India. It was a happy and impressive occasion. On one of those three days Ambassador Keating laid the cornerstone of the new Private Patient Block, which happened to be the first project ever to be funded to a private institution overseas by the U.S. government under its Public Law 480.

The day after his stay in our home, Ambassador Keating wrote Ann and me: "Yesterday was a very proud day for me. I saw much of the best America has to offer the world. It was a wonderful day. . . . It was a great privilege for me to meet you and your associates. Would you please convey to them my special thanks and my admiration for the wonderful contribution everyone connected with your institution is making to the welfare of the people of North India."

Soon after that the U.S. Embassy in New Delhi began sending some of its American personnel to us in Ludhiana for specialized medical and surgical services. Prior to then, such personnel were always flown to the U.S. military hospital in Frankfurt.

In March 1970, Dr. And Mrs. J. Edwin Orr came to Ludhiana as promised, bringing a whole week of spiritual refreshing to a receptive and appreciative medical community at the morning and evening public meetings and to smaller groups within the institution.

At that time a beloved Indian minister friend of ours underwent major surgery and had a cardiac arrest in the recovery room.

He wrote to us when he reached home: "I have returned home with indelible impressions of love, sympathy and concern coupled with efficiency, discipline and services. It is not only physical healing that is going forth, but Christian witness and salvation of souls in the Christian Medical College. One can justly be proud of this institution. May the Lord be more and more glorified through the CMC."

As director of the Christian Medical College and Brown Memorial Hospital in Ludhiana I was, by virtue of my position, also on the council of the Vellore Christian Medical College and Hospital in South India, at times also on its executive committee. Twice every year this meant taking a train to Delhi, then an Indian Airlines plane to Madras, then a bus to Vellore. Coming back two days later, the air trip was usually a night flight through Nagpur. Nagpur was the central spot in India to which small mail planes came from Bombay, Delhi, Calcutta, and Madras, converged at midnight, transferred their loads and passengers, and then flew

Left to right: Dr. J. Edwin Orr, his wife Carol, Mrs. Chandra-Sekar (wife of deputy minister of health, central government of India), and Ann, Ludhiana, 1970.

back to where they came from; this meant, of course, no sleep that night. Despite the tiring travel involved, I looked forward to seeing many other medical missionaries at these meetings and to building friendships with many of Vellore's fine staff, who often contributed ideas helpful to me for operating their sister institution in Ludhiana. At the same time, their situations and ours were quite different; they had problems we did not have, and vice versa.

Another Christian medical teaching center to which I regularly traveled, at least yearly, as a member of their board of directors, was the Miraj Medical Center in western India. Its director was also on our Ludhiana governing body and has for many years been a good friend, beginning with school days in Pyengyang, Korea—Dr. Archie Fletcher Jr. Archie and his wife Huldah were brought up in Taegu, where Archie's father had built up the hospital where Ann and I served during our first term in Korea. At their wedding in Germantown, Philadelphia, I had played the organ for them. While I was a surgical resident in the Graduate Hospital of the University of Pennsylvania, Archie was a surgical resident in the HUP, or Hospital of the University of Pennsylvania. While at HUP, Archie's performance as a surgeon and an academician was so brilliant that his professors begged him to join their permanent teaching staff; instead, he kept his resolve to pursue Christian service overseas. In Miraj he proved his genius also as an administrator. I have always had the highest regard for the Fletchers.

During the fall of 1970, right after India Youth for Christ's head, Victor Manogarom, had conducted a week of meetings in our Ludhiana institution stressing Christian commitment, I went to Poona (Pune) for the Biennial Conference of the Christian Medical Association of India, where I was the opening speaker. To that conference, Ray Knighton, the founder of MAP International (Medical Assistance Program) in America, brought Dr. Denis Burkitt, of world fame in medicine, as our chief speaker. We recalled that Dr. Burkitt, a Christian physician, always fascinating to listen to, had made a major discovery in medical science when he described Burkitt's lymphoma in Central Africa and was the first to relate this malignant tumor to an insect vector. He reached this breakthrough discovery not by sophisticated expensive laboratory research, but solely by means of a jeep, a notebook and pen, and by the alert observations of his own keen mind.

On November 29, 1970, in the city of Nagpur, the Church of North India was founded. The Church of South India had already existed for some years. In a nation where scarcely two percent of the population is Christian, the incongruity of numerous Christian denominations bearing foreign names had become increasingly confusing, if not ridiculous—one Indian Christian saying to another, "I am a New Zealand Presbyterian," or "I am Dutch Reformed," or "I am United Church of Canada," or "I am a Missouri-Synod Lutheran."

It was the Methodists who originally championed church union most vigorously; and with a strong Anglican presence, it was soon agreed that the presiding hierarchy would be known as bishops. It was ironical, therefore, that when most of the Protestant Church bodies throughout most of India (the Church of South India was limited to the deep south) finally agreed to unite to become the Church of North India, the Methodists opted out. This was primarily because Methodist policy stipulated that Methodist bishops worldwide should receive the same salaries no matter what country they were in. So if a Methodist bishop in India were to become a bishop of the Church of North India, his salary would depreciate by some eighty percent; many Methodist bishops in India were unwilling for such a cut.

Being a medical missionary, I never anticipated ever getting involved in ecclesiastical affairs, much less church politics. But when the delegates and leaders of the new Church of North India convened for four days in April 1971 (in Jullundur thirty-five miles from Ludhiana) for their first major administrative meeting since the church was formed, I was officially invited to come as a guest. Before I quite realized what was happening, this body elected the members of its Board of Health Services and then appointed me as its chairman for a three-year term. As chairman of this board, I was automatically on the Executive Committee of the Church of North

India, and I attended its meetings regularly. For awhile, Bob Abrams, our Presbyterian treasurer in Bombay, was the only expatriate besides myself on this committee. This and the board duties took me from Ludhiana more often than I would have wished, but I felt this service to this new church should not be evaded.

One of the more arduous duties of this board was to receive and prioritize the requests for monetary and personnel help being submitted by the scores of hospitals and medical projects affiliated with the Church of North India, since many overseas denominational mission agencies were saying that they would now honor only those requests approved and received through the Church of North India. Fortunately for me, the members of my board were all excellent Indian colleagues, good to work with and willing and able to do what was asked of them.

I must admit that the first several months as chairman kept me hopping, for I was responsible for drawing up the board's constitution and by-laws and for establishing the eight regional boards set up under it to administer the sixty-seven hospitals operated by the Church of North India throughout fifteen of India's nineteen states.

At the same time, our Christian Medical College and Hospital in Ludhiana was trying to respond as best we could to the tragic plight of the some ten million refugees who were then streaming into India from East Pakistan (soon to be known as Bangladesh). We were the first medical college in North India to send medical relief teams to serve among them. Beginning in June, we sent five doctor-nurse teams when cholera was at its height. The refugees had to be vaccinated before they were permitted to enter the refugee camps. At one time, those waiting their turn made a double line two miles long, in spite of the fact that our doctors and nurses, with their three jet injectors, were immunizing two thousand persons each hour. And it was raining hard then, with the monsoons on. (Senator Ted Kennedy was there one day to watch them.)

I don't recall exactly which year it was, but it was in one of the years that Dr. Ram Singh was superintendent of the Brown Memorial Hospital. Dr. Ram Singh was a kindly, gracious, elder-statesman kind of gentleman who knew everybody and was known and respected by everybody, including the general public. One day he informed me that the Maharajah of Naba, who lived some seventy kilometers from Ludhiana, and his maharani had invited him, Ann, and me to spend a day with them at their palace. To us this invitation had the force of a summons, and we quickly accepted.

It was a beautiful day when we arrived there. We were met personally by the maharajah and the maharani, who we found to be a middle-aged and very attractive couple. They showed us around through the whole spacious palace, which was furnished in elegant good taste. Even the crystal chandeliers breathed "home" and avoided ostentation. After a sumptuous luncheon, they took us on a tour of the outlying premises, which included their garage where eight or nine motor vehicles of all vintages, including a 1904 Rolls-Royce Silver-Cloud, were stabled, all spotless and gleaming.

During afternoon tiffin, they stated why they had invited us. They were concerned, they said, for the health care of the people over whom they still bore responsibility, and they wanted to donate their main palace building to the Ludhiana Christian Medical College to be used as a hospital for their people if we would staff it and operate it. They, in turn, liked to travel and would be away much of the time, but would live in one of the smaller buildings whenever they were at home.

Dr. Ram Singh and I looked at each other, wondering how to reply to such an offer, which was obviously sincere and was certainly generous. We had been offered premises before if we would staff them and operate them as a rural hospital or clinic, but the only such offer we had accepted eventually became the Gurbachan Memorial Hospital in Lalton Kalan, a village about five miles from Ludhiana, which was useful for our community health teaching program. Kind-hearted laypeople usually do not realize that there is much more to having a hospital than putting up a building for it to be in; staffing and supplying and managing it are what make a hospital difficult and expensive to operate.

With these realities in mind and with seventy kilometers of poor roads separating the palace from Ludhiana, Dr. Ram Singh and I knew such a proposition was not feasible. But how does one say no to the offer of a palace without giving offense? In Asia one relies on smiling and artful circumlocutions in order to avoid bluntness and so save face. I gave a silent quick prayer, and Dr. Ram Singh, a loving, understanding man with diplomacy in his blood, pulled us through that difficult hole unscathed, parrying for just enough time to avoid hurt feelings and embarrassment. Later we learned that the maharajah and his lovely maharani seemed satisfied and apparently understood why we could not accept their offer.

━━◄►━━

The year 1971 was a particularly difficult one financially for Christian institutions in India. This was not a sudden crisis, but was like a creeping drought. We thought this might somehow be related to the drying up of Christian concern at home for all responsibilities overseas (the Vietnam War was still on), though undoubtedly the growing reluctance and even refusal of the Indian government to grant entry visas to Christian missionaries may have contributed to the cooling of western interest in supporting Christian work in India. "We must take care of needs in our own backyards" was a refrain that became increasingly audible across the oceans.

For example, in 1964 (Ann's and my first year in Ludhiana) forty-two percent of our Christian Medical College's operating budget was met by income from abroad. But by 1970, this contribution from abroad had dropped to thirteen percent; and in 1971, the figure was nine percent. Our then-United Presbyterian Church in that one year reduced its missionary personnel in India from sixty-four to fifty for financial reasons. Many of us in India pledged ten percent of our 1972 salaries to COEMAR (the Commission on Ecumenical Mission and Relations), with the result that the fifty missionaries could be increased to fifty-two— thus sparing the axe for one missionary couple. We heard that missionaries in other countries and supported by some other

mission agencies besides COEMAR also faced similar retrench-
ment. We reflected that the concept of "physician, heal thyself" has
a stunning logic that soon leads to spiritual self-embalmment.

So it seemed almost too much for us to swallow when word
came to the new Church of North India from several mission
boards to the effect that now that the Church of North India had
come into being and was now in charge of its institutions—its
schools, colleges, hospitals, etc.—it could now be expected to
support its own institutions. Of course, it wasn't stated that
bluntly, but the real meaning was unmistakable. We wondered
how anybody in the West could even think such a thing just
because our own wealthier churches in the comparatively affluent
Christian West felt they no longer need to foot the costs of their
own hospitals and colleges. The comfortable fallacy here, we felt,
came from overlooking India's poverty and forgetting that not
more than two percent of its population is Christian.

Besides enduring our own financial belt-tightening in
Ludhiana, we were trying to bear up under the electricity famine
prevailing throughout Punjab State, with an average daily outage
of four to six hours. But even when the current was on, hallways
and rooms in the hospitals remained dark and fanless in order to
lower electricity bills.

Despite the fiscal pressures to reduce our programs at CMC
rather than develop them, a dramatic opportunity opened to
expand our community health program into what we had long
hoped it to be. Around April 1972, Dr. Harbans Dhillon, the
dynamic joint director of health services and family planning in
the Punjab State government, retired from her many years of
government service. But just before she had announced her intent
to retire, the chief medical officer of Ludhiana District gave a
dinner in her honor (she grew up in Ludhiana District), and he
invited me to attend. I was given my seating next to Dr. Dhillon's.
While chatting with her during the dinner, Dr. Dhillon told me she
was retiring very soon. I asked her what she planned to do then,
and she said she would like to settle down in the village of Lalton

Kalan (in Ludhiana District), where many of her family still lived. I told her she was too young and too energetic to put her impressive talents to rest, and I then and there invited her to come to work with us at CMC and expand our community health program. She already knew about our satellite hospital, the Gurbachan Memorial Hospital in Lalton Kalan, her home village.

To my surprise and delight, she said she would like to do that, and she promised to give her decision in a few days, that is, after she had submitted her official request for retirement. Word of her coming retirement spread rapidly, and within a few days I heard that the prestigious Postgraduate Institute of Medicine of the Punjab University in Chandigarh was offering her a full professorship if she would join their faculty and was offering her a salary which we could never match. In our conversations I felt that, even though she and her husband were Sikhs, she really wanted to join us. And in spite of enormous pressures and inducements from the Punjab University and others, Dr. Dhillon eventually decided to join our staff full-time. And for the next several years, as director of our new Comprehensive Health Development Program she worked closely and happily with our own Dr. Betty Cowan from Scotland. They brought about a near-miracle of motivation and success which would have stymied most medical teaching centers in India.

The program Dr. Dhillon was given to direct was soon covering a population of twenty-eight thousand in thirteen rural villages plus a population of fifteen thousand in a slum area within the city of Ludhiana itself plus about eight thousand farmers and factory workers in a suburb of Ludhiana, with special emphasis on maternal and child health. The chief feature of this program was an integrated involvement of medical and nursing students, interns, and residents in practical training at the village and home level. Having pulled in our belts everywhere else, we regarded this program as a feasible responsibility too important to pass up, and we pursued it by faith, though sufficient funds were initially nowhere in sight.

Near the end of 1971, with another war with Pakistan threatening us, we were again making preparations for possible war casualties, just as we did in 1965. The war did indeed take place, with its strict blackouts each night, but mercifully lasted only thirteen days. All our own children happened to be with us then, including our first grandchild, Thayer. That Christmas was our first Christmas together overseas in ten years.

That second war with Pakistan highlighted President Nixon's tilt toward Pakistan, which put us Americans in the doghouse in India. None of us knew then, of course, that this tilt was part of the maneuvering necessary to contact Beijing and open Communist China to the West. The result of this tilt in India was India's coalition with the USSR, and soon "Indo-Soviet friendship" was the buzzword resounding everywhere. Soon Ludhiana industries were exporting ninety percent of their manufactured textiles and bicycles to iron curtain countries.

All this inspired the predominant labor union in India, which was openly Communist-controlled, to begin a determined drive to unionize our 1,400 hospital employees. We knew this labor union had clout, because it already controlled all post office, bank, railroad, telephone, telegraph, and bus company employees in North India, not to mention many employees in private-sector industries and institutions.

This union effort was launched in October 1972 and began with slogan-shouting marchers, thirty to sixty-strong, rallying at the main hospital gate at least twice daily. They were not permitted to enter private grounds, but sometimes they would dump raw, stinking garbage within the gate. Through their daily public agitation meetings at the main hospital entrance, slogan shouting, demonstrations and processions through the city, hunger strikes, posters spreading threats and vicious falsehoods, pamphlets and local newspapers, their object was to intimidate us and wear us down until we should give in and permit their puppet union to enroll our employees, and thus eventually paralyze our institution. Being Communists, their avowed purpose was to discredit anything Christian or related to the West; that is why they always referred to Brown Memorial Hospital as "the American Hospital," though we were an Indian institution with widely international participation. By reducing our hospital to a shambles they would then force the government to take it over and nationalize it, and that would be the end of a distinctively Christian ministry. Their immediate goal was to drive a wedge between India and the West, particularly America.

This effort continued unabated for almost eight months. For example, whenever I crossed the main street to enter the hospital (my office was in the hospital), their leader would call out, "Dr. Scott, *murdhabad*—Dr. Scott, *murdhabad*"; and I would run the gauntlet of his crowd chanting in response, "Dr. Scott, *murdhabad*—Dr. Scott, *murdhabad*," which means "Death to Dr. Scott." I was never harmed, not even touched.

After about six months of this, they set up a small *shamiana*, or tent, on the sidewalk at the hospital's main gate and proclaimed that one of their team was going on a hunger strike in that *shamiana*. They asked that one of our resident doctors examine the man daily and report on his condition. This was done. Later, the doctor told me that the man weighed as much after twenty days of fasting as he did at the beginning.

But one thing this persistent union had not figured on was that hundreds of Christians around the would were praying for us. And God gave us in Ludhiana the boldness to claim His promise in Mark 11:23 (RSV); "Truly, I say to you, whoever says to this mountain, 'Be taken up and cast into the sea,' and does not doubt in his heart, but believes that what he says will come to pass, it will be done for him." We prayed that this towering mountain of evil obstructionism and ill will would be removed and cast into the sea. That prayer was made in May 1973. Within three weeks of this prayer, this whole venomous campaign suddenly folded up completely, and to my knowledge there has never been a ripple since then. We were left with a stronger bond and a finer esprit de corps among our 1,400 employees than we enjoyed before. Surely this was God's doing, and it was marvelous in our eyes!

About that time, in some elections held in Ludhiana, the Communists felt quite confident that they would gain a number of seats. Instead, they did not get any. A bit nonplused, a party official asked a local resident how this could be. The local resident pointed over to the Brown Memorial Hospital and said, "Look, those people are *doing* what you Communists keep saying you are going to do."

Another interesting result of America's tilt toward Pakistan was the widely-spread rumor that our Christian Medical College and Hospital had a number of CIA agents in it. Curiously, it was said that our manager, Tony Bennett, who came from Scotland and not from America, was the top CIA agent for all Punjab State; Dr. Frank Prior, who is English, and Dr. Betty Cowan, who is Scottish, were also mentioned as CIA agents. Interestingly, I, an American, was never referred to as a CIA agent, but for almost two years every envelope coming by mail and addressed to me was routinely opened and rather crudely pasted together again before I received it. (I admit this was disconcerting to me as director.)

In November 1972, I informed our governing body at its annual meeting that I would be relinquishing my responsibilities as director in the summer of 1974. This would give them a full year-and-a-half to find and appoint my successor. Several considerations led to this decision.

1. From the beginning of our missionary career Ann and I were convinced that so far as institutional administrative responsibilities are concerned, a missionary's job is to work himself out of his job. It had been so in Korea. The need to do the same in Ludhiana seemed all the more obvious when we first went there, because at that time almost all top administrative officers and two-thirds of the academic departmental heads were missionaries from abroad—an unwholesome imbalance when we think of today's strong sense of nationhood. We thanked God that by 1971 this awkward disproportion had largely been corrected.

2. In addition, the American tilt toward Pakistan only emphasized the incongruity of an American director presiding over a major Indian institution such as ours—and *that* only seventy miles from the Pakistan border. Despite the heart-eningly genuine friendship and loyalty of our Indian staff

and students, I saw that as director I could easily become an embarrassment to our institution in its wide dealings with the Punjab University, the government of India and the public.

3. We would have fulfilled our original promise to stay with Ludhiana at least ten years. Besides, our daughter Betsy would be graduating from Woodstock School in 1974 and would be entering college that fall, and we wanted to be near her.

Ann and I would be loath to leave our many excellent colleagues and warm friends in a place that had become truly home to us and where we felt that a significant work of Christian witness and service was flourishing (due to God's palpable leading and help through many crises). But everything seemed to indicate that the timing for this decision was right.

In May 1973, Mother died after a short illness. She was almost ninety-five and had been living with Helen and Gordon in their home in Swannanoa, North Carolina, ever since Daddy died. My brother Francis (Laddie to us) sent me a cablegram when she died and also wrote a long letter detailing her final few days and describing her memorial service where Dr. L. Nelson Bell, Ruth Graham's father, made a most gracious eulogy. I never received either the cablegram or that letter—this made me wonder how much of my mail was being lost or deliberately intercepted.

Near the end of September 1973, I had to make another trip to the United Kingdom on Ludhiana business. To save expenses, I flew this time by Air India Charter, which was permitted to go no farther west than Amsterdam. I then had to take a British Airways plane the rest of the way to London. When Guy Constable, who had retired from CMC two years earlier, and his son Mark left me off at London's Heathrow Airport one week later, I checked in at the ticket counter for my British Airways connecting flight to Amsterdam in order to catch my return Air India Charter flight to Delhi. As I settled back in the waiting lounge to await my departure time, I noticed a beginning uneasiness all around me and soon learned that all the British airlines were just beginning a strike and all their flights were being canceled. So how to get to Amsterdam? My two suitcases had already been checked in; but with difficulty I managed to find them in the holding basement where many wagons were piled high with luggage. Dragging my suitcases into a taxi, I drove to another terminal to catch the only remaining seat on the next KLM flight to Amsterdam. Dr. Simon Franken, until recently our Dutch professor of ophthalmology, was waiting for me at the Schiphol (Amsterdam) Airport. Having just learned about the strike, he was about to leave the airport, but decided to wait one more hour just in case I should somehow show up. We had a happy but short visit before my Air India Charter flight was to leave Amsterdam, which was scheduled for 3:15 P.M.

I boarded that plane, a Boeing 707. But then we sat and sat, and after an hour the plane was towed from the gate and we sat some more on the tarmac until nightfall. The air conditioning and lights were turned off to conserve power, and soon the air was so hazy and acrid from the plane full of restless passengers, mostly Indians, lighting up their cigarettes to quiet their nerves that my eyes and nose smarted like fury. I walked toward the galley to get a whiff of fresh air at the open door there, only to find the captain and the crew in very heated conversation. I overheard enough to learn that a Middle East war had broken out and that the plane would not be able to make its usual refueling stop in Beirut. That day happened to be October 6, the day another Arab-Israeli war began.

At about 11 o'clock that night we were bundled off the 707 into buses, taken to a hotel and told to arise at 5:00 A.M., eat breakfast at 5:30, leave in buses for the airport at 6:00, and then fly at 7:00 A.M. We did all this, but it was 10:45 A.M. before we were airborne and on our way. The plan was to fly nonstop all the way from Amsterdam to New Delhi, but due to fuel shortage the flight ended at midnight in Bombay. I cooled my heels in the Bombay terminal hallway until a domestic flight to New Delhi left around 8:00 A.M. When I got back to Ludhiana, I took a good shower and got some needed sleep.

Two days later I had to report to Delhi for a special synod meeting of the Church of North India. Within three weeks the annual meeting of our own Ludhiana CMC governing body was to take place, and well before then we had to complete our institutional budget for 1974—a most difficult task because, unlike the budget of some major government, ours had to balance, and it could not be done without help from abroad.

By the time my last—that is, the last for me—annual governing body meeting was over, I was exhausted, and a simple cold, which ordinarily is over in a week, took a full three weeks for me to get over it. At that meeting, they wanted me to serve on the committee to nominate the next director, but I told them that a retiring director should not be in a position to influence the selection of his successor, though I would be glad to give my opinions and help if asked.

Meanwhile, Ken and Norma and their son Thayer were settling in the U.S. Embassy in Abidjan, Ivory Coast, to begin Ken's first tour of duty abroad as a career foreign service officer. Charles, who had graduated from Princeton University, had entered the University of Chicago's School of Business Administration and was beginning his M.B.A. course in hospital administration. And Betsy was enjoying her senior year at Woodstock School in the Himalayan Mountains.

I was pleased that by the time of my last year in Ludhiana, Indian nationals were now assuming their rightful place of leadership on our CMC staff. Ten years earlier, all eight top administrative positions in the institution were held by missionaries from western countries, and eleven of the sixteen academic departments in the medical college were chaired by westerners. Now, all the top administrative positions except the director were filled by Indian Christians—the principal of the medical college, the director of nursing, the general superintendent, the hospital superintendent, the treasurer, the principal of the College of Nursing, etc. Of the eighteen academic departments in the medical college, fifteen were now chaired by Indian doctors, only three by missionaries. And when I was to leave in July 1974, everyone in the governing body was agreed that the next director should be Indian. Interestingly, the governing body stipulated that the next director should be someone from outside the institution.

Our last year in Ludhiana was a whirl, which accelerated as the weather of 1974 warmed and summer approached. Most of our books and house furnishings we gave to the institution; some items we sold to our colleagues. We donated for use in the hospital chapel the upright piano we had bought from Dr. Kaz Kawata (Dr. Victor Rambo's son-in-law) our first year in Ludhiana. To dedicate this piano and to show our appreciation to our colleagues, I ventured to give a small recital in the chapel, closing with the Myra Hess arrangement of Bach's "Jesu, Joy of Man's Desiring."

In June, Ann and I saw Betsy graduate at Woodstock School. Then the staff and students in Ludhiana gave us a heart-warming send-off at an outdoor convocation, and we were presented with the money to buy a hand-carved, walnut-wood screen of our choosing, to remind us in America of our India friends.

One week before we finally left Ludhiana, I attended an event which was most meaningful to me. Mr. Chhabra, an Indian government engineer in charge of the extensive canal system in Punjab State, was baptized and received his first communion. Five years before, Mr. Chhabra's wife had undergone surgery in our hospital. Mrs. Chhabra eventually died of her cancer. But Mr. Chhabra, a Hindu then, had been so impressed by the caring concern he had seen his wife receive and also by the Good News he had heard in the hospital while visiting her that he gave his life to Christ. He told us at the time of his baptism, "I had never known what mercy was. Now I know, for I have seen it in you people, and Jesus has put mercy in my own heart, too."

Whenever Christians in the West question the relevance of medical missions or think of medical missions simply as a medium for evangelism, I like to quote what the late Dr. Kenneth Strachan of the Latin American Mission said shortly before his death. He said that Christian medical work represents "the spontaneous impulsive expression of the heart that overflows with the indiscriminate love and compassion of God for *all* mankind, poor or rich, friend or foe, responsive or unresponsive." My experience has been that the people we have known are indeed responsive to the gospel whenever caring Christians prove their loving concern for them by a practical response to their felt needs, whether medical or other. Sometimes a person's responsiveness may not be apparent; often it takes time, as with Mr. Chhabra five years after the event which first touched him.

When we left Ludhiana in July, my successor had not yet been chosen. I mentioned that the governing body stipulated that the next director should be someone from outside the institution. But in an extraordinary meeting held in August, the governing body unanimously appointed, not someone from outside, but our own Professor of Neurosurgery, Dr. K. Narayan Nambudripad. This pleased me to no end when I heard about it in America, for my eye had been on him from the beginning. While we were still in Ludhiana, Dr. Nambudripad had become a founding member and the head of a successful Gideon's Camp in Ludhiana, and for three years he had been the president of the Students' Evangelical Union for all India. In 1972 he had been one of the main speakers at the Fourth International Congress of Christian Physicians, which was held that year in Toronto. Some of the other speakers at that Toronto congress were Dr. Paul Brand, Dr. Denis Burkitt, Dr. Tony Campolo, Dr. C. Everett Koop, Dr. Haddon Robinson, and Dr. Paul Tournier.

CHAPTER EIGHTEEN

HOME AND WORK IN
NORTH CAROLINA

WHEN ANN, BETSY, AND I RETURNED TO America, Helen and Gordon were living in Swannanoa, near Asheville in western North Carolina, on the campus of Warren Wilson College, where Gordon taught. They had been there since 1964 after serving thirty years as missionaries in China and the Philippines. In 1971 they persuaded Bunny and Ted to retire among them. When Ann and I returned to the States in 1974, they all—Helen, Gordon, Bunny, Ted,— persuaded us also to join them in Swannanoa. When Laddie and Helen retired from their church in Birmingham, Alabama, in 1978, we in Swannanoa persuaded them to come join us. So for a period of seven years, all four of us surviving Scott siblings and our spouses lived within a few hundred yards of each other—the first time we had all lived together since we were children in China.

When we arrived in Swannanoa in August 1974, we settled into a house belonging to Bunny and Ted. We soon bought it and its adjacent garage-apartment from them. What appealed to us about this house was that it is surrounded by many lovely, huge trees—

oaks, pines, tulip trees, copper beeches, hemlocks, etc., with dogwoods, rhododendrons, and azaleas everywhere. Having lived most of my life in China and Korea and India, where trees were few and firewood scarce, I could now enjoy the luxury of using our living room fireplace without limit and without guilt, because of an endless supply of homegrown firewood. The designer of our one-story home, built in 1960, was the professor of architecture in the now-defunct Black Mountain College, the avant-garde center of free artistic expression, which raised eyebrows in the Black Mountain community while it existed. So our house is quite different from other houses. It has big windows all around it. We like that. We are widely exposed to our sylvan surroundings, and they give us utter privacy. Though the bedrooms are small, our living room is spacious, permitting us to entertain many people at one time without crowding.

I joined the staff of the Western North Carolina Chest Hospital in Black Mountain, the same state-operated hospital where my brother was admitted thirty years earlier and recovered from the tuberculosis he contracted in China. I was delighted to be practicing medicine and taking care of patients again. My eleven years in Ludhiana had removed me from the teaching and clinical responsibilities I had so thoroughly enjoyed before administrative responsibilities crowded them out. My position was that of staff physician. It did not entail surgery (I had done no surgery while in India), but it provided the opportunity I needed to catch up on the newest drugs and procedures being used in America, especially for tuberculosis, since about half the patients in the Black Mountain hospital had tuberculosis, the other patients having other pulmonary problems.

Each physician on the staff also made clinic visits to three or four different county health departments in western North Carolina. When the Western North Carolina Chest Hospital closed its doors in April 1980, as did all the other state-operated chest hospitals, Dr. Ozmer L. Henry, the director of our hospital, and I continued with the state as consultant physicians for tuberculosis. As such, we operated the TB clinics in the health departments of all the forty westernmost counties of North Carolina, including Mecklenburg County and Charlotte (the largest city in North Carolina). This responsibility kept us on the road much of the time; each of us logged at least twenty-five thousand miles a year. This continued until I retired from state employment in May 1990.

Working with Oz Henry was most enjoyable for me, because Oz is a delightful person to be with and work with; this was so before the hospital closed and was even more so *after*. We worked closely together. Before Ann and I returned to America, Oz had served as president of the Rotary Club of Black Mountain; so when I joined his hospital staff, he sponsored me for membership in the Black Mountain Rotary Club, and I have belonged to that club ever since. I had already been a Rotarian in Ludhiana and had valued my contacts there with Ludhiana's leading industrialists and college presidents and others (Ludhiana then had seven colleges and the largest agricultural university in the world). But I found our Black Mountain club even more stimulating and enjoyable.

In 1974, my brother-in-law Ted Stevenson, also a surgeon, began the first free clinic for poor people in Asheville. The First Baptist Church provided basement space for it, and Ann gave her time and know-how as the first nurse to help in this clinic. After a few years proved its usefulness to the community, the Buncombe County Health Department took it over and enlarged its operation, eventually moving this clinic into its health department building. Ann was then free to join the nursing staff of our hospital in Black Mountain, and she worked with my colleagues and me until it closed in 1980.

Many of us were dismayed when tuberculosis sanatoria all over the United States began closing, for we knew that tuberculosis was far from being conquered, and we feared—rightly so, as it turned out—that easing up on its control efforts too soon would result in a resurgence of this universally-prevalent disease, and its management would become increasingly difficult as emerging multidrug-resistant TB bacilli became more common. The appearance of AIDS on the human scene would only intensify the problem of TB control. The general public, accustomed to believing that tuberculosis was a thing of the past, would be in for a rude awakening, but hopefully would finally become aware that TB has been and still is the world's leading infectious-disease killer.

When we returned to America in 1974, Betsy attended Davidson College for her freshman year (or should we call it her freshperson year?). But college life in America produced somewhat of a culture shock for her, especially because Davidson College had become coed only one year before and the men hadn't yet adjusted to having women on the campus and in the dormitories. So she transferred to Warren Wilson College her sophomore year. Her junior year was spent abroad in Agra, India, attending the Institute of Hindi Studies there along with some other American students. As a young girl she had been enchanted with India, but that year in Agra helped to disabuse her of much of that allure. She had now grown up.

After graduating from Warren Wilson College, Betsy attended the College of Nursing of the University of North Carolina at Chapel Hill. With a B.S. degree in nursing, she practiced her new profession for a year in the hospital of the Medical University of South Carolina in the city of Charleston, where, as the locals have it, "the Cooper and the Ashley Rivers join to form the Atlantic Ocean." Soon after, she became a FNP (family nurse practitioner)—I was one of her teachers of that course given in Asheville. Then, as a volunteer in Kenya, she ran the nursing school in the Presbyterian Hospital in Tumu Tumu for over two years. When the severe famine in Ethiopia (then under Communist rule) drew world attention, she was there roughing it in the boondocks with a tent ward full to bursting with severely malnourished kids, usually pulled down further by dysentery, tuberculosis, etc.

In 1987, Betsy married another graduate of Warren Wilson College, John Murphy. In the next few years she earned a master's degree in public health at Johns Hopkins University, and John earned a master's degree in horticulture at Penn State University. Today they are missionaries among the people of Irian Jaya.

Our second son, Charles, a hospital administrator and married, climbed rapidly in his profession, beginning in Reading,

Pennsylvania, then to Council Bluffs, Iowa, then to Tampa, Florida. Today he is the president and CEO of the large St. Joseph's Hospital in Tampa, with responsibilities also for two other hospitals in the bay area.

Ken, our elder son, has become somewhat of an Africa specialist in the State Department's foreign service, having served in Abidjan (Ivory Coast), Douala (Cameroon), Libreville (Gabon), and Dar es Salaam (Tanzania), we hear, with distinction. He has also served in Madras (India) and in Colombo (Sri Lanka).

During my life I have never been paid a fee for medical or surgical services. Only occasionally have I received payment for playing the organ for some church service or wedding. Whatever income I have earned professionally has always been by salary. For a missionary, a salary is in reality a living allowance, given the same to all fellow missionaries regardless of a person's profession or responsibilities. While serving with the state of North Carolina, my background experience, specialty board certification, and my duties and longevity determined my salary. I was happy with this arrangement, for it has always liberated me from the financial hassles of private practice, and I could therefore continue to give my best to every patient without thinking of the patient's ability to pay.

Giving others medical service has always been gratifying to me, and I cannot recall any face-to-face doctor/patient experience that did not give me a sense of personal accomplishment. Moreover, I seem to derive even greater pleasure when I am helping those who I know can never compensate me beyond a simple thank-you. I am especially grateful that the colleagues I have worked with in my life—doctors and nurses and others— have been those who also find great satisfaction in caring for patients in trouble; their joy in doing so has shown itself in their kindliness, and I have been blessed to be their colleague.

In May 1984, Ann and I were urged to go to Wheaton, Illinois, to attend the triennial International Convention on Missionary Medicine conducted by MAP International, a non-denominational Christian medical relief corporation which has been reported by the public media to rank first in cost-effectiveness among American benevolence organizations, religious and secular. We were told that I was to be awarded the Ralph Blocksma Award, the previous recipients of which had been Dr. Denis Burkitt (1978) and Drs. Paul and Margaret Brand (1981). Ann and I went and were overwhelmed when they presented this award to me in the auditorium of the Billy Graham Center at Wheaton College. The brass plaque read

> RALPH BLOCKSMA AWARD PRESENTED TO KENNETH M. SCOTT, M.D. BY MAP INTERNATIONAL IN RECOGNITION OF DEDICATED AND COMPASSIONATE SERVICE TO THE PEOPLE OF THE WORLD THROUGH CHRISTIAN MEDI-CINE—June 3, 1984.

In response I made the following reply, which I wish to quote verbatim because those words express what was then, and still is, on my heart. I said

> This is the third International Convention on Missionary Medicine that I have attended, but this is the first time that my knees have been weak like water. May I make a comment?

> Our Lord Jesus once said, "To whomsoever much is given, of him much shall be required; and to whom men have committed much, of him they will ask the more." I was brought up with every conceivable blessing—godly missionary parents and friends, top Christian schooling overseas and in America, every spiritual and temporal need met, you name it. And ever since junior high school days I have trusted in the Lord with all my heart and have tried in all my ways to acknowledge Him, and He has graciously and wonderfully directed my paths, according to His promise in Proverbs 3:5–6, my life verses. The most I can say about myself, therefore, is "I am an unprofitable servant; I have only done my duty, what was expected of me" [Luke 17:10 paraphrase mine] given all the advantages I have had all my life.

With my wife, Ann, whom I first met in Presbyterian Hospital in Philadelphia where she was a nursing supervisor and I was an intern, things were a little different. She doesn't know I'm going to say this about her, but I'm going to say it, anyway. Ann's immediate family was not the kind that went to church. The nearest relative who did attend church was her grandmother—the family used to call her "Old Hannah." And Old Hannah used to pray day after day that when Ann grew up she would marry a preacher or a missionary. As a young girl, that prayer used to irk Ann and she would say, "Grandmother, why don't you pray for something that has a chance of being possible?" Well, years later when Ann and I were married, Old Hannah sat in the front pew of the church at our wedding with a very pleased, I-told-you-so look on her face. Not long after our wedding, Old Hannah died and was buried, but not before she had seen her prayers answered. I tell you, God does answer prayer.

But the point of my comment is this: Ann once aspired to marrying a doctor and settling down on the Main Line of Philadelphia. But when she knew that I was committed to the foreign mission field, she made no attempt at any time to dissuade me from being a missionary, but went right along and was heartily supportive right down the line. I admire her and love her deeply for this, for I have known of certain Christian women who, after marrying doctors who were headed toward the mission field, dragged their feet and kept them from ever going. And both in Korea and in India, Ann was a first-rate missionary in her own right and was a profound help and encouragement to hundreds of persons her life has touched, both missionaries and nationals.

So, in gratefully accepting this honor you have given me tonight, I include, in my heart, Ann as corecipient, whose loyalty and constant helpfulness I have too often taken for granted.

That's what I wanted to say. Thank you, and God bless you all.

I was delighted when the convention audience then gave Ann a standing ovation and made her get up onto the speakers' platform with me. I had to say what I said about her, and I meant every word of it, feeling that she should be recognized as much as I.

During all our years overseas, malpractice litigation was unheard of. When two patients died in our Brown Memorial Hospital of accidental cyanide poisoning two years before we first went to Ludhiana, nobody was sued. The hospital's pharmacy made up its own cough syrup using ammonium chloride (NH_4Cl) bought from a chemical company in Bombay. However, that company inadvertently sent one jar of ammonium cyanide (NH_4CN) with a "NH_4Cl" label on it, with the result that two hospital patients suddenly died before the terrible mistake was discovered. Instead of trying to cover up the tragedy, Dr. Mel Casberg, then director, immediately, and very wisely, called the media to a press conference and explained fully what had happened. This satisfied the public, and the matter was laid to rest.

It wasn't until we returned to America after serving in India and I began to work with the state of North Carolina's Division of Health Services that I began to appreciate how litigation-prone we Americans are and how vicious malpractice litigations can be. In September 1987, I was served a warrant naming me a defendant in a joint-and-several-liability malpractice suit along with a Charlotte radiologist, the Charlotte Radiology Group, the Providence Radiology Associates, my associate Dr. Ozmer Henry, and the entire Mecklenburg County Health Department.

Many states have outlawed joint-and-several-liability litigation because of its blatant abuse, for under this system if one defending party is found to be at fault, all the defending parties are at fault and must pay up. This is why such suits usually include, as defendants, every conceivable person who might carry insurance or who might have big money. The classical example of a joint-and-several-liability case is that of the drunk driver, driving without a license, who crashes into a telephone booth outside a convenience store and injures the man making a phone call in the booth. The injured man sues the drunk driver *and* the telephone company (for placing the booth too near the road) *and* the convenience store (because the injury occurred on its property). Since the drunk driver has no money and no insurance, the telephone company and the convenience store are required to pay the million dollars or whatever has been awarded in the joint-and-several-liability suit.

In our suit, the plaintiff was the wife of a thirty-three-year-old Charlotte man who was dying of lung cancer. The man was a four-pack-a-day cigarette smoker who had been smoking heavily since he was seven years old. It is significant that the tobacco industry was not included in this joint-and-several-liability suit. His father, with whom he was living, had undergone major surgery for what was expected to be lung cancer but turned out to be active tuberculosis. So all members of his household, being close contacts, were skin-tested for tuberculosis, as required by law, and the Mantoux skin test on the thirty-three-year-old son (thirty-one years old at the time) tested strongly positive for tuberculosis. As required by law, the son reported to the Mecklenburg County Health Department for a chest X-ray and for probable preventive drug therapy.

That's where Oz Henry and I and the Mecklenburg County Health Department came into the picture, since Oz and I were then operating the county health department's tuberculosis clinic. The Mecklenburg County Health Department's policy was that all chest X-rays made there had to be read and reported by a radiologist. (Neither Oz nor I are certified radiologists, but we regularly read all the thousands of chest X-ray films for the thirty-nine other counties we covered.) At the TB clinic, Oz interviewed this man and saw the chest X-ray which showed what the radiologist described as a "small scar," but no evidence of active tuberculosis. So Oz prescribed the usual course of preventive isoniazid for the man. Normally, no further X-rays would be called for. But because of the "small scar" and the possibility that is could represent beginning TB disease, Oz requested a follow-up X-ray film after six months. I saw that follow-up film and saw no change, but I ordered yet another film for six months from then to be absolutely sure. It was that final third film that revealed a discernible increase in the "scar." When I saw that film, I told the nurse to contact the patient immediately and tell him to report immediately for further studies. At no time did I ever see the man or talk with him, nor did I learn of his heavy-smoking history until we suspected that he might have cancer. After all, 99.2 percent of all lung cancers in America occur in patients forty years of age or older, and this man was only thirty-three years old. When he finally came to surgery, his cancer was already inoperable.

A law firm in Atlanta which specialized in physician malpractice and which draws on its own stable of $240-per-hour expert witnesses thought they had a case of wrongful death its lawyers could win. Over many weeks they took extensive depositions from dozens of people, including me. They also videotaped in their Atlanta offices a deposition from their pathetically emaciated victim shortly before he died. But then nothing happened for five years. I had to pay for my own insurance and had bought the minimum one-hundred-thousand-dollar coverage. Oz Henry carried insurance for one million dollars and the Charlotte radiologist was insured for twenty million dollars.

When a court hearing was finally scheduled some five years later, well after I had retired, the plaintiff's attorneys told my lawyer that they would drop my name from the suit if they could have my one-hundred-thousand-dollar insurance money. My lawyer, who told me that in all his twenty-three years of defending physicians he had never seen a malpractice insurance coverage as small as mine, advised me to accept this offer, and my insurance company concurred, saying that court costs of a jury trial could easily come to that much. They also warned me that if a jury sympathetic to a distressed widow with two small boys to support should decide against "those fabulously-wealthy physicians," I could be completely wiped out financially—more so since the company insuring the Mecklenburg County Health Department had by then gone bankrupt, and my own insurance coverage was for only one hundred thousand dollars. I yielded to their advice, though reluctant to do so because this whole business was patently nothing less than legalized extortion. And now I am entered into the national data bank in California as having lost one hundred thousand dollars in a malpractice suit. Does anyone wonder why tort reform is urgently needed in America?

One year after I first knew that I was a defendant in that joint-and-several-liability suit, I myself underwent radical surgery for cancer of the prostate—my first experience of being at the other end of the scalpel. Before I was discharged from the hospital, Helen's husband Gordon Mahy died of a prostate cancer that had spread extensively, and we lost a wonderful member of our family. Two weeks later, while I was still recuperating from surgery, I managed to keep my promise of many months to be the western North Carolina honorary United Nations Day chairman and keynote speaker for 1988. I spoke on the World Health Organization, which was then celebrating its fortieth year of existence. Padded well with diapers inside water-repellent pants, I got through the lecture surprisingly well (I had written it out long before my surgery).

CHAPTER NINETEEN

RETIREMENT—AROUND THE WORLD SOME MORE

I N MAY 1990, I RETIRED AFTER HAVING BEEN A STATE employee for over fifteen years. For many reasons, the timing for this seemed right. My colleagues in TB Control gave me a 35-mm camera at a farewell party, knowing that Ann and I were planning to go around the world in several weeks. Sure enough, in July and August we took a thirty-three-day trip around the world. We timed our trip to attend the Ninth Congress of the International Christian Medical and Dental Association. I had been a speaker at the Second Congress of this same organization when it met in Oxford in 1966, and I had attended the Seventh Congress when it met in Bangalore, India, in 1982, at which time the organization was still called the International Christian Medical Association— the "and Dental" was added since then. A Congress convenes every four years, always in a different country.

In 1990, this Ninth Congress met in Seoul, Korea, and Ann and I were eager to visit Seoul again, which we had not seen for twenty-two years. We were pleasantly surprised when we were met at the Kimpo International Airport by Korean friends we had

Doctors Paul and Margaret Brand in Seoul, Korea, where Paul chaired the Ninth Congress of the International Christian Medical and Dental Association, which Ann and I attended, July 1990.

been in touch with over the years but had not seen since we left Korea in 1963 some twenty-seven years earlier. Those friends were Cho Il-Jae and his wife Lee Hae-Ja, the couple I had married in the wedding ceremony that took place one month before the Student Revolution broke out in 1960. They bundled us into their Hyundai sedan and we expected them to deliver us to the hotel where we had reservations. Instead, they took us to the posh Ramada Renaissance Hotel, recently opened in the new section of Seoul south of the Han River that used to be cabbage fields when we lived there.

"This isn't our hotel," we protested as politely as we knew how. Then Il-Jae told us he had switched our reservations and that he was paying for all our hotel expenses while we were in Korea. He said, "When I last saw you, I was struggling to get enough food for my family. Now I am a rich man. I am the vice president of the Hyundai Corporation in charge of overseas operations and sales. You saved my wife's life. Now, please let me do this for you."

We were smothered with kindness by this busy man and his delightful family throughout our ten days in Seoul. We were in their home and got to know their two grown sons, the elder working in the Hyundai offices, the younger in the offices of Korea's other industrial giant, the Samsung Corporation. The family took us to the best restaurants in Seoul. They drove us to see our former home on the Yonsei University campus where a fourth-generation Underwood missionary-to-Korea was living with his family. Hae-Ja also took us through one of the huge stores of the Hyundai department-store chain. Along the way, we learned that the Hyundai Corporation's largest business was ship building, though they also made war tanks and helicopters, in addition to the automobiles we were familiar with.

We were impressed by how Seoul had grown since we were there before. The population had reached fourteen million. There were subways and elevated express highways—and terrific traffic jams. When we had lived in Seoul, there were only two bridges across the Han River—a railroad bridge and a bridge for every-thing else. Now there were seventeen bridges, and two more were being constructed. In the roof-top restaurant atop Seoul's spectac-ular sixty-three-story skyscraper we had a happy reunion with many old Yonsei University faculty colleagues and their wives.

But our main purpose for this Seoul visit was the five-day Ninth Congress of the International Christian Medical and Dental Association, the chairman of whose organizing committee was a close friend and faculty colleague of mine at Yonsei, Dr. Samuel Y. Lee. The president of this international organization was our friend Dr. Paul Brand, renowned world-wide as an orthopedic surgeon, as a pioneer in rehabilitative surgery for leprosy victims, and as a Christian author and statesman, as well as a gifted speaker always in great demand. He and his physician wife Margaret were there; so were some 350 physicians and dentists from forty-four countries. Over 400 persons had been expected from North America, most of them intending afterwards to visit China; but because of post-Tiananmen Square trepidation and a dilatory promotion in America, only 60 Americans came. As always, the Koreans were superb hosts, and Paul Brand, as usual, made a superb keynote address.

We learned that years before this, a young Korean plastic surgeon had spent nine months with Paul Brand in Vellore, in South India, as one of Paul Brand's apprentices. It turned out that that Korean surgeon's sister was the wife of the President of Korea, Roh Tae-Woo. So when Paul and Margaret Brand came to this congress in Seoul, President Roh rolled out the red carpet for them and gave a formal dinner in the President's Blue House in their honor, also inviting about a hundred of us who were attending the congress. No cameras were allowed. We were escorted to small, round tables where gold-embossed place cards, on which our full names were neatly handwritten, showed where we were to sit. We enjoyed a sumptuous western-style feast. President Roh made a gracious speech, and Paul Brand made a gracious reply. It was a memorable, heartwarming evening.

When our ten days in Seoul were over, Mr. and Mrs. Cho insisted on personally delivering Ann and me to Kimpo International Airport. Flying southward, we spent three days in Hong Kong, a bustling city with a population equal to that of all North Carolina and already tense with foreboding at the prospect of Hong Kong's becoming part of China in 1997.

We continued on to New Delhi, but did not enjoy our two-day stay there because of the heat and humidity of the monsoon season. Maybe American life had spoiled us in the sixteen years since we left India, but it did seem to us that we saw deeper poverty and greater masses of people there than when we lived in India.

Our next flight was to Nairobi. In Kenya we enjoyed a three-day safari in the famous Amboseli National Park with German and French couples as our traveling companions. We relished this experience, not only for itself and the sight of wild animals and birds at close range, but also because we were on our way presently to see our son Ken and our grandchildren Thayer and Audrey in Tanzania. In fact, the whole purpose of our continuing around the world was so we could visit these dear family members in the American Embassy in Dar es Salaam.

We found Tanzania to be a very poor country, badly run by an inept socialist government riddled with corruption. Almost every country had an embassy there in Dar es Salaam, including Iraq, North Korea, and Albania. I spent a full day visiting two hospitals there, the private Aga Khan Hospital and the public Mahimbili Medical Center hospital. The latter had been built for 1,000 inpatients, but it was bursting with 1,900 inpatients when I made rounds there; I had to step carefully between very sick patients lying on the floor and in the hallways. They had almost no drugs available for therapy and almost no laboratory facilities.

It was during our eight days in Dar es Salaam that Saddam Hussein invaded Kuwait, an event immediately applauded in the editorials of the government-controlled newspapers, which all extolled Saddam Hussein as the champion of the world's have-nots. It happened that several months later when the Persian Gulf War was in progress, the American Embassy in Dar es Salaam, barricaded against attacks and its personnel reduced to skeletal strength, became the only one to escape unscathed of the American embassies targeted by Iraqian terrorists for destruction; bombing and bombing attempts occurred at American embassies elsewhere.

By the time Ann and I finally returned to Swannanoa by way of Amsterdam, some thirty-three days after we set out to fly around the world, we were mighty happy to be back in good old America. One needs to see what the rest of the world is like to appreciate properly the good we have in the U.S., imperfect as our nation is.

I was relishing the joys of retirement, relearning piano pieces I used to play in high school and college, and puttering around our premises when I had a heart attack at the end of the year and spent the first ten days of 1991 on the hospital's cardiac floor for what my physicians called a right ventricular myocardial infarction. It was then that I learned that the white tablets I had been taking regularly for years for the Harvard Medical School's Physicians Health Study were not aspirin at all, but placebos. Ever since then I take aspirin regularly. My recovery seemed complete, and Ann and I were able to take advantage of Warren Wilson College's new Olympic-size swimming pool to keep us in shape.

Playing our piano with help from our youngest grandsons, 1992.

When we first came to Swannanoa, there was a felt need among my brothers and sisters and many of our church friends for a weekly Bible class. This we began holding before the Sunday morning church services, and I acted as the moderator. Our text was always the Bible itself, and we began first with one of the Gospels, each person reading a verse or two in turn around our circle and everyone feeling free to make a comment or ask a question at any time. Each Sunday we would begin where we had left off the week before. At one time we had half a dozen ministers attending the class, so we had expert guidance from very knowledgeable saints. The members called me their "teacher," even though Ann and I were usually the youngest in the class. The zest in the class came from the rich participation of everyone in it. By the end of twenty years, we had covered all of the New Testament and much of the Old Testament. In the course of time, most of the many persons who had attended this Bible class left this earth and graduated to Heaven.

With our three children at Fontana Dam, North Carolina, where Ann and I celebrated our fiftieth anniversary, July 1992. Left to right: Ken Jr., Betsy, myself, Ann, and Charlie.

In July 1992, Ann and I celebrated our fiftieth wedding anniversary. It was special for us in that all our children and all but one of our six grandchildren were with us to celebrate it. For that occasion we rented two cottages in Fontana Village beside North Carolina's great Fontana Dam. Charles brought his motorboat from Tampa, and we used that for swimming and cruising all over Fontana Lake.

For the rest of July and most of August, Ann and I joined our friends Charles and Maud Reynolds on a delightful trip to Ireland and Scotland, a trip which included both the Inner and Outer Hebrides. In Glasgow, we had a reunion with retired Ludhiana colleagues Betty Cowan, Tony Bennett, and Jean McLellan, and on Iona Island, with another retired Ludhiana colleague, Nancy Brash. We loved that tour so much that we joined Charles and Maud again the next year on their tour through Ireland and Northern Ireland. We encountered few American tourists in

Northern Ireland because tourists' agents, wary of terrorist violence, were not booking tours there. But our visit there was most pleasant, except for my having to begin taking nitroglycerin for some angina attacks.

The year 1993 was an eventful year for us. In January, I began working for the Buncombe County Health Department half a day each week, running their tuberculosis control program. Then came a great blizzard in March, at which time we became marooned by five-foot snow drifts, and we were without electricity for three days when high winds uprooted a one-hundred-foot fir tree of ours which fell across our power line. So we had temperatures of thirty-five degrees in our bedroom in spite of a continuous fire burning in our living room fireplace, which became the only source of heat for cooking and for keeping warm. To complicate matters, we had special house guests with us, Lee Hae-Ja and her son Cho Hyung-Jin, our dear friends from Korea who had entertained us so royally

On Iona Island, Scotland, August 1992. Left to right: Ann, Dr. Charles Reynolds, Dr. Nancy Brash (former chair of Department of Medicine in Ludhiana), and Maud Reynolds.

At a rare reunion of us four siblings. Left to right: Francis (Laddie), Helen Mahy, Bunny Stevenson, and me.

when we visited Seoul in 1990. Hae-Ja, half-frozen, reminded us wistfully that her home in Seoul was very comfortable. She and Jin had intended to drive to Florida the day after the blizzard struck, but were forced to huddle by the fireplace with us for most of the extra four days of captivity until we could get a bulldozer to plow our way out.

It was during this same blizzard of 1993 that Helen had her first knee joint replaced. That operation in St. Joseph's Hospital was the only surgery performed that day, because hospital personnel trying to reach the hospital couldn't get there, and those personnel marooned in the hospital were too exhausted for more than one operation that day. Helen's replacement of her other knee came months later that year and after she had moved from the Mahy house on college land to the cottage on our premises where Laddie and Helen had once lived. We are glad she is only a few yards from us; it is great to have a wonderful big sister so near.

In September of that same year (1993), I had to have open-heart bypass surgery—another reminder that I am mortal and am living on borrowed time. My surgeon was Dr. George Bilbrey, the same friend who had successfully operated on Gordon and Laddie years earlier for aneurysms of the abdominal aorta. One of our many blessings of life in this beautiful part of North Carolina has been the ready availability of expert and caring professional people to provide superb health services.

In August 1994, Betsy and John and their two boys Gordie and Joey flew to Indonesia for a four-year stint as missionaries supported by the Mennonite Central Committee. They were assigned to Irian Jaya (formerly known as Dutch New Guinea), the Indonesian half of New Guinea Island. This is an area of the world populated by people who until recent years were headhunting cannibals. The penetration of the gospel into some of their most primitive tribes has been vividly described in Don Richardson's best-selling book, *Peace Child*. Betsy and John maintain two homes in Irian Jaya; one in Manokwari, a port city on the north coast and site of a main Japanese naval base during World War II, the other in the elevated Kebar Valley, which is surrounded by rain forests and is accessible only by airplane, so they are dependent on the MAF (Mission Aviation Fellowship) to get them there. The people they serve are poor and malnourished, and malaria and tuberculosis are rampant. Many of these people are now Christians and eager to learn all they can.

In early 1994, Ann and I noticed a small advertisement in our Asheville paper announcing a two-week tour to North China in October under the sponsorship of the North Carolina Center for International Understanding (an organization in Raleigh). What caught our eye was not only the low overall cost but also the fact that the itinerary focused mainly on two cities in Shantung (Shandong) Province. One of these cities was Tsinan (Jinan), where I was brought up; the other was Weihsien (now called Weifang), where Helen and Gordon were missionaries before and after World War II. Tourists do not generally go to these cities. I had not been in North China since 1927, and Ann who had visited Hong Kong many times and Taipei once, had never been in China. So we applied, were interviewed, and were accepted. We attended an orientation weekend in August. On October 15 we flew from Atlanta by Japan Airlines. There were thirty-nine of us Tar Heels in this tour group, including our two close friends and neighbors Al and Edie Fink.

Beijing was our point of entry into China. From the moment of our arrival, we were in the hands of the official government Tourist Bureau and were always under official guides, who took us to see what the government wanted us to see and gave us no time or opportunity to wander on our own or get nosy. So in Beijing we saw the Tiananmen Square, the Forbidden City, the Summer Palace, the Temple of Heaven, the Great Wall of China, and a Chinese opera—the usual routine for tourists.

An overnight train ride took us to Weifang, the kite capital of the world. Here we were taken to a kite museum and a kite factory, where we were invited to buy kites. I inquired about the mission compound where Helen and Gordon and their family had once lived and where the Japanese had crowded together two thousand western civilian war prisoners—men, women, and children from

Our tour group in Tiananmen Square, Beijing, 1994.

many countries—between December 1941 and August 1945. I asked where this world-famous "Shantung Compound" might be (so well described by Langdon Gilkey in his best-selling book by that title), our Weifang guide apparently had never heard of such a place or situation or mission. It seems I could just as well have asked him about Mother Goose; there was not a flicker of recognition or curiosity, and no offer to try to find out.

From Weifang our bus drove us to a farming village-commune which was neatly laid out and built from scratch after the Communists came into power. We were welcomed with a brass band and red banners and firecrackers; the warmth of the hospitality extended to us by the villagers seemed to be genuine. Each couple in our group was assigned to a different home, and there we ate our meals and stayed overnight as house guests. The family Ann and I were with consisted of a young couple with a two-year-old son and a grandfather. The houses were built of concrete and had electricity; water was piped in, but came only during early morning hours. After dark, the entire village and our tour group gathered in front of the communal hall for entertainment—fan dancing by some young school teachers, a martial-arts exhibition by teenage boys, etc. Our tour's contribution to the entertainment was to sing "Carolina in the Morning," and I sang the Chinese Red Army's marching song "Chi Lai!" ("Arise!"), a song which some of us American officers in World War II were inadvertently taught on the *Ile de France* when we were with the Reds' adversaries, the Kuomintang Army.

Our final days in Shandong were spent in the provincial capital, Jinan, where our family had lived until I was ten. Jinan, now with a population the size of Los Angeles, was quite unrecognizable to me except for its lake. The huge city wall was gone; the narrow dirt streets had become wide, paved, tree-lined avenues stretching in straight lines between modern high-rises. I wanted to look up the house where our family had lived, but our strict schedule was so tight and all old landmarks so nonexistent that that hope never materialized. The Cheeloo Christian University, to whose medical college Ann and I were originally assigned to go as missionaries, is now renamed Shandong University. Its medical college was said to be a good one, but we could only drive past it in our bus and not look inside.

We did get a good view of the Yellow River, which flows past Jinan and is almost as long as the Yangtze River. The Yellow River is so named because of the muddy silt it washes down, raising the riverbed until it is higher than the surrounding land and requiring high levees to contain it. Whenever it overflows those levees, the resulting floods are catastrophic; hence the Yellow River is often called "China's Sorrow."

We returned to Beijing by overnight train, and our two weeks in North China were quickly over. I had longed to make some contact with some Chinese Christians, or even just to see a church, but saw none. That gave me a kind of aching void, such as one might experience in a bad dream where God did not exist and Christ had never lived and where one was surrounded by countless human beings everywhere who moved busily about like ants in a giant anthill. To me, it seemed almost as if there had been a conspiracy by the government Tourist Bureau and the guides it employed, not only to keep us too occupied to think, but also to obliterate even the memory of Christianity. In this respect, this visit to China was surrealistic to me and would have left me sad if I had not known that today, in China, there are millions of Christian brothers and sisters whose faith shines bright and clear in spite of stifling adversity.

Ann's and my next trip overseas was in March 1995—this time to India. The occasion for this visit was to help celebrate the one hundredth anniversary of the founding of the Christian Medical College in Ludhiana, where I had been director for eleven years. Two years before this visit, the Christian Dental College had been founded and added to the medical and nursing colleges existing when Ann and I were there. We were astounded to learn that the city of Ludhiana, which had a half-a-million population when we lived there, today has a population of over two million.

The crowning celebration was on March 24 (the birthday of Dame Edith Brown, the founder and first director), when the

Celebrating the one hundredth anniversary of the founding of the Christian Medical College, Ludhiana. At the final convocation, the governor of Punjab State presents a Distinguished Service Award to Dr. Mary Mathew, retired chair of Department of Medicine. The present director, Dr. Richard Daniels, at left, looks on, March 1995.

governor of Punjab State presided at the Founders Day Convocation and made a fine speech and conferred the degrees to the graduating doctors and nurses. Two days later (on Sunday), a worship and Communion service led by the Bishop of Delhi closed the celebrations. At this service, I played on the rebuilt grand piano once owned by Queen Mary (wife of King George V) and donated to the Christian Medical College while Dame Edith Brown was director.

This visit to Ludhiana was a joy to us because of all the friends and colleagues we knew and saw there, both those serving there currently and the many who came from other countries to celebrate this centenary, most of whom were now white-haired. We were especially happy because the current director, whom we knew well, is the first of our own medical alumni to become director of this interdenominational Christian medical teaching center.

As if one trip abroad wasn't enough for one year, Ann and I made another trip overseas in 1995, this time to Indonesia to visit with Betsy and John and their boys, Gordie and Joey, in Irian Jaya. We left home on Ann's birthday, October 16, and spent two delightful days on the way seeing Bunny and Ted and Lad and Helen in Westminster Gardens Retirement Center in Duarte, California. It was good to see many long-time friends there, too.

The flight from Los Angeles to Jakarta was a long one and was followed by another all-night flight to Biak, an island north of Irian Jaya. John met us in Biak, and together we flew in a small Twin-Otter plane across the ocean to Manokwari, the main town on Irian Jaya's Bird's Head. There Betsy and the boys engulfed us with excited jubilation, while a crowd of black-skinned, fuzzy-haired native Papuans looked on with great curiosity.

In Manokwari, their family lived in a rented house built on high stilts. It was in this modern town that sits on a beautiful bay that the Japanese had their main naval base during World War II.

In 1858, the first missionary to Irian Jaya, a German Moravian, came to Manokwari and founded this church—the first Christian church in all Irian Jaya.

Ann and Betsy, Gordie and Joey—seen in this Japanese war memorial in Manokwari. Manokwari, on the equator, was the site of Japan's principal naval base during World War II.

Most of the heavy luggage we brought with us consisted of food items, school supplies, books, and other presents for the boys, not only for their birthdays, which we celebrated during the two weeks we were with them, but also for Christmas and beyond.

Betsy and John also maintained a second home up in Kebar Valley, a valley some 1,800 feet above sea level and surrounded by 6,000-to-9,000-foot, rugged, rain forest-covered mountains. The only access to this valley was by small airplane. John and I were able to get there in the one Cessna assigned by Mission Aviation Fellowship to the Bird's Head, which is a territory about half the size of North Carolina. Our MAF pilot, Phil Nelson, expected to pick us up from Kebar and take us back to Manokwari the following day.

The people in Kebar Valley, I found, were poor and poorly nourished, their staples being, typically, cassava root and sago palm, both miserable foods. John wanted to introduce more nutritious

John Murphy talking to Mission Aviation Fellowship pilot Phil Nelson in the Cessna plane carrying us to John and Betsy's home in Kebar Valley, accessible only by air.

plants to grow there and then, hopefully, encourage these to catch on. The people seemed eager to learn and to cooperate, for I could see he had already won their hearts and confidence. They were already beginning to grow peanuts, and John was trying to work out a way to press out peanut oil for their own cooking needs and for cash export.

The health problems there were formidable, tuberculosis and malaria being major causes for the people's shortened life expectancies. The villagers quizzing John about my age gasped with surprise when John told them that I was almost eighty years old. I became an instant celebrity when they insisted that I must surely be the oldest human being ever to have set foot in their valley.

The next day, while I was wandering about and taking in all the sights and sounds of Anjai (the main village in the valley) with my camera at the ready, John got a radio message informing us that after flying back to Manokwari, Phil had accidentally ripped open the front of his leg and the top of his foot with an electric tile cutter he was using at home; this would now ground him for weeks to come. John and I wondered, "What now?" Later that day another radio message told us that Victor, another MAF pilot in Irian Jaya, would be coming for us, and the message urgently requested me to see Phil in his home as soon as we got to Manokwari and evaluate his condition.

While we were waiting for Victor to pick us up, the village fathers brought several patients to John's front porch for me to see, and within one hour I had diagnosed two women as having far-advanced, cavitary, pulmonary tuberculosis. John proved to be an excellent interpreter. One of these women, the wife of the church leader there, had been told she had tuberculosis, but had not been able to get any proper medicines for it. She showed me a two-year-old X-ray film made in Manokwari which revealed a cavity even then. Several weeks before Ann and I arrived, Betsy had witnessed the delivery of twin babies in Kebar Valley whose mother soon thereafter died of TB, and the patient I was now seeing was taking care of one of those twins in her home, using baby formula Betsy was providing. (I saw both those twins while there.) Later, when John and I got back to Manokwari, I was able to buy all the ideal drugs most recommended for a six-month intensive treatment course for tuberculosis, and Betsy would administer and supervise them when she next got to Kebar. Such a course cost me two hundred thousand rupias, or about one hundred dollars. Drug treatment for tuberculosis must be done right, or not at all.

Holding impromptu medical consultations on the Murphys' front porch in the Kebar Valley while waiting for the MAF plane to return us to Manokwari, October 1995.

The other woman patient's diagnosis I could not verify, though I strongly suspected TB, for TB and malaria are known to be most prevalent in that area of the world. I didn't have even a stethoscope, much less a microscope or X-ray machine. I know John had to smile when he saw me trying to use the cardboard core of a spent toilet-paper roll as a stethoscope, while the whole village stood around watching.

Needless to say, we were relieved to see Victor finally land and taxi right up to John's house, one room of which still served as the church office, the church itself being next door. I marveled that Victor—all six-feet-five-inches of him—could squeeze into that little Cessna cockpit, but he did. We were glad to get back to Manokwari, and we went straight to Phil's house near the runway. What we found when we saw Phil was that his wounds had been carefully stitched together in the local hospital with thirty-six stitches, many of them buried—far too many for his contaminated, mangled tissues to cope with—and his wounds were already grossly infected. So I removed all readily-accessible stitches, began continuous hot-wet soaks and started Phil on Augmentin by mouth (the best antibiotic that Betsy had on hand), and made sure that his leg was kept elevated. I saw him daily while we were there; then Betsy took care of him when Ann and I left Irian Jaya. Besty was happy to report to us later that Phil was making decent progress at home and did not have to be evacuated. But all trips to and from Kebar Valley had to be canceled for weeks.

We all learned to appreciate what Mission Aviation Fellowship is doing and the high standards and dedication of its pilots and their families—also how indispensable their services are. (The local people call MAF the "Missionary Air Force.") Phil told me that for Irian Jaya alone, MAF currently was maintaining twenty pilots and sixteen aircraft. There were vast territories still wholly uncharted and, no doubt, tribes still to be discovered in Irian Jaya hidden beneath the impenetrable rain forests covering the ruggedly mountainous and swampy island that is New Guinea, the second-largest island in the world (after Greenland).

When given the chance to hear the Christian Good News, these Irian Jayan people have avidly embraced the gospel and have repeatedly demonstrated the dramatic transformation of whole people-groups from being the treacherous, violent, head-hunting cannibals they once were a few decades ago, to the friendly, cheerful, likable people we were now seeing. But they still need the help and guidance and encouragement of godly people. If such helpers are to be allowed by the Indonesian government to enter from abroad, they will have to come as tent makers.

Our two full weeks with Besty and John and their boys passed by all too quickly. Ann and I were grateful for every moment of our visit with them and their friends there. We thanked God for what we had experienced; but by the time we had retraced our long, tedious air routes back to Swannanoa, we were glad to be back home.

CHAPTER TWENTY

ANN'S ILLNESS

AS MY EIGHTIETH BIRTHDAY DREW NEAR AND Ann and I were wondering how we could make it special, Ann came upon a page in the 1996 *Christian Tours* catalogue which caught her eye. On it appeared this item: "Panama Canal & Caribbean—San Juan, La Guaira, Panama, San Blas, Curacao, Martinique, St. John, St. Thomas," all this to take place in March, my birth month. "That's us," we said when she showed it to me. We had never been to the Caribbean or to any place in Central or South America. Here was our opportunity par excellence, we thought—everything arranged and provided for us, with no hassle or red tape involved. We had liked our previous experiences with Christian Tours. A phone call to them that day confirmed our reservations for the twelve-day cruise scheduled for March 4–15. When the time came, a Christian Tours bus picked us up just 1.8 miles from our home and took us to the Charlotte Airport; there we joined the rest of our Christian Tours party of thirty retired persons like ourselves.

In Charlotte we walked through long concourses to reach our airplane. In San Juan, we again walked long distances from plane to bus to shipside, so that by the time we reached our cabin, Ann was in agony with pain in her left hip and extending down into her knee. That evening, walking the length of the cruise ship for dinner was almost unbearable to her, in spite of all the ibuprofen she took for it. The next morning I borrowed a wheelchair from the ship's hospital, and from then on for the rest of the trip, Ann went nowhere except by wheelchair. Any weight-bearing seemed to get progressively more painful as the days and nights went by, yet there was no hint of fracture or arthritis anywhere. The medicine the ship's physician dispensed did not help at all. We never left the ship throughout the entire cruise.

One thing we had looked forward to on this cruise was a visit with our niece Dorothy and her husband Peter Muilenburg in their home on St. John Island and going sailing in their boat. That was not to be, but we did see them briefly on board our cruise ship. We were thankful not to miss them completely.

After returning home, Ann underwent many diagnostic procedures, including a total bone scan, and an MRI (magnetic resonance imaging) study. Two months after we began our cruise, she had surgery on her spine. The neurosurgeon removed a two-inch-long mass which was wrapped around the spinal nerve roots. When local pathologists could not identify this mass, the specimen was sent to Duke University and then to Johns Hopkins. Two weeks later, they reported an inflammatory process, but no evidence of tumor. But what was it?

Ann had dramatic decrease of pain immediately after surgery, and she was discharged from the hospital to our home on the third post-operative day. But her pain never quite disappeared. It steadily increased over the next weeks, requiring stronger and stronger pain-killing drugs around the clock and much attention from myself. Many thoughts were running through our minds. Was our loving Heavenly Father wanting to sharpen our own perspectives? Perhaps His purpose in this was to draw us closer to

Himself through greater trust and deeper commitment to Him and thus to learn more experientially that His grace is indeed sufficient for every need and stress—certainly, continuous bodily pain is stressful, especially when the pain confined Ann to bed.

Where was I to fit into this picture? As a physician, I was stumped. However, as Ann's husband, I knew for sure that I owed her every *bit* of personal attention I was capable of giving—gentle, loving, tireless care. She needed me now more that ever for emotional support. Often she would plead with me not to leave her alone in the house. If ever she needed the reassurance of my love, it was now, and I was thankful that I was in good enough shape to try to show it. After all, she had devoted herself to me all the many years of our life together, and now here was a unique opportunity for me to do for her what she had been doing for me all these years. I could sense also that the real test of my loyalty to Ann would come after the initial flush of chivalry began to wear off with time. If her suffering and disability should increase, as well it might, would I be able to weather that storm?

My great inspiration in all this has come from Dr. Robertson McQuilkin of Columbia, South Carolina, the Christian leader and educator who gave up the presidency of Columbia International University in order to care full-time for his wife, who had become helpless with Alzheimer's disease. I greatly admire him for his decision to do this—a truly Christian decision—because it was fulfilling the solemn vows he had made before God and the many assembled at their wedding years before, as a true "promise keeper" before that term was to become popularized. I will always honor him for his fidelity—fidelity not only to the letter, but also to the spirit of those vows. My own commitment to Ann was considerably easier than his, for Ann did not have Alzheimer's disease, and I had the hope that she would eventually get well and not need anymore to be waited upon around-the-clock.

In any case, it would have been pointless and non-productive for me to wail, "Why? Why?" and bang my head against the wall. Rather, I should seek to discover what it was that God was telling *me*, trusting Him to do what was best for us all and submitting to

His loving child-training. Already I was convinced that He wanted to make me less caustic, less cutting, less insensitive, less egocentric, and less impatient and derogatory of others—in other words, more loving. I had already gone long enough through life with certain characteristics that would be incongruous in Heaven, my ultimate home. Now that I was eighty years old, I realized that Heaven couldn't be very far away. I had better learn fast while there was yet time.

Meanwhile, Ann's general condition slowly worsened, and she began slipping mentally. She was taking almost nothing by mouth, her blood pressure was soaring to dangerous levels, and she was becoming more and more disoriented and restless. Little noises annoyed her, such as the chirping of a small bird outside her widow or the bark of a distant dog or the singing of critters in the summer air. For three months I did not touch our piano. The television was rarely turned on, and then it was kept hardly audible and with the hall door closed. More and more frequent doses of stronger and stronger opiates were required to control the increasing pain in her back and hip and leg. From early July on, her pain confined her to bed rest. During all those weeks, I was by her side, day and night.

With Ann's neurosurgeon's arrangement and with our son-in-law John to accompany me, I drove to Duke University for consultation with its Chairman of Neurosurgery, along with an armful of films and medical records. He recommended a nine-hour spinal operation to restore stability to parts of the spine that seemed to be melting away.

At this point, the Session of our Warren Wilson Presbyterian Church designated 7:00 o'clock on the evening of July 24 as a time when our church family could join in prayer together for Ann. Our children all made plans to come home. Betsy and John had already arrived on their two-month furlough from Irian Jaya. Ken Jr. stepped up his October leave from Ivory Coast and arrived on August 9 to be present for the nine-hour spinal surgery that was now scheduled for August 13 in Asheville. Charlie would arrive from Tampa on August 12, when Ann was scheduled to enter

Memorial Mission Hospital. All along, many wonderful friends and neighbors, including the very supportive members of our church, were filling our lives with countless expressions of love and too many kindnesses to possibly count.

But Ann's condition then deteriorated so rapidly that she had to be admitted earlier to the hospital, on August 8. A family conference was scheduled to consult with her neurosurgeon Sunday morning, August 11, to decide whether that hazardous surgery should take place as scheduled or should be canceled. Charlie and Marjorie drove from Tampa all Saturday night to be present at that consultation. At about 3:30 that Sunday morning, I awoke and prayed beside my bed. I had already surrendered Ann to God's will, so that whatever He planned for her, no matter what it was, I would accept. I remember with great clarity that I made two specific requests. I asked, first, that the decision our family would be making that day—whether to operate on Ann as scheduled, or to cancel it—would be the right decision. Second, I prayed that as a sign that we were making the right decision (like a "Gideon's fleece"), *all* of us would be in complete agreement on that decision, whatever it was. In retrospect, I am convinced that the Holy Spirit prompted me to make that particular prayer, because when I rose from beside my bed, I felt a heavy burden lifted from me. I then dressed and drove to the hospital to relieve Betsy, who had been staying all that night with Ann in her hospital room.

Charlie and Marjorie arrived just in time to join the rest of us in the X-ray reading room where we were reviewing with Ann's surgeon the various studies made on Ann—bone scan, myelograms, CAT scan, MRI studies, etc. The surgeon outlined for us, thoroughly and candidly, what her nine-hour spinal surgery would involve and what might be expected from it. He then left us in the conference room to make our family decision whether to operate or not.

All our three children and their spouses were with me on that unforgettable Sunday. We opened our family discussion with a prayer that we would make the right decision, still not knowing what that decision might be. Meanwhile, our two oldest grand-children, Thayer and Audrey, stayed with Ann in her room, since she could not remain unattended. As we talked together, I was suddenly aware that we were all of one mind—not to operate. And as suddenly, every eye brimmed with tears at the realization that, by our decision, we were probably saying good-bye to Ann. We notified our surgeon that we were canceling the surgery scheduled for August 13, and we began to talk about hospice arrangements for Ann's coming days.

It was not until the next day that the seemingly bizarre possibility seriously surfaced that an over-producing parathyroid gland was the major culprit accounting for Ann's downhill course over the past six months. So on August 14, a parathyroid adenoma—a benign tumor the size of a small pea—was surgically found and removed from Ann's neck. (A normal parathyroid gland is about the size of a pinhead.)

The next day, Ann was almost a new person. Her severe pain was gone, she was smiling, and her mind was clear. Our family and friends were ecstatic. We were especially grateful that God clearly, we strongly believe, kept Ann from a traumatic operation that would not have helped her. And all this in the nick of time. Two days later, she returned home from the hospital.

Had someone "goofed" by not recognizing this problem earlier? Not at all. Ann's medical situation was far too complex for such a thought. The best consultants had been enlisted, and I fully concurred in every conclusion and decision they reached. If faced with an identical situation all over again, even with the benefit of hindsight, I do not think we would have done differently. Besides, Ann still had a serious spinal problem to cope with, the answer to which was not clear nor the prognosis assured. One thing was certain: God had graciously touched our lives, enriching them with a greater love for Him and for one another and a new tenderness toward each other.

Ann soon regained a measure of well-being after that close call in mid-August. However, all of us physicians knew her original spinal problem had not yet been fully addressed, simply because we still did not really know what her diagnosis was. So a biopsy needle was poked into her back to again try to identify her disease. It hurt her much, but it only pointed again to some chronic and acute inflammatory process (the same as reported after the surgery in May). Betsy and John and their boys had to return to Irian Jaya before their reentry visas expired, but they were able to leave America with peace of heart because Ann continued to get better.

A number of weeks later, however, left hip and thigh pain began to recur and slowly to increase, so that by the beginning of October Ann became confined to bed again and required opiates to give her relief. When pain started to appear also on the *right* side and after another CAT scan demonstrated total bone destruction of her third lumbar vertebra, it became plain that the difficult spinal surgery originally scheduled to be done August 13 (and was canceled August 11) had to be done now without delay. We were grateful that Ann was no longer in the precarious shape she was in before her parathyroid tumor was removed. So on November 5 and 13, in a two-stage procedure—seven hours for the first operation, five hours for the second—the disintegrating lumbar vertebra was removed and a metal prosthesis put in its place and her lower spine stabilized with metal rods secured in place with large nuts and bolts and screws. Again, the material removed at surgery was sent to the Duke University and Johns Hopkins hospitals for diagnosis. This time the report they gave was Hodgkin's lymphoma, even though Hodgkin's disease of the bone is considered extremely rare.

Ann's post-operative recovery included a month in Thoms Rehabilitation Hospital, for she had to learn all over again how to walk. A bivalved body brace was made for her, and she soon became known among her friends as Mrs. Ninja Turtle. This brace was to be worn for the next eight months whenever she was out of bed. The month of rehabilitation was followed by radiation treatment to her lower spine—twenty-two doses in all.

Sometime during the spring of 1997 after a period of well-being, Ann noticed pain in her left flank, which slowly increased and returned her eventually to bed rest and opiates to relieve it. Then in early June, a chest X-ray revealed a considerable amount of fluid in her left pleural cavity. A look-see (thoracoscopy) into her left chest and biopsy of her pleura (lining of chest wall) confirmed the diagnosis of Hodgkin's lymphoma, and a course of chemotherapy was begun July 3. From the next day onward, all pain disappeared, which encouraged us all immensely.

God knows what lies ahead. Ann's oncologist says her chances of a complete cure is sixty percent. I have been with her in it all, leaving her side only for some Sunday morning worship services and Rotary meetings, short trips for food, and several swims each week in the Warren Wilson College pool. I have been grateful for enough good health throughout Ann's ordeal to permit me to be close to her to help. We are grateful that we still have each other to appreciate and cherish. And everywhere friends have helped us much and have prayed for us both.

We are happy in the Lord and, come what may, we are ready for our travel to Heaven—any time He wants us there.

Our home in Swannanoa, North Carolina.

There may be some who think that a person is able to praise and worship God only when life is gloriously unruffled. Job refuted that idea. Scripture records that on the day calamity struck and he lost everything, including any encouragement from his wife, Job "fell to the ground and worshipped." In fact, it is the unruffled person who is most in danger of ignoring God. Moses had to warn the Israelites, "When you eat and are satisfied, be careful that you do not forget the LORD . . ." (Deut. 6: 11–12 NIV). The sleek and pampered are rarely inclined to give God the worship and praise and thanksgiving due Him.

Through our experience we all were learning more fully to accept what we cannot change, whether good or bad. When Job's wife said to him, "Curse God and die," Job replied, "Shall we accept good from God, and not trouble?" Too many Americans have the idea that they have the right to expect a lovely, trouble-free life with everything going their way, and anything blocking that expectation demands that they go on a rampage or at least sue somebody. I imagine that some people would sue God if they could figure out how. But Jesus never promised anybody a life of smooth sailing. He did promise His presence, His peace, and His grace.

EPILOGUE

IDENTIFY MYSELF—AND GLADLY SO—WITH THOSE millions of American Christians who have been described by the *Washington Post* as "largely poor, uneducated, and easy to command." I am sure that newspaper would include me because I am one of those who can't understand how anyone could doubt the existence and the importance of God. For if there were no God to create this vast and complex universe with its perfect order and obedience to the many laws of nature we keep discovering, there could be no existence of anything—only a total blank for all time, a total nothingness. The expanding discoveries of medical science alone and their insights on life's intricate and balanced, interlocking processes—as a physician I appreciate this especially—all proclaim with a mighty chorus the amazing wisdom and ingenuity of the master designer, to say nothing of His awesome power to bring it all about initially and then make it keep functioning. Nobody should be so conceited as to think that because he does not fully understand something, it cannot be so. Most people believe what they want to believe, and whenever those beliefs are derived from unworthy motives, they will stoutly deny any solid evidence to the contrary.

I have never doubted the reality of God, and I have never doubted that the Bible is God's inspired Word and is wholly reliable and relevant for today. I am convinced that nobody knows enough to decisively gainsay what the Bible tells us. The carping and criticism leveled against it has arisen, I believe, from ignorant and bigoted suppositions. What I cannot prove objectively with my own eyes must be accepted by faith. Yet true faith is not blind faith, and whenever there is something said in Scripture that is inexplicable or that appears contradictory, I simply reserve judgment for the moment. So very often a satisfying explanation will in time surface and clarify that matter; meanwhile, I am willing to wait. Some people are so cocksure that they have all the answers that they will condemn Scripture without hesitation. Thus Chuck Templeton has accused Billy Graham of intellectual dishonesty simply because Billy Graham will not harbor doubts about the Bible and is willing to wait until he gets to Heaven to have his questions answered.

⇒·◈·⇐

I am amazed that so many persons, seemingly intelligent, scoff at such concepts as natural laws and teliology and sin, even though we are immersed daily in these phenomena, both their reality and their consequences. This blindness reminds me of the fish swimming in the ocean and asking, "Where is the water?"

⇒·◈·⇐

God has given everyone the privilege of free choice, without which we would all be automatons, puppets, incapable of loving or having fellowship with anyone. God loves us and longs for us to love Him. That is why He gave us freedom to choose and with it the ability truly to love, since love is a function of the will and is not merely a passive feeling. The greatest mystery in life is the mystery of evil: why do we choose to be selfish and greedy? Why do we choose to rebel against God, to disobey Him, to ignore Him, even to hate Him? Only the Bible gives a clue to this mystery—a mystery which remains quite unfathomable to the philosopher and the moralist.

———

Evolution, as it is being taught in our public schools, should rightly be labeled a philosophy and the hypothesis that it is, since it has not been proven scientifically. At best, it might be called a theory. Certainly, in the light of what science is now telling us, it is not a fact. The credence given to evolution has arisen from the desperate desire of fallen mankind to dismiss the existence of God and His work in creation and therefore to dismiss any responsibility to Him. One of its fatal flaws has been its failure to distinguish between mutation, which is seen commonly, and transmutation, which has never been observed, and then begging the issue by throwing time back by millions of years—out of observation's reach.

———

People who say, "You leave me alone and I'll leave you alone," forget that the world operates on the federal system, which means that what one person does will affect other people. Thus, when a pervert contracts the HIV virus and passes it on to others, such as to a baby or a hemophiliac or a transfusion recipient, these innocent victims will suffer. A madman like Hitler or Saddam Hussein can bring incalculable destruction and misery to many people. And one person's blunder, well-intentioned though it may be, such as at Chernobyl, can bring death to multitudes for decades to come. This is why the world has been called a global village. I am indeed my brother's keeper—in more ways than one.

I am really not a hatemonger, and I am not a homophobe. I do not condemn a person for being attracted to others of the same sex. And my Christian orientation constrains me to love such people, for they are as much my neighbors created in God's image as anyone else. But for such to have sex with each other is wrong in God's sight, just as sex between a man and a woman outside of marriage is wrong, as the Bible explicitly states. The fact that many persons ignore God's laws without compunction does not make their actions right or acceptable. At the same time, I may not point a holier-than-thou finger at those who sin, because I am myself a sinner who has fallen far short of God's standards and who needs to repent and be forgiven just as much as the most deviant pervert needs to repent and be forgiven. The amazing thing is that nobody is beyond the reach of God's love and restoring grace; He loves us all and is saddened whenever we ignore Him and fail to ask His forgiveness and to love Him in return.

In my generation, divorce was unheard of among my acquaintances. Family solidarity was the backbone of life, especially for us who grew up on the mission field. "Divorce can never happen to us." But it did. In fact, divorce happened among the children of my two living sisters and among my brother's children and our own children. How could this be? Has the concept of commitment disappeared from our society or does that promise no longer have the staying power it once had? It seems that the marriage-vow phrase "as long as we both shall live" has mutated to "as long as we both shall love." Ann's heart and mine ache for each of our family members who have experienced the trauma of divorce. As far as we are concerned, our former daughters-in-law are still dear to us and continue to be members of our family. God loves them; why should not we? Still, we are most fortunate in that all our children and grandchildren are living and well and are loving and responsible and successful individuals that we are proud of. And all of them have steered clear of tobacco, alcohol and drugs, and other hurtful entanglements. This is a great mercy to us.

———•◦•———

I, for one, have been given every conceivable advantage in life: godly, loving parents and brothers and sisters, a Christian schooling and other welcome Christian influences, as well as a wonderful family and many friends. My temperament has never been a rebellious one, and so I have been spared many unnecessary heartaches and frustrations. Because of these many advantages, I may not claim credit to myself for anything good in my life. Jesus' quotations, "Unto whomsoever much is given, much is required," and "I am an unprofitable servant; I have only done what was expected of me"—these certainly apply to me. Therefore, I find nothing about me to crow over.

I have tended to be somewhat self-centered and lazy—inclinations I have always had to fight against. But early in life, I determined to be strictly honest in matters of money and possessions, and this has been most liberating to me. Not envying what others may have or wanting more things for myself than I need has made me truly carefree. Happily, I have never known want or worried about the future, thanks to God's loving care over the years.

———•◦•———

I long that Christian people everywhere shall soon come to recognize afresh the primacy of Calvary's cross. I am saddened when one of the most poignant hymns ever written—Cecil Frances Alexander's "There Is A Green Hill Far Away," beautiful in its simplicity and understanding of Jesus' death for our salvation— has been deleted from our current Presbyterian hymnal and replaced by blander, more triumphalistic offerings of recent hymn-smiths. And even some of Charles Wesley's incisive masterpieces have been reworded so as to take the teeth out of the gospel lion. Happily, some new hymns are now being written which are gloriously worshipful and Christocentric, and so I take hope. And speaking of the Cross, no single volume written in this century on that pivotal subject can surpass, I believe, John R. W. Stott's true labor of love, *The Cross of Christ*, scholarly and inspiring, which was published some ten years ago. I rejoice that there are still people today who understand and who marvel with head bowed.

——————

Writing my life story as I have, primarily for my children and grandchildren, is one way for me to express my deepest desire for their spiritual welfare, for I love each one of them and want only the best for them. It would pain me to see many of these dear family members miss, through neglect or unbelief, the *joie de vivre* and fulfillment that have been mine through trusting in God and seeking His honor. My greatest longing is that all my loved ones shall, in time, join me in Heaven. As of this writing, not all have yet committed themselves to Christ and His will for them, and this saddens me. So I continue praying for them daily, and I am confident that God hears and answers prayer and that nothing is too hard for Him.

Dr. James Dobson of Focus on the Family has said it all better than I could ever say it when he wrote to his son Ryan these words, as he anticipated eternity in Heaven, "Never forget that this is what I want most for you: I want you to BE THERE."

INDEX